THE UN'S LONE RANGER

THE UN'S
LONE
RANGER

COMBATING INTERNATIONAL
WILDLIFE CRIME

JOHN M SELLAR OBE

Whittles Publishing

Published by
Whittles Publishing,
Dunbeath,
Caithness, KW6 6EG,
Scotland, UK

www.whittlespublishing.com

ISBN 978-184995-103-6

Printed by
Latimer Trend & Company Ltd., Plymouth

For Alison, Caroline and Michael

CONTENTS

Prologue ix
Acknowledgements xi
Foreword xiii

1 BECOMING THE UN'S LONE RANGER 1

2 CITES, CONSERVATION AND CRIME 7

3 WILDLIFE CRIME AND ORGANIZED CRIME 12

4 COMMITTING THE CRIME 16
  The structure of poaching 16
  Sophistication of smuggling techniques and routes 21
  Sophisticated forgery and counterfeiting of documents 25
  Use of fake or 'front' companies 27

5 MANIPULATING PEOPLE AND CIRCUMSTANCES 29
  Provision of high-quality lawyers 29
  Exploitation of local communities 29
  Exploitation of civil unrest 30
  Use of 'mules' 32
  People in high places 34

6 CORRUPTING, THREATENING AND KILLING 45
  Corruption of judicial process 45
  Bribery and corruption 46
  Corruption of law enforcement personnel 54
  Violence towards law enforcement personnel 56

7 THE WORLDWIDE WILDLIFE WEB 61
  Fraudulent advertising of wildlife 61
  Financial investment in technology 63

8 SPOT THE GANGSTER 65
  Previous convictions for other types of crime 65
  Inviolability of those involved 67

Payments to organized crime groups 69

Organized crime's ownership of wildlife 69

Huge profits 70

9 WILDLIFE CRIME AND TERRORISM 73

10 THE CAVIAR CRIMINALS 77

Examining Caspian crime responses 82

Controlling caviar commerce 93

Caspian hospitality 104

11 ELEPHANTS AND IVORY 109

There's no pleasing everyone 111

Making sense of illegal trade in ivory 115

Improving our response 123

To trade or not to trade? 129

12 TIGER TRAFFICKERS 132

From bad to worse for tigers 146

Tigers: to trade or not to trade? 151

Political will at last? 157

13 RHINO RACKETEERING 164

Why rhino horn? 164

Rhinos in peril 168

An apparently unceasing demand 174

Is an end in sight? 176

14 WHAT MIGHT WE DO BETTER? 179

15 RIDING OFF INTO THE SUNSET 189

Annex 201

Official CITES missions 201

PROLOGUE

I switched on the light for the main room again but then stood with my ear to the still-closed bathroom door for almost half a minute. Not the slightest sound came from within. It did not make any sense at all. 'What on earth can they be doing?' I wondered. 'They' were the head of the national fishery protection agency and the president of a caviar-producing company.

Mystified, I made my way back into the bedroom area, just in time to see that the Miss World candidate, her back towards me, now had her jeans and panties around her ankles and was in the process of pulling her right leg free of them whilst her left arm was on the bed, steadying herself in this unbalanced position.

Not for the first time, I found myself thinking, 'How the hell did I end up here?'

I will leave the Miss World Candidate for the moment and focus on just how I did end up in the bedroom of a Soviet-style and Soviet-era hotel on the shores of the Caspian Sea with my grand title of Chief of Enforcement of the Secretariat for the Convention on International Trade in Endangered Species of Wild Fauna and Flora. It was just about as bizarre as what was happening in the hotel room in the early hours of that morning, especially given that I have never been particularly interested in wildlife. I had watched the David Attenborough documentaries on television and my wife and I had always enjoyed visiting sea bird colonies on the high cliffs of Scotland, but I am certainly not a twitcher. I can tell the difference between a tiger, an eagle and an elephant but my identification skills are quickly exhausted if I'm asked to distinguish between any lesser-known species. It was not at all unreasonable, then, that I, and probably many others, questioned how on earth I landed up as a senior United Nations official, travelling the globe for 14 years, devoted to wildlife crime matters.

This book will reflect on just how that happened and also, I hope, provide some insight into wildlife crime and the sometimes shockingly poor way in which the nations of the world respond. Here, too, will be some examples of the excellent work that also goes on to protect the natural resources of the world. It will be for you to decide if an effective balance is being struck and whether or not the good examples make up for the bad.

ACKNOWLEDGEMENTS

When I first sat down to write this book, I decided that I was not going to name the guilty, so it seemed appropriate not to name the innocent either, or those in between. But it would be remiss of me not to identify certain individuals, without whom my life between 1997 and 2011 would have been dramatically different.

Firstly, the Chief Constables of Grampian Police, its Police Authority and the Scottish Office deserve my thanks for agreeing to the initial secondment that took me to the United Nations and my subsequent continued service there.

I served with three CITES Secretaries-General, one Interim Secretary-General and one Deputy Secretary-General and thank each of them for their support and encouragement:

Ambassador Izgrev Topkov, who truly was larger than life; the late Rueben Olembo who, I'm pleased to say, I managed to introduce to a different perspective on policing; Willem Wijnstekers, who ensured, from our very first meeting until his retirement, that life would never be dull; John E. Scanlon AM, who must have been very surprised by how crime-focussed his life would become and I thank him most sincerely for his Foreword to this book; and Dr Jim Armstrong, who showed why the post of Deputy S-G deserves to be funded by the parties.

I enjoyed support from each of the Standing Committee Chairmen. I particularly treasure the comment by one, who professed his admiration for my ability to word criticism so carefully and diplomatically that delegates would thank me for censuring them.

Too many people served in the Geneva offices during my time there for me to acknowledge them all personally. However, the secretarial and research assistants who supported me, Virginia and Maritza, need to be singled out as, especially, does Penny, who put up with me from start to finish. Ger and Steve taught me what I know about the regulation of wildlife trade, while just knowing Jonathan Barzdo enriched my life.

There are many conservationists, working nationally and internationally, and individuals in NGOs who do so much for wildlife and who did so much to aid my work. You have my admiration. I so wish that I could name all the people, in national CITES and law enforcement agencies, who provided help over those 14 years but the list would be almost endless. I am confident you know who you are and several will recognize scenarios described in these pages. Those of you who wear a uniform or who carry a badge to work deserve not just my gratitude but that of the whole of society. Special thanks go to counterparts and colleagues in IGOs, particularly those who helped establish ICCWC.

I am grateful to friends, former colleagues and relatives who commented on draft passages and whose input improved them. I am very grateful for the confidence shown in me by Whittles Publishing and trust that this will prove to have been well-placed.

As for Alison… well, Helen and Alan produced a beauty there, in all senses of the word.

FOREWORD

John Sellar started his career as a Police Cadet in Scotland in 1973, the same year that the Convention on International Trade in Endangered Species of Wild Fauna and Flora (CITES) was adopted in Washington, D.C. Perhaps this coincidence in timing was a sign of things to come, with John going on to end his career with the CITES Secretariat as Chief of Enforcement Support, in 2011.

John blazed a trail for the Secretariat in the fight against wildlife crime. He meticulously helped CITES Parties respond to threats, build enforcement capacity, and develop a vast body of decisions and resolutions on enforcement. Mission by mission, report by report, meeting by meeting for over 14 years John helped build the foundations that continue to guide our enforcement work today.

John describes himself in this book as being "Scottish from head to toe" noting that Scots "are known for our frank and blunt speaking". John's time with CITES certainly reflected his own self-assessment and, while he may have occasionally ruffled some feathers, his commitment was always respected.

John preferred the field to the office and he relied on his instincts before academic reports. He is well-known for his story telling prowess, as is reflected in this book, which is a 'warts and all' account of his 'on the road' experiences from CITES missions across 60 countries. This offers us a very personal insight into John's assessment of the challenges we face, and the promising opportunities that exist, in the fight against wildlife crime.

John highlights four broad areas that he helped drive at CITES, issues that we continue to pursue today, namely: the need to prioritize enforcement efforts; the added value of collaboration and collective effort; the importance of connecting policy with practice; and the need to secure core financing for wildlife enforcement officers at all levels. As someone who has served in the front-lines in the fight against crime as a Police Cadet, uniform Sergeant and Detective Constable, as well as an international civil servant, John's reflections warrant our close attention.

John's most enduring legacy is perhaps the establishment of the International Consortium on Combatting Wildlife Crime (ICCWC), which he conceived and crafted together with senior officials across each partner institution - INTERPOL, the UN Office on Drugs and Crime (UNODC), the World Bank and the World Customs Organization (WCO). The initiative ultimately found favour with the executive head of each agency in 2010. ICCWC is today serving as an international model for the cross-agency collaboration that is needed at all levels – national, regional and global – to better confront the highly organized criminals who are increasingly moving into wildlife crime.

This timely publication is released as we experience a serious upsurge in the illegal killing and related illegal trade of wildlife. It will undoubtedly be of great interest to anyone with a passion for wildlife and to those concerned with the implications of illegal trade for the survival of some of our most charismatic species in the wild, as well as many other lesser known plants and animals.

Thanks in part to John's efforts to raise the profile of enforcement issues, CITES has moved beyond just having a 'lone ranger', and together with its long-standing partners is today investing additional resources to combat wildlife crime. The significant contribution that John has made over many decades in fighting wildlife crime received high recognition when he was made an Officer of the Order of the British Empire (OBE) in the 2013 Queen's Birthday honours list.

John E. Scanlon AM
Secretary-General, CITES

BECOMING THE UN'S LONE RANGER

In April 1973 I was appointed a police cadet in what was then the Scottish North Eastern Counties Constabulary, but which would within a few years become Grampian Police, following its amalgamation with Aberdeen City Police. I would simply have laughed had anyone told me that I would, some 38 years later, end my law enforcement career in Geneva.

For 24 years, from 1973, I carried out a wide range of policing duties but a significant part of that period was spent as a detective constable, investigating just about every crime there is in the book. I also spent considerable periods of time working at what was then Scotland's maximum-security prison at Peterhead, because of major riots and several very serious prisoner-on-prisoner and prisoner-on-prison officer assaults there. The prison at that time, in the late 1970s and early 1980s, held some of the nation's most vicious criminals, including convicted Tartan Army members, armed bank robbers and the worst of Scotland's sex offenders. Battles for supremacy within the inmate population were common and it was also the period of the 'dirty protests'. In my latter years as a detective, I was regularly selected to undertake investigations into allegations of brutality on the part of prison staff and this led to the development of a relationship with some inmates of 'The Big House' (as Peterhead prison was known among the criminal fraternity) that was out of the ordinary. Ruthless criminals, who would normally have shunned any contact with a law enforcement officer, suddenly found themselves co-operating with me as I looked into their allegations of having been assaulted by 'screws' or claims that their human rights had been abused. Just how ruthless some of these men had been was illustrated in a conversation I had with one prisoner, a man serving a life sentence, who had participated in the hold-up of a wages delivery. He described how he, armed with a sawn-off shotgun, had warned a security guard to move aside. The guard had refused to do so and, in the words of the inmate, 'decided to commit suicide.' I was later to discover that organized crime could be just as brutal elsewhere in the world.

Not long after my arrival in Geneva, a UN administrative officer mentioned he had noticed in my file that I had investigated murders and said he presumed, due to the nature of the work I was to start, that this referred to animals. 'No,' I replied, 'it was people who'd been killed.' I was to learn that the United Nations did not have many staff members with operational law enforcement backgrounds and the organization's decision-making processes and views of how laws might be enforced sometimes made that all too clear.

In the late 1980s I was stationed as a uniform sergeant in that area of northeast Scotland known as Royal Deeside. Here is Balmoral Castle, the holiday home of the British Royal family since the days of Queen Victoria. As its name suggests, it is also home to one of the world's best-known salmon fishing rivers, the Dee, and it was this which led me to the combating of wildlife crime. In those days, the Dee was suffering from the attentions of well-equipped and well-organized salmon poaching gangs travelling from the south of Scotland. So sophisticated, organized and successful were these gangs that some of them were travelling north with refrigerated vans to deal with the quantities of salmon they were netting under cover of darkness. Knowing of my years spent in the Criminal Investigation Department, the officer-in-charge of Deeside asked me to use my experience to tackle what was happening.

I worked with the District Fishery Board committee and staff and we were able to reduce poaching substantially. We also introduced River Watch (based upon the successful but usually urban-based Neighbourhood Watch), the first of its kind in the UK. When, a couple of years later, Grampian Police decided to appoint a Wildlife Liaison Officer, I was asked to take on the role. Since Scottish police forces had very few officers undertaking such work at that time, it was no great surprise that I began to represent my country's police service on UK-wide committees and consultative bodies.

I was, for example, involved in steering groups that would lead to the establishment of the UK's Partnership for Action against Wildlife Crime (PAW), which brought together various governmental, statutory and non-governmental organizations (NGOs) to co-ordinate a response to what seemed to be an increase in offences involving, or directed at, wildlife throughout Britain. I also became involved in several international investigations relating to the smuggling of endangered species from Scotland to mainland Europe and, in one case, to Australia and New Zealand. In 1995, I represented Scotland at a meeting of the Interpol Wildlife Crime Working Group and was trained in relevant international law at that organisation's headquarters in Lyon. Even then, though, I had no inkling of what was to come and had no particular desire to focus on this field of law enforcement.

Indeed, at that time of my life I was maybe better known, both inside and outside the police service, as someone who was dedicating a lot of his hours to the subject of mountain and ski safety and had been honoured and privileged with the award of a Churchill Fellowship to study this in Canada and the United States of America. I was, though, aware that policing, wildlife and mountain safety were all too large an area of interest to be compatible with each other and that either wildlife or mountain safety was going to have to go. It was not long before I was nudged into making a once-and-for-all decision.

It was in early 1997 that my secretary asked me to take a call from someone in the UK government, an individual whom I had met at many committee meetings. By that stage I was Area Inspector in charge of Deeside, one of the prime appointments in Grampian Police as it brought a wide range of considerable responsibilities and a posting in one of the most beautiful regions of Scotland. The phone call was to radically change my life and that of my family.

I was asked to undertake a secondment, for one year only, to the secretariat of the Convention on International Trade in Endangered Species of Wild Fauna and Flora (CITES, pronounced 'sigh-tees'). The UK had been paying for the position of Deputy Enforcement Officer in the CITES Secretariat's offices and had transferred funds to cover a three-year period. The British customs official who was currently there, however, had expressed a wish to leave after two years and it had been decided that I might be the best person to plug the remaining twelve-month gap. After talking to my wife and the Chief Constable, the former being, of course, the more important, it was agreed. For legal reasons, I was formally loaned to the United Nations by the Secretary of State for Scotland.

On 1 October 1997, I walked into the CITES office. It was to turn out to be my workplace for the next 14 years. In that time, I would be promoted to Senior Officer, Anti-smuggling, Fraud and Organized Crime and would eventually retire as Chief of Enforcement. While it would have been laughable to suggest that I would ever focus solely on wildlife crime, I'd have told you not to be so damn silly had anyone suggested that I might hold diplomatic status, get a tour of the White House courtesy of the US Secret Service and the US Capitol Building courtesy of its police force, spend five days crossing the Tibetan Plateau to visit anti-poaching squads at over 5,000 metres, interview inmates of Zimbabwe's Central Prison in Harare, join patrols and investigators in the mangroves of the Sundarbans, the jungles of Sumatra, the savannahs of east and southern Africa and the rainforests of the Amazon, engage in light aircraft and helicopter patrols over the plains of Africa, travel on jet-boats used by federal border guards and fishery inspection departments on the Caspian Sea, provide testimony to the US House of Representatives, chair a committee during a Heads-of-State forum hosted by Vladimir Putin, draft and negotiate multi-national agreements, make presentations to the UN Crime Congress and to international organized crime and terrorism seminars and help establish the International Consortium on Combating Wildlife Crime, a partnership between CITES, Interpol, the UN Office on Drugs and Crime, the World Bank and the World Customs Organization to support countries, especially in the developing world, in protecting their natural resources. My subsequent enforcement-related travels amounted to over 2 million kilometres, equivalent to circling the globe 50 times, and I visited 66 countries in all, many time and again.

Throughout those 14 years I was the only member of the CITES Secretariat dedicated solely to enforcement matters. For a significant part of that period, I was the only official in any international governmental organization (including Interpol, the UN Office on Drugs and Crime and the World Customs Organization) who was devoted to wildlife crime. It was therefore perhaps not surprising that, having given an interview to an international press agency, I subsequently read an article about me headed 'The UN's Lone Ranger'.

I was extremely privileged over the course of almost a decade and a half to be given a detailed insight into international wildlife crime, which I believe few others have gained. Some of what follows in this book will be recognized by parts of the law enforcement and conservation communities but will be expressed in language, and with a frankness, which I have not been able to use in the past. Many of the criticisms, which I regard as constructive, have been included in formal reports that I have presented to hundreds, and sometimes thousands, of delegates attending international meetings and conferences. Then, though, they were couched in the diplomatic prose of the United Nations. Almost every formal document I drafted was subject to editing in the corporate style of the CITES Secretariat. It was perfectly right and proper that it was but this does, inevitably, inhibit the ability to express oneself freely.

It is not my intention to ridicule or disparage in any way what is taking place in some parts of the world. Neither is it my intention to embarrass any particular individual, country or organization. I trust readers will be informed and even entertained by the descriptions of some of the more bizarre encounters I have had. I dare say that those who are very familiar with wildlife law enforcement or CITES will be able to identify some of the countries, and perhaps even individuals, I describe but I do not see that anything is gained by my naming them, except where it would be utterly pointless not to. In a similar vein, I have deliberately restricted any specifically negative portrayals to incidents or experiences that are now more than a decade old. Such depictions should not be taken to reflect what might be found today - at least, I sincerely hope the same could not be found today.

A period of retirement has enabled me to reflect on what I did and also on what the agencies I was associated with, or collaborated with, did. It has provided me with an opportunity to consider where I, personally, may have missed opportunities to make more progress, and also where the national and international response to wildlife crime might be improved and enhanced. Hindsight offers perspectives that are not available when one is caught up in the frenetic daily routines of a job. I have found myself wondering why I did not take certain actions sooner, or why I did not raise certain issues during my period of UN service. As a retired United Nations official, I am bound by the following regulation:

> Staff members shall exercise the utmost discretion with regard to all matters of official business. They shall not communicate to any Government, entity, person or any other source any information known to them by reason of their official position that they know or ought to have known has not been made public, except as appropriate in the normal course of their duties or by authorization of the Secretary-General. These obligations do not cease upon separation from service…

I have, in writing this book, studiously attempted to comply with this requirement. In my opinion, nothing in the following chapters discloses 'information' which might be considered confidential. In the course of my United Nations service, I was privy to significant amounts of private, restricted or classified material. None of that is replicated, repeated or disclosed here. I have, however, recounted experiences of a curious, interesting or relevant nature which might not have been open to experience by anyone other than a UN official. I do not believe the UN regulation quoted above was intended to gag its staff from describing instances that might contribute to the enhancement of the general understanding of issues that are worthy of greater public and political attention.

I would dearly love to name some names and some countries and to describe some of the utterly appalling things I saw or heard about. But it would not be fitting for a retired UN official to do so. I also have to bear in mind that doing so would, in some instances, place specific people at great risk. My repeated visits to particular nations allowed me to establish close working relations with certain individuals, often government or institution employees, who ended up showing me a degree of trust and confidence which I treasure but which I cannot now, or ever, break. They provided insights into realms of corruption, abuse of authority and wickedness that were sometimes horrendous. Those responsible deserve to be named and shamed but I cannot do so without jeopardizing my contacts. I have shaken the hands of, and even dined with, a number of individuals around the world who I would certainly never allow to enter my own home. They presented a public face of being dedicated and caring politicians, government officials or employers while actually being self-serving, hypocritical, manipulative and abusive characters; several of them were worse than people I had put behind bars in Scotland. One of the things I learned when I was a detective was that policemen and criminals can often spot each other in a crowd. There were several people with whom I shook hands who, when they looked me in the eye, knew that they weren't fooling me, while I knew that my diplomatic pleasantries were not fooling them either. I can only hope that government or regime changes will remove such people from power and influence.

It was, though, my great pleasure and honour to meet many individuals who dedicated themselves, often in the face of opposition or despite a lack of support, to enforcing their nation's laws and protecting their country's natural resources. I saw, many times, just how much could be achieved by a few stalwarts. I also saw, though, a failure to grasp how serious wildlife crime has become in recent decades and was frustrated by this and by the lack of a truly co-ordinated response at both national and international levels. This frustration helped prompt me to write this book in the hope that it may stimulate some reflection on the part of those who can influence policy- and decision-making.

The unlawful exploitation, theft, illegal trans-border transportation and eventual illicit trade of natural resources have been noted, in recent years, to have evolved into significantly profitable activities, attracting organized and sophisticated criminal alliances and networks. There are increasing grounds to believe, too, that some groups engaged in rebel and terrorist actions may be participating in the illegal harvest and trade of fauna and flora to fund activities that threaten national, regional and, potentially, international security.

However, to date, the overall reaction of the international community has not been at a similar level of organization or sophistication, allowing it to present a fully adequate response or offer a meaningful deterrent. In many respects the response has been haphazard: across the political spectrum and among decision- and policy-makers, on the part of national and international law enforcement agencies, in the acquisition of sufficient insight into what is driving the apparently ever-increasing criminality, with regards to identifying and bringing to justice those individuals responsible for directing and controlling criminal acts and in the provision of financial, logistical and technical support to those nations most seriously affected by these crimes.

That the response to date might be assessed as being haphazard should not be taken to mean that it has necessarily been random, hit-and-miss or arbitrary. There have been many examples, across and throughout the areas noted above, of excellent work and initiatives. However, the overall response has perhaps been unsystematic, irregular and insufficiently targeted. To a significant extent, the response in the past and today has inevitably been haphazard in nature due to factors such as a lack of awareness of the problem or its gravity, insufficient appreciation on the part of potential stakeholders of how they might contribute, inadequate communication, co-ordination and collaboration at national, regional and international levels and, perhaps most importantly, inadequate resources or an inefficient use and deployment of existing resources.

No one can change the world overnight. We will never right all the wrongs in this world. But if we do not make a better job of combating international wildlife crime soon, we may have to say goodbye to a number of endangered species. And the number of species entering high-risk categories seems to increase with every passing year.

CITES, CONSERVATION AND CRIME

Given its formal title — the Convention on International Trade in Endangered Species of Wild Fauna and Flora — it is little wonder that the treaty is more commonly spoken of as CITES. It is sometimes also referred to as the Washington Convention, particularly in French-speaking countries, the text of the treaty having been agreed at a meeting in that city on 3 March 1973.

This agreement between governments is intended primarily to ensure two things: firstly, that any animal or plant specimen regulated by the Convention's provisions will have been obtained in accordance with national legislation, i.e. it is of legal origin, meaning that one cannot trade items that have been poached or illegally harvested; and secondly, that trading the particular animal or plant will not have a detrimental impact upon remaining specimens in the wild. I would always use parrots as an example. If a country has only three parrots left from an entire species in the wild, and two of them are female, one could not trade the male, as that would lead to extinction of the species. That is, of course, ridiculously simplistic, as no nation would engage in trade if a species had reduced to only three individuals, but it makes the point.

As with any form of legislation, CITES incorporates some complex conditions, together with exclusions and exemptions. It also suffers from a considerable degree of misunderstanding. Perhaps the one I used to come across most regularly related to CITES itself. I would be asked, 'Why doesn't CITES do…?' or 'CITES has failed to…' as if CITES were an organization. It is not. It is international law. Consequently, if the Convention succeeds or fails in regulating trade, the success or failure results from the way in which it has been implemented, either by individual countries or through countries working together. The provisions of the Convention can be adapted or adjusted, but it cannot, in and of itself, do anything.

Another misunderstood aspect, one very relevant to my activities, related to the scope of the Convention. CITES applies solely to international trade. While the parties to the Convention, 'parties' meaning the nations that have agreed to be bound by its provisions, may make recommendations in relation to domestic trade, the legally-binding obligations of CITES apply only to international cross-border movements of wildlife. When one is considering crime, of course, it makes no sense to consider such cross-border aspects in isolation. Contraband that is being smuggled from one nation to another must, firstly, be obtained within one country and will subsequently be traded within another. This involves a chain of criminality and it is senseless to focus on just one or two links of that chain. The CITES community needs to consider both poaching and domestic consumption in designing its strategies, even if the text of the Convention focusses mainly on what takes place at borders.

Another misunderstanding arose in what is meant by 'trade'. This was frequently interpreted as meaning some form of commerce. In fact, the Convention defines this as export, re-export, import and introduction from the sea. As a result, by way of example, if one botanical garden wishes to make a gift of a plant to another, located abroad, the movement would still fall within the terms of CITES, even though no money may change hands. The word 'wildlife' also causes confusion. For CITES purposes, this means both fauna and flora, although many may not associate the term with plant life. Nomenclature can be a complicated subject and I also struggled, in the early days, to get to grips with what can be an all-encompassing CITES approach. In later years, I would still come across such confusion or misunderstanding. I found, for example, that even if people I met in the law enforcement community were already aware that the Convention included 'flora', they did not associate that with timber and, so would not appreciate that CITES had considerable potential in relation to the combating of illegal logging.

Although it is often described as the 'UN Convention on...' this is not strictly correct. CITES did not evolve through UN processes and its activities are not reported upon to UN bodies such as the General Assembly. There is a link with the United Nations in that its secretariat is provided for, and administered by, the United Nations Environment Programme. As a result, my colleagues and I were all UN officials. The work programmes of the Convention and the secretariat were decided upon, and overseen, by what was termed the Conference of the Parties, a rather formal phrase describing meetings of the countries that use the provisions of the Convention to regulate trade. In between those meetings, which take place every three years, a form of executive body, called the CITES Standing Committee, monitors everything.

Each CITES Party must establish a national management authority to administer the Convention on a day-to-day basis and a scientific authority to determine whether trade can be sustainable and not pose a threat to wild populations. These national management authorities, if they choose to consent to trade, do so by issuing permits and certificates which must accompany shipments. Information concerning all authorized trade must be submitted on an annual basis by each CITES country.

The Convention does not control trade in all wildlife, but instead has three appendices listing animals and plants which warrant regulation, and it is their level of endangerment or degree of conservation concern that determines in which appendix they will be listed. Additionally, it is the impact of trade upon a species that, strictly speaking, determines these listings. Some species are in danger of extinction because of influences and impacts other than trade, such as loss of habitat or global warming. They will not be listed. A good illustration of this arose at the most recent CITES Conference of the Parties, in March 2013, when it was proposed that the existing listing of polar bears should be altered. No change did take place, as the meeting decided that it was not trade which was increasing the level of conservation concern for the species.

The first appendix lists those species at greatest risk of extinction and this, essentially, means that no commercial international trade is allowed. Tigers, for example, are listed there. The second appendix incorporates those animals and plants that might be threatened by extinction, if their international trade (commercial or non-commercial) were not strictly regulated. In most cases, if a species is listed, this has the effect of regulation taking effect regardless of what form of trade takes place, i.e. whether the animal is alive or dead or if it has been converted into some form of product. An example of this, for the second appendix, would be trade in caviar. The word caviar does not appear in the appendix, but the product is regulated because it is made from the eggs of sturgeon, which are listed. The third appendix contains species that individual countries have chosen to list because the specific geographical populations of those animals or plants are at risk of national extinction and the countries wish the rest of the CITES community to provide regulatory assistance.

Perhaps not surprisingly, a good deal of my focus related to species listed in Appendix I, not because of legal trade, which was prohibited, but because the animals were being poached or, in the case of plants, illegally harvested and entered into illicit markets. The Convention requires parties to penalize movements of species which violate the terms of CITES, and my main role was to assist them in that process. The CITES appendices list over 30,000 different animal and plant species. Fortunately, only a relatively small percentage of them are regularly in legal trade and, better still, even fewer are affected by illicit trade. Unfortunately, it is the latter that tend to be most endangered.

Historically, customs officers have been the frontline in enforcing and implementing the Convention since it is they, in the law enforcement community, who control cross-border movements. Consequently, CITES looked to customs authorities not only to regulate the legal trade but also to intercept illicit wildlife shipments. Police agencies have, though, become increasingly involved in CITES enforcement, since illegal trade in wildlife can only be combated effectively if both ends of the criminal chain are targeted. It was logical, therefore, that I had regular contact with Interpol, the world's policing body, and the World Customs Organization (WCO), the international agency that represents customs' interests. As time passed, I would also work with the United Nations Office on Drugs and Crime (UNODC), since its staff devote much of their time to combating organized crime.

One of the things I discovered, very soon after my arrival in Geneva, where the CITES Secretariat has its offices, was that both the Secretariat and parties seemed to have evolved a view in which 'compliance' and 'enforcement' often appeared intertwined or, worse, to my way of thinking, were thought of as almost one and the same. In my opinion, compliance should be defined as whether or not an individual or country has conformed to the provisions of the Convention. In the case of an individual such as a wildlife trader, compliance could be measured by his or her acquiescence with the rules of CITES. Had a permit been applied for before wildlife was moved cross-border, for example? In the case of a country, were its officials ensuring before issuing a permit that wildlife to be moved internationally was of a legal origin? By comparison, enforcement can be thought of as an action taken to ensure compliance. For example, the police enforce speed restrictions by the use of cameras or radar devices and this encourages drivers to comply with the speed limit.

While compliance and enforcement will inevitably come together at times, I found that, to a degree, a significant number of parties viewed the enforcement-related activities of the Secretariat as focussing upon whether they, the CITES nations, were complying with their obligations. This appeared to have built up areas of substantial sensitivity and I noted that this could particularly be seen in something of a reluctance on the part of some States to communicate information, especially confidential information, relating to illegal trade. Although I recognized that part of my work would have to involve assessing countries' compliance with their obligations, I believed I ought to concentrate on helping them to enforce the Convention in combating illegal trade. I also thought this to be the best use of my particular skills and experience. I noticed, for instance, that communication between the Secretariat and the parties was something of a one-way street. We encouraged countries to advise us about instances of smuggling but we were not then using the information to good effect. I already knew from my first career that police officers are sometimes discouraged from contributing to centralized intelligence databases if they get nothing in return. As a result, I devised intelligence bulletins, drawn up using national data, which were distributed worldwide and intended to help countries respond to wildlife crime. I also increased the sharing of intelligence with counterpart agencies, such as Interpol and the WCO. Another idea I copied from back home was to introduce a Certificate of Commendation scheme which recognized exemplary enforcement actions by countries. These proved very popular among recipients, just as a Chief Constable's Commendation had been welcomed by my police officers.

I learned that CITES had two technical committees, the Animals Committee and the Plants Committee, which operate using volunteers on a part-time basis to bring scientific and conservation expertise to bear in monitoring trade. A significant remit of both committees is to review whether trade in fauna and flora is being conducted sustainably. I also learned that the notion of an Enforcement Committee had been suggested in the past, but that it had been rejected, due to the parties' concern that it would be some form of compliance supervisory body. In due course, I would be able to obtain agreement to the establishment, instead, of CITES Enforcement Task Forces and the CITES Enforcement Experts Group. The former allowed the secretariat to bring together relevant law enforcement officials, from a variety of agencies and from each region of the world, to examine species-specific illegal trade. These people would be drawn from countries where illegal trade originated, nations through which wildlife was smuggled and countries where illicit trade was occurring. The Expert Group consisted of similar individuals but their role was to look at general or specific enforcement issues. In the case of each, it was stressed that they had no mandate to consider compliance by individual countries.

In 1997, relatively few people, whether in the conservation or law enforcement communities, acknowledged the serious scale of international wildlife crime, the involvement of organized crime groups and networks or the level of profit that criminals were making. There also seemed to be a significant failure to appreciate how drastically such crimes were impacting upon particular endangered species. Much of the 14 years I would spend with CITES would be spent trying to raise awareness of crime, alongside attempts to strategically and operationally support countries and national enforcement bodies in their efforts to combat criminal natural resource exploitation. This book outlines the nature of wildlife crime, both in general and in relation to specific species, yet wildlife crime is so far-reaching, especially in the range of animals and plants involved, that I have had be selective in the species I consider here. The fact that a particular species may not be mentioned does not mean that I have ignored it or am not aware of illicit trade affecting it.

The CITES community, its Secretaries General and the CITES Secretariat have done sterling work to combat illegal trade, especially given that secretariat staff numbers reduced constantly throughout my period of service. Counterpart international organizations have also participated considerably and the range of contributing bodies has increased significantly. I also witnessed the expansion of regional wildlife enforcement networks, which have brought neighbouring countries together in a collaborative fashion and which have encouraged the development of national multi-agency responses. These networks have achieved, and continue to achieve, worthy successes and it is very pleasing that new ones are being created across the globe. Specific multi-national projects and operations have met with commendable results in relation to seizures and arrests. Yet, despite this, wildlife criminals have persistently outpaced everyone.

Estimates of the value of illegal trade in wildlife range from the equivalent of between ten and twenty billion US dollars per year. Since these figures do not include illegal harvesting of marine or timber species, the actual sum will be much, much more. Natural resource crime may be the third or fourth most important form of crime in the world today. And profits, numbers and their position on league tables aside, these crimes are pushing several species toward extinction. The smuggling of animals and plants across national borders also brings significant risk relating to the spread of disease. Infections can have serious consequences for both human and plant life in countries through which, or into which, wildlife contraband passes. The ebola virus that affects primates, for example, can also infect humans and there is currently no cure for this invariably fatal disease. Invasive alien species can have devastating effects upon indigenous fauna and flora, sometimes taking over and wiping out national species. Illicit harvesting, such as the illegal logging of forests, can lead to total deforestation of areas, with the subsequent impact on global warming or the destabilization of landscapes and hillsides. The seriousness of wildlife crime, the profits illicitly generated and the number of species adversely affected increased constantly throughout my career. it does not make for contented reflection from my position in retirement.

WILDLIFE CRIME AND ORGANIZED CRIME

I remember very clearly the days when I was representing Scotland on UK committees considering wildlife crime, and our frustrations when we tried to get central government, in the guise of the Home Office, to take the subject seriously. Home Office representatives would invariably ask for statistics to demonstrate that such crimes were prevalent or rising. Data was everything and no decision could be taken in its absence. At that time, in the early to mid-1990s, and to this day, all police forces were required to submit annual crime figures, from which the Home Office collated crime statistics. Those forces did not, though, throw everything in the direction of Whitehall but only reported what had been designated, by the civil service, as 'recordable' crimes. These were what one might have expected: murder, rape, robbery and assault, for example.

The problem, for us, was that crime involving wildlife was not recordable. That did not mean that individual police forces were not keeping some form of records in relation to such crimes but they were not storing them in the way they did for mainstream crimes. And, importantly, they were not providing any statistics on an annual basis to the mandarins of Whitehall.

And so we found ourselves in the crazy catch 22 position where the Home Office was insisting upon the production of figures which it, itself, had determined that the police did not have to keep. We were getting nowhere fast.

This was partly a historical problem. Crime records were closely associated with, and to an extent determined by, complaints. To a significant degree, the police learn about crime because someone complains that they have been the victim of one. Not everyone, though, contacts the police when they become a victim. This may be because they feel it is a minor matter, such as vandalism, and they think the police either will not be interested or will not be able to do anything about it. Or they may, in the case of rape victims for instance, feel that they do not want to face the trauma of an investigation which will inevitably involve intrusive questions, a medical examination and, in due course, perhaps a trial.

The police and civil service have long appreciated that not all crime is reported and that is what prompted the Crime Survey, an effort to try and capture a true picture of how much crime is being committed, rather than what is reported.

It is the absence of formal complaints that leads to difficulties in both recording and measuring wildlife crime. In Scotland, if someone steals an egg from the nest of a peregrine falcon, intending that it be hatched out and illegally traded for falconry, neither of the parent birds is likely to turn up at a police office to report the matter. If an elephant is shot in a savannah area of Africa and has its tusks hacked out, no matriarch from the herd will make her way to the nearest Ranger Station to complain. The relevant authorities may never learn that such a thing has happened.

In Africa, the authorities, in this case rangers or wardens from a Wildlife or Parks Department, may subsequently stumble across the carcass during the course of anti-poaching patrols or population surveys, but this could be weeks or months later. In some parts of the continent, aerial surveys are sometimes the only effective way for such departments to discover carcasses, but some departments only have the necessary financial and logistical resources to conduct this type of counting every few years.

In Scotland, it would be pretty well unheard of for a police officer to come across, in whatever manner, the theft from a falcon nest site. Many nest sites are monitored by Raptor Study Groups, ornithologists who visit nesting sites to conduct population studies, but these too can be irregular. And, unlike in Africa, there will be no carcass remains to indicate that anything is amiss. Eggs, furthermore, can be taken from nests by animal or bird predators, so the absence of an egg or eggs (if their presence had previously been observed by a Group member) may not necessarily indicate that a crime has occurred.

With all this in mind, it was extremely difficult for us to convince the UK civil service that wildlife crime was serious and that more needed to be done, both to respond to and combat it. The figures that were available tended to be from the NGO community. The Royal Society for the Protection of Birds, for example, had been recording suspected incidents of bird persecution, egg thefts and the like for many years but the civil service and sometimes, too, the police, tend not to trust 'unofficial' data.

This was the situation in the early 1990s. In 2012, the UK House of Commons Environmental Audit Committee published a report, having conducted a review of wildlife crime. It noted that a central database to record all such crimes, which it had called for in 2004, had yet to be introduced. Is it any wonder that we do not have an accurate overview of crimes involving fauna and flora? In a nation as advanced as the UK, this is an absolute disgrace.

But we are not alone. I think it can probably be argued that India suffers from much more significant wildlife crime than Britain, crime which is potentially devastating in terms of species extinction. And yet, for most of my time with CITES, the Central Government of India had no effective overview of what was happening, for example, to tigers. I have seen several cases of government officials in New Delhi, responding to questions from members of parliament, having to rely on statistics provided by the Wildlife Protection Society of India, an NGO as well known in that nation as the RSPB is in the UK.

The same lack of data will probably apply in most countries of the world. And collecting it, or starting to do so, is further complicated by the fact that, in many parts of the globe, the agencies who deal with wildlife matters are not seen as part of the law enforcement community and have nothing to do with recording crime.

Having encountered data collection problems in Britain, it was not a surprise when I moved to Geneva and found that international statistics were sadly lacking. I also found, though, that decision-makers across the world, in the political and law enforcement communities, were tending to adopt a stance that was becoming ever more prevalent in the UK. It was not enough to produce statistics demonstrating that there was a lot of crime (whatever type of crime that might be) - one had also to convince the people who held the purse strings or who determined priorities that such crime was 'serious' or 'organized'.

By the end of the 1990s, another consideration had been added – was a crime type linked to terrorism, or might it be linked?

I was therefore faced with trying to convince those who mattered, at national and international level, that wildlife crime deserved attention, yet had no figures to back up my appeals. And what was not helping was that Interpol, when asked by the media if wildlife crime involved 'organized crime', was tending to reply in those days that it had no evidence to demonstrate such involvement. This was really frustrating for me.

It is probably worth taking some time at this point to look at what is meant by 'organized crime'. Understandably, the layman tends to think that this means groups or families of criminals like the mafia, be they American, Italian or Russian, Chinese triads or Japanese yakuza. Well, yes it can mean that, but it is much more complex a story. There has been, and continues to be, great debate about the meaning of the phrase 'organized crime'.

Article 2 of the United Nations Convention against Transnational Organized Crime contains definitions that provide useful guidance:

> (a) 'Organized criminal group' shall mean a structured group of three or more persons, existing for a period of time and acting in concert with the aim of committing one or more serious crimes or offences established in accordance with this Convention, in order to obtain, directly or indirectly, a financial or other material benefit;

> (b) 'Serious crime' shall mean conduct constituting an offence punishable by a maximum deprivation of liberty of at least four years or a more serious penalty;

Given the number of people that are usually needed to carry out a cross-border wildlife crime, definition (a) would appear to be easily fulfilled. Definition (b), however, causes considerable problems for some countries, as their national legislation dealing with wildlife crime – for example the smuggling of endangered species – does not include any term of imprisonment whatsoever as a sentencing option. Indeed, in some nations, it is not even a crime but purely an administrative matter for which a monetary penalty will be imposed by, for example, a customs officer.

Fitting in with legal definitions does not really help when one is attempting to set wildlife crime into a clearly recognizable organized crime context. I realized that I had to try and make it plainly understandable.

What also did not help was that, worldwide, there were very few cases that had been brought to court where the circumstances illustrated an organized nature. All too often, and this still applies, those who ended up being prosecuted were minor links in the long chain of criminality that stretches from one end, where fauna or flora is illegally harvested, to the other, where it is sold to the consumer. They might otherwise be the small links in the middle, the men and women engaged to transport animals, plants or products from one country to another.

The people who formed the links close to, but importantly far enough removed from, both ends of the chain were hardly ever identified, let alone brought anywhere near to justice. These are the people who control and direct what happens and it is these links that reap the real rewards.

Until now, as far as I am aware, few countries have managed to prosecute anyone who had already been known to the authorities to be a member of an organized crime group. No individual has ended up in jail in the manner of, say, John Gotti. He became the head of the Gambino mafia-like crime family in New York, an organized crime group that controlled activities ranging from loan sharking to extortion to illegal gambling. He was eventually convicted after other criminals gave evidence against him. He died in prison in 2002. (As an aside, it is worth noting that one of the crimes of which he was convicted was 'racketeering', a charge that has also been used effectively recently by the authorities in South Africa when dealing with those involved in poaching of and illegal trade in rhino horn.) But I, and others like me, did not then have cases which we could hold up as examples to demonstrate that natural resource crimes were truly grave.

Eventually, I decided that I would have to take a different approach and, in the early 2000s, came up with the notion of using something that was being employed elsewhere in policing and political circles. This was the concept of 'indicators'. In the UK, performance indicators had been introduced as a means of assessing how well police forces were carrying out their duties. Several were straightforward, such as how many crimes had been detected in the course of a given time period. Had the person responsible been identified and reported for prosecution? How long was it taking for officers to arrive at the scene of an incident after an emergency call had been received?

It struck me that if indicators could be used to illustrate the success or failures of the police, then they could surely also be used to demonstrate the success, sophistication or organization of criminals. I created a list of subject headings, under each of which could be described practical illustrations, demonstrating the level of organization involved. I must have been heading in the right direction because this approach was subsequently used by the United Nations Office on Drugs and Crime and the United States Department of Justice.

The indicators I developed were not intended to be an exhaustive list and neither were they laid out in any particular order. The following chapters incorporate the indicator headings I used and include examples not only of organized crime issues but also of some of the day-to-day hurdles which face the enforcement community.

COMMITTING THE CRIME

The ways in which wildlife-related crimes are carried out tell us much about those behind them and what is needed to combat them.

THE STRUCTURE OF POACHING

It may be useful to examine first what is meant by poaching, especially as there are countries - and Britain is one of them - where the term 'poacher' can conjure up the image of a likeable rogue sallying forth into the countryside to bag a pheasant or salmon from the estate of some absentee landlord in what might be viewed as a blow for the working classes. Such a jolly jape, set in the picturesque landscape of a Constable or Landseer painting, is in total contrast to the violent and bloody illegal harvesting occurring in Africa or Asia and may be one reason why poaching may not immediately be thought of as serious crime.

Poaching is generally regarded as the taking of animals without the legal right to do so. The manner of the taking varies considerably. Its simplest form, perhaps, is the setting of a wire snare on the path regularly used by the target species. The snare is designed to encircle either the animal's leg or neck and strangle it or hold it in place until the hunter comes along to kill it with a firearm, club or knife.

Snares are used throughout the world and have been for centuries. In some countries, such as Britain, their use is legal under certain conditions and to take specific species.

There are a range of other forms of trap into which animals and birds are lured by food, using either live or dead bait. Our image from the movies might be of a large pit, sometimes with spikes placed at the bottom, covered with vegetation through which the passing animal will fall. I cannot think of any instance of such a trap being used in recent years: they involve too much work and the end can be accomplished by much easier means.

Nets strung in appropriate places can be effective but require time to erect, can be hard to conceal and also need to be checked frequently, which can be present problems for poachers.

If the hunters want the animal's body parts for anything other than human consumption, then poison is a very effective killing method. Meat, or occasionally vegetable matter, laced with an appropriate toxin, is placed either on a path used by the target animal or in the area where it will feed or graze. Poisoning becomes especially effective when the target is a species which is used to having humans contribute to their diet. In some of the private reserves, game ranches and safari parks in Africa, the management (either regularly or at certain times of year) will distribute fodder or other dietary supplements for their animals. This practice has been exploited by poachers, with several incidents in South Africa in recent years in which rhinoceroses have been killed by poisoned cabbages or pumpkins, placed where they were used to finding food supplements.

An added bonus in using poison, from the poacher's perspective, is that it is noiseless. A firearm brings the considerable risk of shots being heard by anti-poaching patrols or by local residents who may contact the authorities, and for this reason the use of tranquilizer darts has made an appearance in southern and eastern Africa in recent years. But the darts, the rifles that fire them and the tranquilizing chemicals themselves are not easy to acquire. The fact that some people have done so demonstrates the increased organization and sophistication that has entered into these criminal activities.

One horrendous side-effect of the employment of tranquilizers in rhino poaching is that, once unconscious, the creatures have their horns literally hacked out of their heads by the poachers and wake to face a slow death by bleeding.

Poison is also in widespread use in what are sometimes described as revenge attacks on animals. Such incidents - not, strictly speaking, poaching, but worth mentioning here - occur when villagers are motivated to rid themselves of species that may be preying upon them, their livestock or their crops. As might be imagined, they are commonly carried out on big cats and will be deployed to target, for instance, tigers in India, leopards in Nepal or jaguars in Brazil. Poison is also laid in parts of Africa and Asia in response to crop-raiding elephants.

It is usually easy for local authorities to distinguish revenge or deterrent cases from true poaching incidents, as the animal carcass will be found intact. That is not to say, though, that there are not also occasions where a villager, having been moved to kill a 'pest' animal, will subsequently strip the carcass of, say, its skin or tusks. After all, if you are living in poverty it may be silly to look a gift horse (or tiger or elephant) in the mouth, so to speak.

Poaching can also involve some rather bizarre methods. There have been many cases in India in which hunters, but also villagers in revenge incidents, have either re-routed overhead live electricity cables or run wires from them, so that they stretch across paths followed by elephants. In the late 1990s, in northern Cambodia, I was told of poachers who had set mines on jungle trails used by tigers. This was favoured in some areas because of the high number of munitions left over from the days of the Khmer Rouge. This method was apparently also used occasionally in Vietnam, again because of easy access to military weaponry. I have not, however, heard of mines being used in recent years.

Munitions are certainly not quiet and seemed only to have been used in the most remote areas. They also risk causing very considerable damage to the target animal, since they detonate when the animal's paw or pad presses down upon them. In the late 1990s, when it was the bones of a tiger that poachers sought, the damage caused to its head and skin when the mine exploded did not matter too much. However, as the skin trade became increasingly valuable and important, this method was just far too destructive.

I have been told that mines have also been used against elephants but, as with tigers, they can prove devastating and almost inevitably damage, if not destroy, the tusks.

Marine species are illegally harvested using several of the methods described above, especially - and not surprisingly - netting. They too, though, can be poached using poison and explosives, although nets are normally needed to sweep up the resulting dead or stunned fish.

17

The biggest disadvantage of all these tactics - because few poachers will care that they often cause very considerable suffering to the animal - is that (with a few exceptions and only with very careful placement) they are indiscriminate. If poachers set a snare for a tiger or rhinoceros, that is what they want to catch. If they have had to sneak, perhaps over a long distance, into a well-patrolled national park, probably in the dark, at risk of animal attack or other natural hazard, and have then to repeat the journey the next night to inspect the snare, the last thing they want is to discover that it is holding onto a worthless wild pig or deer.

Consequently, the killing approach favoured by most poachers is the same as that used by legal hunters: the firearm. Although one will occasionally encounter poachers using a bow and arrow or a crossbow, it is rare. Handguns are rarely used for poaching. Revolvers or semi-automatics, despite what you see in Westerns or cops-and-robbers films, are very inaccurate except at close range. Consequently, poachers will opt for long-barrelled weapons.

These can be either shotguns or, more popularly, rifles. A shotgun is more effective in the hands of the less-skilled shooter because its pellets spread out and so are more likely to hit the intended target. They have a lower physical impact, though, which also reduces with distance, so a shotgun is good for bringing down a bird in flight but will certainly not stop a rhino or tiger unless the shooter is very close - the last thing he wants to be if the animal can quickly close the gap and gore or claw him to death.

A rifle, by contrast, expels a bullet that can travel very considerable distances and which will punch into even the thickest-skinned creatures. Its force is such that the shock of the impact alone can knock it over and rip apart or fatally injure its brain, heart, lungs or other major organs, so that death quickly follows. In the right hands, a rifle can be extremely accurate.

Rifles vary. In single-shot rifles, a fresh bullet has to be loaded into the breech after the trigger has been pulled, while rifles fitted with a magazine hold several bullets. In semi-automatic rifles, a bullet is loaded into the breech after each pull of the trigger, while in fully automatic weapons, bullets continue to be fired as long as the trigger is pulled back and until the magazine is empty.

The majority of poachers use semi-automatic or fully automatic weapons. In some of these, the semi-automatic feature can be converted to fully automatic at the simple flick of a switch. The majority of such rifles were originally designed for military purposes. In most areas of the world where poaching is rife, these weapons are left over from armed conflicts, either within that nation or in neighbouring countries. In many of these places, weapons are widespread, commonly kept in homes, and can be acquired very cheaply. A survey in 2012 estimated that 650 million weapons were in the hands of civilians around the world, while military, police and other government officials had 225 million.

The type of weapon favoured by poachers is sometimes referred to as an assault rifle, the type of gun which have been used in several of the multiple death and injury shootings that have occurred, for example, at schools in America in recent decades. These incidents have illustrated just how quickly, and morbidly efficiently, one person can bring another's life to an end or change it forever.

Perhaps the world's best known assault rifle is the Kalashnikov AK-47, named after its Russian inventor. As the model number suggests, it was developed in 1947 and became the standard weapon of the Soviet army. As the influence of the USSR spread around the world, so too did its armaments and AK-47s can now be found across the globe and particularly in the developing world. They are somewhat clumsy and not especially sophisticated but they are reliable, easily repaired and cheap to buy, while the ammunition for them is also widely available and inexpensive. The standard AK-47 magazine holds 30 bullets (rounds). When fully automatic mode is selected, the Kalashnikov can in theory fire 600 rounds per minute. If that were not firepower enough, the AK-47 can also be quickly adapted to fire grenades, which is not something that anti-poaching personnel like to come up against. Many have, though, particularly those in the Kenya Wildlife Service, who regularly encounter very heavily-armed poachers entering from neighbouring Somalia where all sorts of weapons may be readily obtained.

The AK-47 has been copied and is now manufactured in many countries other than Russia, which has made the weapon cheaper. The most modern model, the one favoured by Osama bin Laden and which he was pictured holding in videos, can sell on the black market for the equivalent of 2,000 US dollars. In the Niger Delta, an older model AK-47 might cost as little as 75 dollars.

Less common, but seen more frequently in recent years, are the latest model high-powered military-style weapon or the high-quality hunting rifles that are designed specifically for big game hunting. These are equally efficient, effective and deadly. The hunting rifle, though, will always be the more accurate, especially in the hands of a true marksman.

When these weapons are combined, they become particularly lethal to man and beast. Some poaching gangs making intrusions into South Africa's national parks in search of rhinos, for example, have been seen to be armed with a mixture of guns. The most accomplished marksman in the group carried a hunting rifle and it was his job to kill the animal. His companions, maybe three, four or five in number, had automatic assault rifles. Although they could assist the marksmen in killing rhinos, they were primarily there to protect him and their job was to kill any rangers or other law enforcement officers that might intercept the gang.

This brings me to the first of the organized crime indicators and the structured nature of endangered species poaching.

Even if its cost is as low as 75 dollars, an AK-47 will remain beyond the pocket of most rural residents of Africa or Asia. When one then considers that a big game hunting rifle, capable of firing a .375 Holland and Holland or .416 Rigby bullet, the calibres favoured by those who want guaranteed 'stopping power', will cost anywhere between 1,500 and 20,000 dollars, then that's a whole new ball game.

And that is just for the gun. It is of no use without bullets. AK-47 ammunition can be bought cheaply, several bullets for the equivalent of a dollar. However, rounds for a hunting rifle are a different matter, especially as there is not such a ready black market for those calibres. Good-quality big game ammo can cost 90 dollars for 20, but even if all the poacher needs is AK-47 bullets, he is going to need many of them and this, again, involves money he probably does not have.

This is where organized crime comes in. Someone further up the criminal chain seeks out an individual who lives where the target species can be found. Ideally, it will be someone who already has experience in illegal hunting, probably of a subsistence nature, poaching to put food on the table. Throughout the world there are families, and sometimes whole tribes, with a centuries-long tradition of hunting. The skills have been passed down from father to son (it is usually the men who hunt) and involve not just killing or capturing the animals but tracking, skinning or dissecting them, and being able to move quickly and quietly around the land – an area they know like the back of their hand - avoiding detection by the authorities.

Hunting skills can also be found in the developed world. There is an often-told story in Scotland of a German field sportsman visiting Moray who had been guided, over several hours, by an estate stalker to within shooting distance of a red deer stag with an impressive set of antlers. This was a true trophy animal. The German sighted along his rifle and pulled the trigger. The bullet landed but not cleanly on target. The deer began to limp away. Grabbing his client's weapon, the stalker reloaded, aimed and fired. The stag dropped stone dead. The client gushed compliments on the guide's marksmanship and asked how he had ever achieved such expertise.

'It's simple,' the local man replied. 'My grandfather was head stalker on this estate, my father was head stalker and now I'm head stalker. I've been doing this, except for a break of five years, for over thirty years.' 'What did you do during those five years?' enquired the visitor. 'I killed your ancestors!' came the reply.

Hunting, legal or not, can also be a cultural and macho practice. A survey conducted in Africa many years ago found that males in a tribe loved nothing better than to head out into the bush for several days at a time to escape from their womenfolk. It provided an opportunity for them to gossip, drink home-brewed liquor, swap stories and tell dirty jokes that they wouldn't get away with at home, just as English men head for soccer games on a Saturday afternoon or American men are drawn to bars 'where everybody knows your name'.

Recruiting a lone individual for poaching will usually not be enough. For one thing, the finest tracker may not be able to hit the proverbial barn door if you give him a gun. It is not just about skills, though. Someone who can hunt down an elephant, and then efficiently aim at it and shoot it, is faced with the plain physical problem of extracting the tusks, which will mean bringing an axe with them, and somehow carrying two large tusks, the axe and the rifle back out of the park, perhaps over many miles. It simply is not practical for one person.

I have already described how some rhino poaching gangs operate in South Africa and one can see that there is a significant financial input required to equip them. Perhaps the finest example of this particular indicator can be found thousands of miles to the north and east in an environment that, in many respects, could not be more different from the savannahs where the elephant and rhino roam.

The Tibetan Plateau in western China borders Bhutan, India, Myanmar and Nepal. It is home to one of the world's most remarkable creatures, the Tibetan antelope. This antelope roams across a harsh and forbidding wilderness at heights of between 3,250 and 5,500 metres. To protect it from this tough environment, nature has endowed the antelope with a coat of hair that is regarded as the finest in the world. Not only is its habitat sparsely populated by other animals, it is also sparsely populated by humans.

The small numbers of people who do live full-time on the plateau tend to occupy settlements below the 4,000 metre level and are relatively nomadic, moving about to find grazing for their yak herds. A few other humans enter the region temporarily from time to time for specific purposes - to engage in illegal mining, for example - as the area is rich in a range of mineral deposits, including gold.

The locals are poor, simple people. They live hand to mouth, governed by the weather and the seasons. There is no money for luxuries on the plateau. It is these inhabitants who are sought out, recruited and equipped by organized crime groups.

There is probably no illegal animal harvesting anywhere in the world, apart from trawling for marine species, which calls for as great a degree of organisation as the poaching of Tibetan antelope. Gangs of men - up to twenty at a time - are required to kill the antelopes. Each will bring a particular skill, as a driver, a cook, a tracker, marksman or skinner. Each gang will have between four and seven 4x4 vehicles, carry hundreds, if not several thousand, rounds of ammunition and will usually use Chinese-manufactured AK-47s. Most gangs will have at least one AK-47 weapon per vehicle, but will often carry more, often single shot rifles. The weapon of choice will depend upon the marksmanship of gang members. AK-47s are *de rigueur,* however, because they are the best response if anti-poaching patrols appear.

The bands spend a month or more on the plateau and need appropriate quantities of fuel and food rations. Interestingly, although it would presumably offer a source of protein, the meat from poached antelopes seems hardly ever to be consumed. Some gangs will be equipped with GPS devices and, very occasionally, satellite phones, and will need appropriate clothing to cope with the temperatures on this, the world's most elevated and extensive highland area, ringed by the world's highest mountain ranges. Winter temperatures can drop to -40 C, but the wind chill factor will take temperatures considerably lower.

The people who live in this realm cannot afford, even if grouping together, to equip themselves to engage in this level of sophisticated poaching expedition. It is organized crime networks who recruit, pay, equip and direct them. And it is those same groups who subsequently take possession of the Tibetan antelope skins and arrange for them to be smuggled out of China to neighbouring countries where they will be processed into shawls that can each attract prices of up to 35,000 US dollars once they are moved to consumer nations.

The Tibetan Plateau was certainly the harshest environment I visited in my 14 years of international wildlife law enforcement, and the poaching there was more extensively organized than any I encountered elsewhere. That said, the use of light aircraft and helicopters during recent rhino poaching incidents in southern and eastern Africa has probably displaced the Tibetan antelope as the most complicated illegal target. It is a sad reflection of the seriousness of wildlife crime that we can now start to draw up this kind of poaching league table.

SOPHISTICATION OF SMUGGLING TECHNIQUES AND ROUTES

The customs officer in America who was checking parcel goods in a terminal several years ago must have wondered about the strange things people want to collect when he opened a package from southeast Asia and found many large, dead, beetle-like creatures. Not being an expert on species identification, he may have acknowledged that their colourful carapaces, horns and multiple spindly legs made for unusual and exotic specimens. Knowing that CITES regulated trade in endangered species, he sought the assistance of a wildlife inspector.

The inspector was able to tell that these creatures were not CITES-listed but picked one out of the package to examine it more closely. It was then that he and the customs official discovered that the hard shell of each beetle had been packed with amphetamines.

A few years before that incident, an officer in Miami noticed snakes arriving from South America had had cocaine wrapped in condoms forced up their rectal passages. Since not many border control officials relish a close physical inspection of venomous reptiles, it was an effective smuggling method.

It is not common to find wildlife and narcotics being smuggled together, but wildlife smuggling techniques are as colourful as the human imagination itself. Elephant ivory is stained to give it the appearance of wood or may be baked inside an outer covering of clay, to mask its true nature. Tusks are stuffed into containers full of smoked or dried fish, in the hope of masking its odour from the sniffer dogs increasingly often used at major ports. Primates are wrapped in adhesive tape and then drugged, so that they will lie motionless inside passenger hand baggage during long-haul flights. Rare birds are painted or dyed to make them appear drab, to allow them to be passed off as a common or less-regulated species. Small reptiles are hidden inside men's briefs or women's bras as they are carried cross-border. Birds' eggs are transported in vests fitted with many pockets, which are worn next to the smuggler's skin. Not only do such vests conceal the eggs from the gaze of border control staff but their presence next to the smuggler's body provides sufficient warmth for them to continue to incubate en route.

In Kathmandu, I saw a vehicle that had been stopped by forest department officials as it made its way from India to a final destination in China. Its rear compartment had been reinforced to enable it to transport a large amount of valuable and rare timber. More impressively, a switch fitted on the dashboard, when activated, changed the front and rear number plates. The car's true Nepalese registration plate would rotate to display a plate purportedly allocated to that of a foreign embassy in Nepal. The officials had received specific intelligence about the smuggling attempt but admitted that, without it, they would not normally have stopped any vehicle displaying diplomatic CD plates. The smugglers presumably got this idea from the gadget-packed Aston Martin which featured in a James Bond film many years ago.

Rare, highly-prized poison arrow frogs have been smuggled from Amazonian regions to Europe inside plastic 35mm camera film cases. These beautiful, highly-coloured creatures get their name from the toxic mucus that covers their bodies. It protects them from predators and members of Amazonian tribes have traditionally rubbed their arrows on the frogs' bodies before setting out on hunting trips.

Air waybills and cargo manifests are forged to conceal the true origin of contraband. Sea-going shipments will transit through various ports before arriving at their final destination. In some cases, the cargo will be off-loaded and perhaps repacked before continuing on its way. This makes determining the true country of origin difficult and some shipments will go round and round for weeks and months at sea before finally reaching the true destination.

Contraband handovers between smugglers occur in the transit lounges and terminals of airport hubs, so that a different individual travels the final leg of the journey, using a route or airline that is less likely to be targeted for passenger inspection at the final destination.

In Hong Kong, a customs marine patrol intercepted a fishing boat smuggling ivory. A concealed compartment built into the hold of the vessel would swing aside when an electric current was connected. The same current was used to power a hydraulic lift that raised the ivory to deck level.

It is at its container terminals that Hong Kong Customs tend to find themselves busiest with regard to smuggling. Each year, over 24 million containers pass through the port. Not surprisingly, it has historically acted as an important entry point to mainland China for both legal and illegal cargo. Customs officers there benefit from some of the most advanced screening equipment available. That said, they still face a huge task in determining just which containers to pass through the large X-ray machines. And, as with any other X-ray, it takes a well-trained and experienced operator to pick out the sometimes very subtle and hard-to-distinguish clues that indicate that something is amiss inside the 40-foot steel boxes.

Hong Kong Customs have developed a particular expertise when it comes to sniffing out ivory smuggling. One of their best detections came through the X-ray screening of containers. Their risk-assessment work made them suspicious of a container declared as transporting sheets of timber from Cameroon; the supposed cargo did not justify the cost of the shipment. The X-rays confirmed that the box seemed to be full of what it was meant to hold, yet at the far end of the container, opposite its doors, there was an area reaching from floor to ceiling which was full of tightly-packed objects, showing on the X-ray screen as of a dense material. Their initial concerns now justified, they decided to unpack the whole container.

And yet, when they had unloaded what were indeed hundreds of sheets of timber, the container stood empty. Puzzled, they ran it through the X-ray machine again. Again they noticed the dark objects, but they could see for themselves that nothing remained inside. More puzzled than ever, they measured the outside of the container and the floor space inside, and found that the two figures did not match. They were looking at a false wall, welded in place so carefully that it was almost impossible to discern with the naked eye. It took a long time and oxy-acetylene cutting gear to remove the partition, but it was worth the effort, as it was concealing more than three tonnes of elephant tusks.

We helped the authorities in Hong Kong pass word of the interception to their counterparts in Cameroon. Subsequent enquiries there led to the company responsible for the shipment and to the discovery, in the company's compound near the seaport of Douala, of two further containers, both also fitted with false walls. Checks of the company's export records showed that it had been organizing similar shipments for several years. Goodness only knows how much ivory had been smuggled successfully using this method.

I was, though, somewhat surprised when I received feedback that customs in Cameroon had never seen, or heard of, this concealment method. On reflection, though, I realized that this should not be too surprising. In the West, we tend to think of customs officers as being part of the law enforcement community but that is not necessarily how they see themselves in developing nations. There, their focus is very much on gathering taxes and duties, reflected in the fact that many agencies are called 'The (country name) Revenue Authority'. It also means that their focus, in relation to cargo, tends to be on what is entering the country, because that will be where most tax is liable.

The sheer volume of cargo and passengers that travel by land, sea and air each day make distinguishing between legal and illegal a daunting task for customs and other border control officials. It is why risk assessment, targeting and profiling are so essential. The exchange of information and intelligence is utterly vital and yet that exchange can be abysmally low.

For well over a decade, I regularly attended meetings of the World Customs Organization at its headquarters in Brussels. In the beginning, it was a surprise for someone with a police background to see how greatly the role of customs could vary from region to region and what impact that had on their priorities.

I had expected the WCO to be the Interpol of the customs community but it certainly was not. Indeed, its constitution prohibited its secretariat from acting as a conduit for information in which the details of an individual or company suspected of smuggling could be exchanged. It was the early 2000s before the WCO began to adopt policies with regard to the gathering, analysis and exchange of intelligence.

This change of focus was, in large part, driven by the events of 9/11. Indeed, had those terrorist attacks not occurred, I think the customs community and its representative body would not have joined the enforcement community nearly as effectively or as speedily as it has done. Today, the WCO is one of the strongest supporters of CITES and it is customs officers who truly are at the frontline of implementation and enforcement of the Convention. I treasured the working relationships I developed with WCO staff over the years and I seemed to become a well-known face in its Brussels offices and at seminars and conferences involving senior customs officials from around the world. The fact that I came from a policing background was also well known. This, and my twisted sense of humour, led to an incident that still makes me smile.

Having the status of 'observer' at WCO meetings, my place was at the back of the conference hall. In the main, I kept my interventions to CITES-related matters but, from time to time, I would comment or make suggestions during discussions where I thought my policing experience might be of help. It was during deliberations regarding an intelligence policy, which the Organization wished its members to adopt that the chairman acknowledged my request to speak.

I made a suggestion relating to the point in hand, added that CITES was very supportive of the adoption of an intelligence policy and then finished by saying that, as an ex-police officer, I could not help observing that the phrases 'customs' and 'intelligence' did not seem naturally to go together.

There was a silence in the hall, made all the longer because half of those present were listening to an interpretation of what I had said. Finally and thankfully, the laughter broke out, especially amongst those who had been used to my presence for several years. I could see several delegates, though, who hadn't a clue who I was, thinking, 'Did that guy just insult us?'

As the laughter died away and someone else began to speak, I could see the Director of the Compliance and Facilitation Directorate – the number three in the WCO hierarchy – scribbling on a pad beside him and then tearing off the sheet. He beckoned to one of his staff, handed him the note and pointed at me. The staff member made his way to the back of the room and passed me the piece of paper. Unfolding it, I read the words, 'You personally have just been designated as an endangered species.' Touché!

Sophisticated forgery and counterfeiting of documents

If you are an organized smuggling or illicit trade network and you want to introduce your illegally-harvested product into legitimate markets, then it has to appear *bona fide*. This may involve the counterfeiting of invoices or bills of lading that will help convince your customers that the goods are of a legal origin.

But the falsified documents that I encountered most commonly were the CITES permits and certificates that countries use to authorize trade in fauna and flora. This fraud took various forms. On many occasions, unscrupulous traders would apply to a national CITES office and obtain a genuine permit. The permit would then be altered, perhaps by changing the number of, for example, birds that could be exported or by adding more species to the document. Sometimes the trader did this himself. However, I also saw instances where the apparently legitimate trader was selling the genuine permits he was obtaining to criminals and they would then alter them to cover whatever illegality they were involved in. Because it was not unknown, especially in countries with limited capacity or poor export controls, for no check to be made on how the permits were being used, this type of fraud could take place time and time again.

And poor controls further down the chain could make life easy for the criminals too. When a shipment of CITES specimens arrives at its destination, the original permit should be surrendered to customs. If it is not, then the trader can potentially use it again and again.

Unfortunately, technological advances have really worked against border control officials in recent years. When I first started CITES-related work in 1997 it was relatively easy for the trained eye to spot a permit that was not an original. However, as colour printers, and, in particular, scanners started to become almost as commonplace in the home as any other electrical appliance, the sophistication of forgery multiplied many times over. And if distinguishing between genuine and fake was difficult for me, who had spent hours poring over relevant documents, just imagine how problematic it was for the average customs officer, who maybe only saw a CITES permit or certificate once every few months.

The time will come, I hope, when this will no longer be a major problem. E-permitting, where applications for permits and certificates, their issuance, their inspection, and their endorsement are all carried out electronically, ought to eliminate most of the opportunities for fraud. But such systems will inevitably be at risk from hacking and I cannot envisage wildlife trade ever becoming free of fraud. Indeed, the sophistication of organized crime has always meant that the law enforcement community is in a constant state of catch-up and organized groups are certainly now operating in cyber-crime.

While e-permitting may make it harder to gain corrupt access to genuine permits and certificates, it is an unfortunate fact that the reliability of almost any system depends upon it being administered by honest officials. I regularly saw, or was advised of, cases where CITES officials had accepted money or other forms of bribe to provide genuine permits, stamps or licences, or had sold their signature on documents. The CITES Secretariat was also advised of instances where permits were stolen from offices in different parts of the world. While some of these were no doubt genuine reports, I personally suspect that several involved officials who were covering up for the fact that they themselves had either sold them or corruptly issued them.

I also encountered situations where corrupt officials frustrated my attempts to combat counterfeiting and forgery. When the illegal caviar trade was at its height in the late 1990s and early 2000s, the misuse, abuse and forgery of permits was rife. Some national CITES authorities affix an additional, anti-fraud security measure to their permits at the time of issuance. These are adhesive stamps that incorporate a number of anti-tampering and other measures which prevent their copying or duplication. A colleague and I had worked with the company in Switzerland which designs and prints passports and currency for many countries around the world, creating an improved version of this measure, which had been around in CITES for a very long time. Unfortunately, technological advances had made the original model too vulnerable to forgery and counterfeiting. Although we advised countries that used the new stamps of some of the measures incorporated into them, we kept one or two measures secret. We did so because, to be frank, we had learned that some national CITES authorities simply could not be trusted.

In September 2000, I introduced what became known as 'CITES Alerts'. These were bulletins we published to advise national CITES management and enforcement authorities of emerging wildlife crime trends, new smuggling concealment methods and other items of intelligence that they could use in their risk-assessment, profiling and targeting work. Initially, these were sent to all CITES Management Authorities by mail and they were encouraged to disseminate the information to other relevant agencies. But one incident in particular led to us changing our approach and making the Alerts solely available through a restricted-access online system.

I had noted that several suspicious shipments of caviar were accompanied by extremely high-quality counterfeit permits. They were almost impossible to distinguish from the real thing and we had to contact the issuing authority to discover if they were genuine. It could sometimes take a long time to get a response. In the meantime, the shipment would be held in refrigeration by customs in the intended country of import. Not only was this inconvenient and expensive, but the customs authorities were invariably coming under a lot of pressure, including threats of litigation, to release the caviar and clear the shipment for import.

One day, when examining the copy of another counterfeit that had been faxed to our office, I noted that a security stamp was attached. It also appeared to be a first-rate forgery. Then I spotted that it had obviously been produced separately from the permit itself and had been added subsequently, as the real thing would have been. But I noticed that it had one feature, if you looked really closely, which did not match the genuine article. I realized this was going to make life much easier for border control staff and we quickly issued a CITES Alert, describing how to identify a fake stamp.

To my disgust, and within a matter of weeks, a copy of another counterfeit permit landed on my desk; this one also bore a stamp and I saw that the forgers had corrected the earlier flaw. I simply do not believe that there is any other explanation for the counterfeiters moving to correct their mistake other than that the information in the Alert was leaked by corrupt officials. And although I could never prove it, I am convinced I know which office was responsible.

A chain, then, really is only as strong as its weakest link. To suggest that there weren't several weak links in the CITES chain would be delusional. While many of the links have been strengthened over the years, the chain remains open to fracture.

USE OF FAKE OR 'FRONT' COMPANIES

Organized crime groups will create businesses and enterprises, often on a short-term basis, through which wildlife can be laundered or marketed and through which profits can be filtered. Since any details that may be required to register these corporations, obtain licences and so on will be false, it will subsequently be difficult for investigators to discover who is truly behind the operation. Alternatively, at least one 'front' man or woman will be employed to be the public face of the business and to conduct day-to-day activities, accept deliveries to any premises, act as sales staff or handle deliveries. Like the mules recruited to carry out smuggling, or the poacher to kill animals, these people are essentially disposable and expendable if customs or the police come calling.

Of course, these people know little, if anything, about those further up the chain and will usually be well paid to compensate them for the potential risks. I can think of one man, based in Singapore, whose job it was to co-ordinate the shipping arrangements from Africa to Asia for containers which concealed large quantities of ivory. His orders came by phone and he knew nothing about those who issued the instructions. He had a mobile telephone number to call in case of an 'emergency', such as a consignment being intercepted by the authorities, but the number related to a pay-as-you-go mobile in Hong Kong, whose owner was untraceable. When the man in Singapore was arrested, he could genuinely claim that he did not know who his employer was, did not know what cargo was being transported (although he had a hard job denying that it was suspicious in nature) and, since he had no criminal convictions, only faced a fine when he was brought to court.

Fake companies also provide organized crime groups with the opportunity to make money in ways aside from trading in wildlife. Their establishment presents the chance to engage in what the policing community has known for decades as 'long firm fraud'. The way this works is for the company to gradually, over time, build up credit ratings and perhaps even take out bank loans and mortgages. As its primary business of merchandizing - caviar, for instance - progresses and the profits flow, those credit ratings will rise. This allows the firm to branch out into other commodities and order goods, but without having to pay upfront. Even routine business supplies, computers, printers, laptops, mobile phones, corporate entertainment goods and the like can be acquired on credit and quickly sold. By the time creditors come calling, the firm's premises are an empty shell and everything has gone. Why profit from just one thing if you can sell more?

Customs in Azerbaijan stumbled across a fake company one day when they noticed a large shipment of tins being imported. These were identical in size and construction to those used to pack caviar at the end of its processing and production phase. The very nature of the tins indicated there could be no other plan for them. But, interestingly, the company to which they were headed was not one of the country's licensed caviar producers. The company found customs officers, rather than the tins it had ordered, arriving at its doors.

One fake company that made me smile came to my notice when an airline contacted me in the early 2000s. It was one of the world's largest and the head of its catering services phoned to ask my opinion about a fax he had received. He sent me a copy.

It consisted of a very impressive letterhead, allegedly that of a private investigation agency. The message explained that the firm had been contracted by the United Nations Environment Programme to probe illegal trade in caviar and had uncovered that the airline's current supplier was dealing in illicit products. It recommended that the airline immediately sever its contract with the supplier and provide the investigation agency with copies of all paperwork relating to its business with the company.

The whole thing was a complete scam, presumably carried out by a rival illicit caviar trader. But the fax was imposing and convincing and I could imagine how airlines might have been taken in by it. If successful, it could have proved profitable as the airline and cruise companies were very significant customers for caviar, which was used to pamper clients in their first-class and stateroom cabins.

Fake companies can be work both ways. The US Fish and Wildlife Service, for example, has conducted several highly successful 'sting' operations, establishing businesses to which poachers and unscrupulous dealers have been hoodwinked into selling their ill-gotten gains, or duping them into meetings with special agents, only to have handcuffs slapped onto their wrists. It is nice to see organized crime's own techniques used against the criminals.

MANIPULATING PEOPLE AND CIRCUMSTANCES

PROVISION OF HIGH-QUALITY LAWYERS

I have described how crime syndicates will recruit, equip and pay poachers. I have also explained how the poachers will commonly come from communities living on or below the poverty line. It is this background that, at first sight, might make people wonder what is happening when some of these poachers are brought before the courts. In India, for instance, I was told of poachers who had been arrested by the Forest Department after killing a tiger.

In court the following morning, forestry officials and the local magistrate were astonished to see that a well-known barrister appeared to represent the hunters, a lawyer who was more used to arguing cases in front of judges in the courts of New Delhi. This was not someone known for taking *pro bono* cases out of a desire to help the needy. There was simply no way on earth that the accused standing in the dock could afford to pay the fees that a criminal defence lawyer such as this would charge.

It was a first-rate example of how organized crime looks after its own. Unfortunately for most poachers arrested by the authorities, and probably fortunately for most prosecutors, such examples are few and far between. The vast majority of those caught poaching are simply abandoned to their fate by those further up the chain who recruited or equipped them.

EXPLOITATION OF LOCAL COMMUNITIES

Much of what I have described in relation to poaching illustrates how the skills, and particularly the local knowledge, of those living alongside species wanted for illegal trade are utilized by organized crime networks, groups or syndicates. But I believe this goes further, into the realm of exploitation.

Those people who control the illegal harvesting and trade of endangered species do not want to get their hands dirty. Neither do they want to expose themselves to the wide range of hazards, both natural and law enforcement-based, that such activities will incur.

Poaching animals, capturing exotic birds or harvesting rare plants invariably requires those at the frontline to enter habitats that will be awash with natural hazards. Some of these will be physical, as in coping with difficult terrain (the climbing of cliff faces, for example, to access bird nests), some will present risks to health through diseases such as malaria or dengue fever, others will expose poachers to attack by the very animals they seek (tigers, elephants and the like do not welcome humans entering their territories) and all offer the chance of being arrested and prosecuted.

Organized crime also exploits the fact that many rural communities are living so close to, or below, the poverty line that they will do almost anything to achieve incomes beyond what they and their neighbours might normally expect. Consequently, they will encourage villagers to gather rare plants, for example, for a pittance. The few dollars paid for each orchid may be welcome income for the harvester but will bear no comparison to the thousands that a collector in Europe might subsequently pay.

Perhaps the most blatant and callous exploitation of local communities, however, is the manner in which organized crime groups have recently recruited the poachers of high-profile and high-value species. Historically, elephant and rhino poachers have been paid relatively little for their work, certainly in comparison with what their product will fetch once the final consumer purchases it. But some of these activities, especially rhino poaching in South Africa, have become really high risk. In the first quarter of 2011, 14 poachers were shot dead by the enforcement authorities. Many more were injured.

Organized crime has responded. It is rumoured that 10,000 US dollars were being offered per kilo of rhino horn in 2011 and that some gangs were being promised such a fee, regardless of success, for each incursion they made into South Africa's parks. For poachers to be paid such sums is absolutely without precedent. Although crime syndicates might expect 70,000 dollars per kilo for horns sold in far east Asia, it was unknown for them to divide their profit base with the first link of the chain of criminality in such a manner. But it certainly reflects, and emphasizes, the seriousness of wildlife crime.

Dangling such amounts of money in front of those in desperate need clearly meets any definition of exploitation. They vastly exceed what any rural resident in Africa could hope to acquire, not just in one year but maybe in a lifetime. And they illustrate the manipulation of those who live in poor communities. In early 2013, I spoke with a South African law enforcement official who told me that their criminal intelligence sources indicated that for every poacher killed, a queue of other potential recruits was waiting, metaphorically speaking, to take his place.

EXPLOITATION OF CIVIL UNREST

Several studies, including the research conducted and data collected under the CITES Monitoring of Illegal Killing of Elephants project, have shown that a lack of governance or absence of the rule of law in countries makes life easier for poachers. It also, of course, makes for an ideal setting in which organized crime, and even terrorist groups, can make the most of situations where law enforcement can, on occasions, be more or less absent.

I remember having a conversation with a customs officer from Myanmar shortly after I had been provided with rough footage, due to be part of a documentary illustrating trade in wildlife along a particular part of its border with China. In the video, one could see tiger skins and other exotic species' body parts openly on sale on stalls and in markets within the Burmese border town. On its outskirts, bears were being kept in captivity and milked for their bile.

This is a particularly unpleasant practice, involving the insertion into the animal's gall bladder of a steel tube through which bile is drained off at least once a day. This practice remains legal in some countries, such as China, but at least there it takes place in licensed 'farms' where the bears' health is meant to be monitored and where the insertion of drains and the bile extraction should be undertaken by skilled people. Bear bile can be used effectively in the treatment of some medical conditions in humans, but the active ingredient in bear bile can be synthesized in laboratories, so equally efficacious alternatives are readily available. There are consumers, though, who continue to believe that only 'the real thing' is truly effective and some who believe that only 'the real thing' from wild animals will do. And so the killing of wild bears for their gall bladders continues, despite the existence of captive breeding and farming of bears.

The video also showed people walking across from Myanmar into China, several hundred metres from the official border control post, in plain sight of officials who seemed oblivious or who just did not care. Apart from establishing wildlife trade operations, entrepreneurs in the Burmese town had built large casinos there, which were attracting large numbers of patrons from the Chinese side.

The Myanmar customs officer knew exactly where I was describing when I recounted what I had watched on screen but explained that this was part of his nation that was essentially beyond government regulation. He said that it was under the control of a high-level officer who had retired from the military government of Myanmar and who had, to all intents and purposes, established his own little kingdom in that area. There were rumours that this 'governor' even taxed the illicit trade which crossed into neighbouring China. 'My colleagues and I have no authority to enter that part of the country, which is why you will never see Myanmar Customs at the border there,' he explained. He also told me that trafficking in drugs, weapons and humans was commonplace too.

Crossing continents, it has long been recognized that, years ago, rebels in Angola poached elephants and sold the tusks to fund their activities and it seems that modern-day groups such as the Lord's Resistance Army, together with rebel groups linked with or operating from Rwanda and Somalia, are doing likewise.

In the unrest-ridden north and east of the Democratic Republic of Congo, armed militias and rebel gangs have poached elephants and rhinos, subsequently trading their ivory and horn. But they have also slaughtered many other species for their meat, including highly-endangered gorillas. Great ape meat is prized in some parts of Africa and some tribes have culturally and historically treated it as something that must be served to distinguished guests. But rebel groups, having killed adult members of ape families for human consumption, are also thought to have then sold live juvenile animals to be smuggled out of the country to enter the private exotic species collections of wealthy individuals.

At one point in the mid-2000s, park rangers who were battling rebel groups poaching elephants were told that if they did not back off, the much rarer gorillas in the park would be killed instead, simply by way of revenge. Gorillas, then, became the hostages of guerrillas. And as it happens, further gorillas were killed regardless.

Use of 'mules'

I once saw an individual described in the media as being a 'kingpin' of wildlife crime. Not long afterwards, this same person was arrested after the luggage he was using to smuggle pythons between two Asian countries burst open on an airport baggage conveyor belt. I believe the phrase 'kingpin' was utterly inappropriate. It was equivalent to suggesting that Al Capone, at the height of his power in Chicago, might have been caught driving a truck loaded with bootleg liquor across the American-Canadian border. It would be nonsensical.

The only thing the senior figures in organized crime groups like to get their hands on are the profits. Even then, if they have any sense (and most do) it will be only after the money has been laundered. The Mr Bigs of the criminal world do not get their hands dirty and do not leave their fingerprints where they can be found by the police.

That is why they recruit expendables to harvest the wildlife and, similarly, recruit people to transport it across borders and often within countries too. These couriers, who were originally termed 'mules' in relation to narcotics trafficking, will sometimes be recruited in the country of final destination and dispatched to the country of origin to bring the contraband back. Vietnamese mules are paid to travel to South Africa, for example, to return with rhino horn, and occasionally they will also participate in the harvest.

I was told in Ho Chi Minh City, for instance, of a man whose usual job was taking photographs of tourists in a popular city park. He was recruited to fly to South Africa, pose as a *bona fide* big game hunter, shoot a rhino, and then head home with its two horns. He had also managed to acquire another on the black market whilst in South Africa. He came to notice as he arrived at his home airport because he had a CITES permit for only two of the horns. He subsequently was sentenced to three years in jail.

Frustratingly, he was never interviewed to find out who had financed the trip. There was no way he could have funded it personally. For a start, he probably could not have afforded the flight, but he undoubtedly could not have afforded the tens of thousands of South African rands required to get a hunting licence and then hire a professional guide. Customs in Viet Nam were not interested in anything other than the import offences. They had got their man and he had gone to jail. Job done. They were happy. The police in Viet Nam were not interested either. They saw it as a customs case. The culprit was now behind bars. Case closed.

Customs and police did not liaise or co-operate with each other. The glaring fact that this person must have been recruited by someone else, someone who could afford to finance such an operation and who would have taken control of the rhino horns if the mule made it out of the airport, someone who must have either been part of, or maybe controlled, an organized crime network, was overlooked or, worse, ignored.

I have seen so many examples of wasted opportunities like this that I am afraid to say I am no longer surprised. I am even approaching the stage where I am no longer disappointed or frustrated. I simply shake my head in resignation.

Most smugglers, though, are purely there for the transportation. Many are poor people who are identified as likely candidates to accept some extra cash. Some are expatriate workers or foreign students who will be given a plane ticket so that they can have a free holiday home to see their families. Elderly tourists were once popular as mules, as they used to be regarded as low risk in the profiling conducted by border agencies, but this has changed, especially after drug traffickers began to use them. They are now more likely to be stopped and checked.

Smugglers may be provided with cash to bribe relevant officials. I used to be amazed at the number of ivory smugglers that were caught, particularly arriving in Bangkok for some reason, with two or three suitcases absolutely laden down with tusks or pieces of tusk. These sometimes weighed several hundred kilos altogether. The smugglers were often women. If they could not find a luggage trolley (and this sometimes led to their discovery), they were almost trapped in the baggage reclaim area, as there was no way they could carry the bags out under their own strength.

I suspect most of us have had the experience of arriving at check-in and being told we are suffering from that infuriating and potentially very expensive condition known as 'excess baggage'. Try bribing your way out of that at a British Airways counter in Heathrow or Delta desk in Washington D.C. and you are unlikely to get very far. Regrettably, the reality is that money talks more loudly at some check-ins elsewhere in the world.

Sometimes the couriers know what they are carrying, sometimes not. But they will certainly know at least something about other links in the chain. At the very least they know, or can describe, who recruited them, who gave them the contraband and who they are meant to give it to at the end of their trip. That knowledge is intelligence. It helps identify the other chain links. That intelligence needs to be extracted (by asking questions, not by any more sinister means) from the smugglers. And then it needs to be disseminated to others in the enforcement community who can use it, whether that is to one's own colleagues or counterparts in other national agencies, to the countries across which the contraband chain stretches, to regional and sub-regional enforcement bodies or to international customs and police agencies.

However, if questions were being asked, I used to see precious little sign of the information being shared. Frankly, I think a lot of the time the questions were not being asked. To be fair, I think some of this was down to the lack of basic training. To try and address this, I asked Interpol to work with me in preparing a 'Questioning Wildlife Smugglers' manual. The World Customs Organization helped too, and it was translated into Arabic, Chinese, English, French, Russian and Spanish and promoted as widely as possible. Has it made a difference? I am not in a position now to judge but, when I retired, there seemed a long way to go in many parts of the world.

I suspect, too, that many law enforcement officers are too parochial. I know I used to be guilty of that. When you make a good seizure or capture, it is all too tempting to be pleased with yourself (maybe deservedly so) and to sit back thinking 'Job done!' before moving on to catch up with your other work. If we are to really make a difference, particularly when it comes to disrupting organized crime networks, we must exploit each and every opportunity to the utmost. From what I could see, that was happening only rarely.

It is also important to speak to the people you arrest, aside from specifically seeking targeted intelligence. It helps you understand them, to understand what drives them to engage in criminal activities, how they were picked out for recruitment and also to understand the nature of the trade itself. Months and months passed before we understood what was prompting the increased illegal trade in rhinoceros horn in the late 2000s. It is vital to understand the big picture and it is often only those at the international level, in organizations like the CITES Secretariat, Interpol, the UN Office on Drugs and Crime and the World Customs Organization who are able to get the 'helicopter view' that provides an overall appreciation of what is taking place and, importantly, enables them to think about how best to respond.

Back in the early 1980s, before drug addiction became a major driver of all sorts of crime in the UK, I remember spending time one night talking to the leader of a group which had broken into the pharmacy in a small town in northeast Scotland. Prescription drugs were what they were after. They had been caught red-handed and there was no need for a formal interview. I was just chatting with the burglar and asked him whether he was a drug-user. 'Christ, no!' he replied. 'You won't catch me putting any of that stuff in my body.' I had seen from his criminal record that he had been involved in many break-ins in the past, to a wide variety of premises, but never before to a chemist shop. Why this choice of target, I wondered? 'Simple,' he explained, 'Drugs are the only thing that, once you've stolen them, increase in value.'

I have often seen fellow law enforcement officers engage in no conversation with people they had arrested beyond what was formally and officially required. I sincerely believe that to be another wasted opportunity. While most judicial systems throughout the world follow the principle of 'the right of silence', meaning that a suspect is not bound to answer any questions, it does not mean that a customs or police official is prohibited from asking questions. Many criminals who may initially respond with 'No comment' or 'I'm saying nothing!' will provide answers if questioned effectively.

PEOPLE IN HIGH PLACES

There are countries around the world where politicians and successful business people have an influence far beyond that of their counterparts in Europe or North America.

I will never forget a very simple, but very telling, example of this fact, which I observed during one of my visits to Astrakhan in the Russian Federation. The city has been built up on either side of the River Volga and there is one major bridge that offers an outstanding view of both the city and waterway. A small group of us were being shown around the city, accompanied by a number of local officials. Our convoy of three vehicles drove to the middle of the bridge and parked, and we were ushered out and to the side to take in the view. Not surprisingly, the three cars we were travelling in caused quite an obstruction and a considerable traffic jam built up.

Before long, a police patrol car appeared, its lights flashing, and one of the officers came across to remonstrate with us. He had no sooner started speaking, though, when the most senior local official, who I think had a title equivalent to something like 'assistant governor', pulled out an identification card, thrust it towards the cop and barked something at him. One did not need to be a Russian-speaker to know that the policeman was being told to bugger off. To my amazement, and deep disappointment, the officer meekly turned away, slunk back to his patrol car and drove off. The local official looked very pleased with himself.

In the West, we are used to the autonomy of law enforcement officers and, for the most part, a freedom from influence. It is frequently very different elsewhere. Indeed, I have often seen how in parts of east Asia, for instance, it is very much politicians who determine the priorities for the police, in particular, and who, aside from routine day-to-day matters, decide what and who will be investigated. Time after time, officers have told me that their ability to be proactive and undertake self-initiated investigations is strictly regulated. Sometimes this is even enshrined in national legislation.

I know of one country in Asia where enforcement agencies could not execute a search or arrest warrant without prior notice being given to the relevant city mayor or provincial governor's office. Sometimes, not surprisingly, when the law officers arrived at the premises in question, the bird (be it the contraband or the criminals) would have flown.

This abuse and misuse of political authority and position seems particularly prevalent where countries are administered at provincial levels. There are parts of southeast Asia, for example, where provincial governors and military and police commanders appear to operate fiefdoms and seem to be answerable to no one at central or federal level. Some of these people even appear to flaunt the fact that they perceive themselves as being above the law. I was told of several provincial heads in both Kalimantan and Sumatra in Indonesia who kept juvenile orang-utans as pets and made no effort to conceal their possession of these animals.

Orang-utans were not simply kept as pets, though. I was told of one village in Kalimantan where a female orang-utan was kept as a form of sex slave, rented out by its keeper as a prostitute to local men. So used had it become to this treatment that, if approached by a man, it would turn onto its hands and knees, ready to be penetrated. It was finally rescued by the authorities but it was to be months of rehabilitation before it got out of this habit. The villagers where it had been kept were so reluctant to give the animal up that they initially prevented forest department officials from seizing it and threatened them with violence. The presence of armed military police was eventually required to warn off the local people.

I witnessed several examples of successful Asian businessmen who, amongst their various enterprises, operated public entertainment venues. These people had acquired juvenile orang-utans in such numbers that it seemed unbelievable that this could have happened without the knowledge of wildlife law enforcement agencies. And they certainly did not hide the animals from view. The orang-utans had been trained to engage in boxing matches, ride bicycles and perform other stupid circus tricks. I am sure the fact that some of these venues were major tourist attractions, both for nationals and foreigners, and employed large numbers of local residents, had a bearing on the fact that no action had been taken by the authorities until the CITES Secretariat was alerted by NGOs. Although it was outside my remit, I was disgusted to be told off-the-record by the staff of one facility that more than one juvenile orang-utan had died there when, with cattle prods used to train the animals, they were given too many electric shocks. I have also witnessed examples of bizarre species inter-breeding; in one safari park there were large cats on display which appeared to be a cross between a tiger and a lion.

One of the entertainment venues I visited was in Cambodia, close to its border with neighbouring Thailand, where gambling was illegal. It was a huge facility, incorporating a large casino, hotel and self-catering complex, children's amusement park and what was called a zoo. The zoo, though, was more a collection of performing creatures and visitors would have been wasting their time had they gone there to learn anything about the animal kingdom. The whole complex had been designed to attract as many visitors from Thailand as possible. The Thai baht was used as the currency inside the facility, rather than the Cambodian riel. The owner of the facility had initially indicated he would meet with me and a colleague but then cancelled at the last minute.

A quick internet search on his name threw up some incredible results. Umpteen media articles and blogs alleged that he was a mafia crime boss who was, by birth, a national of the neighbouring casino-barren Thailand and who had bought himself the position of 'senator' in his new country of residence. It was alleged that he had paid for military units to clear farmers and their families off land which he had subsequently developed, and that he was engaged, without environmental impact assessments, in building major roads and bridges from the nation's capital to his facility. When completed, this would reduce the travelling time by several hours, as the casino was situated in a remote corner of the country.

I was sorry I did not get the chance to meet someone who sounded fascinating. Perhaps he thought I was there to arrest him. His absence certainly made life difficult for his staff, as they faced a very uncomfortable questioning session, trying desperately to explain their possession of endangered mammals and marine species. But if it led me to shake my head at what this person had allegedly accomplished by criminal means, I also shook my head over how apparently easily and brazenly he had got away with it.

In the Middle East, it was not unusual for a small number of sheikhs or members of ruling families to have built up large personal collections of exotic species. Such people, along with large numbers of the general citizenry, were also heavily involved in falconry, a centuries-old tradition in that part of the world. Questions had seldom been asked about how these animals and birds had been acquired and few ever passed through the border controls that would have been in place elsewhere. To be fair, this acquisition and possession of wildlife had started long before these nations acceded to the CITES Convention.

In the main, once countries in that part of the world did begin to regulate trade in fauna and flora in compliance with international standards, most people (including national rulers and others of high status) also played by the rules. There were, of course, exceptions.

Part of the problem lay in the traditions and cultures that are in place there and it is hard to change the practices of many lifetimes. It was, for example, customary for the members of Arabian tribes to visit their sheikhs and to describe their experiences after sorties into the desert. They would habitually bring with them a gift for their tribal leader. This custom continues in many places today, so that even the rulers of some Gulf States set aside time throughout the year for audiences with community members in a way that would seem remarkable to the presidents of European or American nations.

The gifts presented to sheikhs nowadays follow the traditional practice but are semi-salutary, in the way that one might take a bottle of wine, flowers or chocolates when going to visit friends and relatives. They can, though, be considerably more valuable and are offered in the hope of receiving something similar in return. This is because, again in accordance with tradition, visitors to the sheikh's palace would never leave empty-handed. Presenting something that the sheikh might especially treasure could lead, on occasions, by way of return, to a position in government or other honour.

This background was referred to one day in the early 2000s when an informant phoned me about two juvenile gorillas that had been smuggled into a Middle East country and then presented as a gift to a Crown Prince. The person responsible, knowing of the prince's private exotic species collection and having his eye on a particular government contract, hoped to curry favour with this bizarre offering.

I made some checks and the information appeared to be corroborated by an incident that had taken place in central Africa. There, a gorilla family group, which was regularly monitored by conservation researchers, had been observed a few weeks previously to have two new babies. However, during their most recent visit to the group's territory, the researchers had found all the adults shot dead and the babies missing.

I contacted the enforcement authorities in the Middle East and asked them to investigate the informant's intelligence. I was told that the gift had indeed been made to the Crown Prince but that he was horrified by it, as he was aware that the removal of juvenile gorillas would necessitate the killing of their parents and perhaps all other adults in the group. However, tradition and custom prevented him from refusing the present. Many weeks passed and it was hoped that the local CITES authorities would be able to take possession of the animals and send them to an appropriate rescue centre or rehabilitation sanctuary in sub-Saharan Africa. Unfortunately, the young gorillas could not be traced. My contacts in the Gulf were satisfied that the prince no longer had the animals but did not know what had happened to them. When I expressed frustration at the lack of progress with this investigation, they explained that there was no way they could seek to interview the Crown Prince and the matter went no further. Since my informant insisted that I did not disclose his identity, I had no hard evidence with which to pursue our concerns formally and the local enforcers were similarly hampered as they had nothing but intelligence with which to seek court action. To this day, I have no idea whether or not they survived.

Sometimes an individual will exploit not their own high status, but that of someone to whom they are connected. In the late 2000s, there were signs that an illegal trade in rhino horn was becoming a major problem. During the same period, but not necessarily connected, it seemed that the poaching of elephants and the smuggling of ivory were also reaching really serious proportions.

While the two illicit trades appeared to be driven by different demands, I noted that one particular name seemed to be appearing in connection with both. This was someone who was apparently head of a trading company based in southeast Asia. Both the man's name and the company name were featuring regularly on a range of documents associated with intercepted contraband shipments. I asked one of our partner agencies if their national office could investigate this person and the company.

The reply I got back was, essentially, to forget it. 'This person is a very close personal friend of the Prime Minister and there's no way anyone will authorize an inquiry.' Regrettably, it was not the first response of that type I had received and it was something that I had to learn to live with.

This, then, is a two-way street – heading in one direction are individuals abusing their positions for personal enrichment, while heading in the other are criminals making use of those individuals for their own ends. But the history of crime is awash with examples of criminal networks that have made use of politicians, for instance, in order to gain access to favourable business connections or to circumvent government regulations or judicial processes.

Officials in national CITES offices not uncommonly found themselves overruled by those above them. A trader might apply for an export permit but would be refused, perhaps on the grounds that that year's export quota had been met. The trader would then go to someone further up the government ladder and either plead his case, offer a bribe or bring some other influence to bear. An instruction would then arrive on the CITES official's desk ordering that the permit be issued.

I recall one incident where a government in Asia decided to make a present of a rhino to another country as some form of bizarre diplomatic gift to improve or cement relations between the two states. When consulted, as they had to be, both the CITES management and scientific authorities advised against it. Their advice was ignored and the animal was shipped off.

I was really sympathetic with those on the ground whose best intentions were frustrated by managers upon whom they should have been able to rely for support. While attending a meeting in a major city in Central Africa in the early 2000s, I came downstairs on the first morning and passed some time by wandering through the souvenir shops in the hotel lobby. My accommodation was part of an international chain of high quality hotels. Several had large quantities of ivory carvings openly on display. I knew the domestic sale of ivory was completely illegal in that country.

Later that day, I recounted what I had seen to the head of the provincial wildlife law enforcement body. I could tell immediately that this was not news to him and he looked very embarrassed. He described how, a few months previously, he and a colleague had inspected the shops and that their findings had matched mine. Working on the principle that a warning should be issued before moving to initiate prosecution proceedings, the team leader had told the shopkeepers to remove all the items from display and that his men would be back to collect them for destruction.

The following morning, the team leader received a call from the head of the wildlife department, based in the capital city. He was ordered never to go near the hotel again. He asked what had prompted this directive. His boss explained that the general manager of the hotel had called the mayor and complained about law enforcement officials entering his premises. This was not what his guests wanted to see, moaned the manager. The mayor phoned the provincial governor. The governor phoned the Minister of Tourism. The Minister phoned the head of the wildlife department.

It must have been terribly frustrating for the head of that team and his officers to have their work interfered with in that manner. It must be equally dreadful, however, for him and his staff, when they read (as they must often do) criticisms in the international media, in reports prepared by non-governmental organizations and, indeed, in documents presented at CITES committee meetings and conferences, that the country in which they live and work is not doing enough to crack down on illegal trade. It is all too easy for us in our ivory towers to lambast others. It is all too easy to fly into a nation, conduct market surveys, be appalled by the findings and then prepare disapproving comments.

CITES undoubtedly benefits by having compliance procedures and, in the main, it makes effective use of those sanction processes. But when I sat and read or listened to calls for trade bans coming from people, some of whom did not have the slightest inkling of what life was really like at the coal face, it really irritated me on occasions. The fact that many of those people were white and enjoyed lifestyles unimaginable to law enforcement staff in the Third World also infuriated me.

I have written many critical reports over the years and was probably one of the people in the Secretariat who most regularly recommended that compliance procedures be instigated. However, I like to think I did not do so until I had reached the point where I believed it was the only way to make a difference and that sanctions might generate the political will that had, up until then, been absent. I hope I never forgot what a kick in the teeth such criticism must have been for the individuals, even if they were only a few, who really had been trying to make a difference and were carrying out their sworn duties in an honest, dedicated and committed fashion, many of them bravely in the face of violence, threats or attempts to corrupt them.

Although it was one of the several reasons why I opted for early retirement, I generally coped well with the many criticisms that were directed at me by those who felt I did not do a good job, that I was biased, that I was blind to what was happening in some parts of the world or that I was corrupt. Having said that, I believe the United Nations is poor at defending or standing up for its staff. I can think of several instances where utter untruths about me, including allegations of corruption, appeared in print, either in emails or on websites. No action was taken. Had similar comments been made during the other period of my law enforcement career, the Police Federation would have sued those responsible. As I write this, I have in front of me a print-out from a website page referring to a 'UN official' (many of those who read the article at the time immediately recognized me in that description) who acted in exchange for bribes '... which I am told totaled (sic) over a half-million dollars,' writes the author. While the allegation is utterly ludicrous and the sum quoted equally so, I imagine there will be people who read the piece and wondered whether or not it was true. Indeed, the author of the piece clearly believed what he had been told. I am sorry to disappoint him and his source but nowhere in the decision-making process leading to my early retirement did it occur to me that I would need the extra years free of work in order to spend my ill-gotten $500,000.

One memory that will never leave me, though, is that of my teenage daughter who read an allegation of corruption directed at me on a website. 'Is that true, Dad?' she asked. 'No, of course not,' I replied. 'Then how can someone say it and get away with that?' It was not easy to explain. But it was relatively easy for me to cope. I was handsomely paid by the United Nations. I lived in a nice house and drove a decent car. My children were privately educated and we enjoyed good family holidays together. I had a reasonable pension to look forward to.

An awful lot of wildlife law enforcement staff do not enjoy such benefits. Imagine how demotivating it must be for them to hear such criticisms. Apart from the fact that they probably have, at least, a semi-reliable government salary, there must be a considerable temptation to ponder why they bother and to go find something else to do which involves much less hassle. I doubt whether the people levelling the criticism would be willing to carry out those duties on occasions.

And it probably gets even worse for the team leader. I can imagine, if CITES does invoke or threaten sanctions unless more is done to eradicate illegal trade, and the necessary national political will is finally achieved, he will end up receiving another call from his boss. I can picture him, phone in hand, saying to himself, 'Oh right, *now* you *do* want me to do something.'

To try and, in some way, help the wildlife team leader I did some web browsing when I got back to Geneva and noted the addresses of the head offices of the world's major hotel chains and the names of their CEOs. I wrote to all of them, politely pointing out the law relating to wildlife trade and how their guests might unknowingly fall foul of this if they innocently (or otherwise) purchased holiday souvenirs, only to have them confiscated by customs when they returned home. I also drew their attention to the fact that, depending upon national legislation, their companies might be liable to prosecution if illegal sales were taking place in their premises. I think we sent off about ten letters in all. I never received a single acknowledgement.

Without doubt, the abuse of position that frustrated and infuriated me the most during my time with CITES was that displayed by diplomats. People with diplomatic status are, to all intents and purposes, immune from prosecution while carrying out their duties. There are good reasons for this, which I would not quarrel with, and it provides a degree of protection that can be essential if they are to operate free from influence or interference. As a United Nations official, I benefited from the same immunity.

And it is not just the diplomats themselves that are free from action by law enforcement officers or prosecutors but also their personal baggage and goods as they are transported between missions and embassies. What several diplomats have failed to realize over the years, though, is that the immunity which applies to them is not quite as wide ranging when it comes to their luggage or 'diplomatic pouches'.

This field of law is dictated by the Vienna Convention on Diplomatic Relations, which has existed since the early 1960s. It was an area of law that I highlighted at every training event I attended, since it provides an important provision that all law enforcement officers, especially border control officials, need to be aware of. Article 36 of the Convention contains the following significant wording: 'The personal baggage of a diplomatic agent shall be exempt from inspection, unless there are serious grounds for presuming that it contains articles not covered by the exemptions mentioned in paragraph 1 of this article, or articles the import or export of which is prohibited by the law or controlled by the quarantine regulations of the receiving State.'

The 'serious grounds for presuming' might emerge from various sources, including intelligence. The most common source was the X-ray machines used in passenger and cargo terminals at air and sea ports. On several occasions I learned of diplomatic baggage passing through airport security X-ray screening and observed to contain highly suspicious items.

I happened to be in an African country when just such a scenario arose. Three military-style metal footlockers were X-rayed shortly before being loaded onto a flight to Asia. Airport security saw that each was packed with objects that were shaped exactly like elephant tusks.

The passenger under whose name the boxes were being transported was summoned from the airport terminal transit lounge and was asked to open them. He refused. He produced a diplomatic passport in his name and bearing a photograph that matched him, which had been issued by a nation in far east Asia. He insisted that the metal boxes were diplomatic baggage and were immune from search.

The police and customs were sent for but were wary of forcing entry to the boxes. Officials from the national wildlife agency were then called. Fortunately, because CITES had, for many years, publicized the abuse of diplomatic immunity, they felt confident enough to take action and they broke open the boxes. Each was packed solid with whole tusks or tusks cut into pieces so as to fit inside. Over half a tonne of ivory was divided between the three containers. The diplomat and the boxes were taken to the agency's headquarters arriving, by pure coincidence, at the same time as me. I was in town for a meeting elsewhere but was simply making a courtesy call at the headquarters.

I reassured them that their actions were legal and congratulated them on their seizure. I then helped them search the boxes thoroughly and examine the contents, which produced some interesting clues as to where the ivory might have originated. I saw the diplomat in custody but took no part in interviewing him. As it happens, he refused to speak and defiantly declared that he should not have been arrested nor his property searched.

Somewhat to my surprise, the prosecution authorities decided to keep the man in custody overnight and brought him before a court the next morning. Personally, I thought they may have been going too far, since the Vienna Convention does offer the individual total immunity. It seemed that the court may have shared my concern, as the magistrate released the man on bail whilst his status as a diplomat was confirmed, but made him surrender his passport. Within the coming days, he fled to a neighbouring country, was issued with a fresh diplomatic passport by his country's embassy there and made his way home. He never has been prosecuted, but neither has he ever seen his metal boxes or ivory again. That, though, is not the end of the story.

On my return to Geneva, I described to the CITES Secretary-General what I had seen. I also went on to explain that this was the third occasion in eighteen months when large quantities of ivory had been detected in luggage or cargo declared as 'diplomatic pouches' headed for the same country. The others had occurred in Western Europe and in the Russian Federation. We agreed this had gone on long enough.

Since Geneva is the European headquarters for the United Nations, most countries of the world have Permanent Missions based there, staffed by senior diplomats who will represent their nation's interest at UN events. The Ambassador of the country in question was invited to come and meet with the Secretary-General. I was present for the encounter.

My boss began to read out details of the three seizures from a briefing note I had prepared for him and had just started to express his concern when the Ambassador interrupted him. He loudly denounced the information as lies and was adamant that no diplomats from his country would ever have anything to do wildlife smuggling. Calming down somewhat, and presumably remembering that he too was meant to behave diplomatically, he said that he expected some mistake had taken place and that his country had been confused with some other. The Secretary-General looked at me and gestured that I should take over.

'Mr Ambassador', I began, before going on to describe what I had experienced just days before in Africa, including having seen the alleged diplomat himself and the document that had every appearance of being a diplomatic passport issued in his nation's capital. I, too, was interrupted. But this time there was no holding the Ambassador back. He began to rant, telling me that I was a lackey of the United States' Central Intelligence Agency and was clearly being paid to spread vicious smears against his proud and honest country. Rising from his chair, he then stormed out of the Secretary-General's office. We never saw or heard from him again.

The Secretary-General's gaze switched from the back of the disappearing diplomat to me and he smiled. 'Well, John,' he said, 'I think that went really smoothly, don't you?'

One explanation, but certainly not an excuse, for this type of behaviour can be found in how diplomats were, or sometimes still are, designated. Some nations, in times past, tended to appoint their ambassadors by way of honouring individuals. Such people were not career civil servants or individuals with experience of international diplomacy but might instead have supported or endorsed heads of state prior to their election. In most cases, they were wealthy people and needed to be, as often no salary or budget accompanied the appointment. Whilst diplomats representing most 'developed world' countries are officials with long service in the relevant Ministry of Foreign Affairs or State Department, the same is not true for all personnel in the many embassies around the world. Some, especially those representing developing countries or countries with economies in transition, still find themselves appointed without salary and must rely on exploiting their position to fund both their official and personal expenses. This can, and has, prompted some to engage in illicit activities.

I suspect the diplomat in the incident described above was probably acting on his own behalf, one reason being that he held a very senior position in his State's embassy in a country in West Africa. But some people with diplomatic status, usually junior embassy employees, are undoubtedly used by organized networks either to collect contraband from poachers or to transport it out of the country. They are essentially mules with a diplomatic passport. This scenario has certainly been seen in South Africa, where its government declared two Vietnamese 'diplomats' *persona non grata* in relation to the handling of poached rhino horn, and both individuals had to leave the country.

I mentioned how, as a UN official, I also had immunity. I like to think I never abused it. But I did exploit it and in what might, at first sight, seem a strange way. As a police officer in Scotland, especially during my service as a detective, I regularly dealt with informants. The recruitment and handling of informants, if properly and legally conducted, can often be one of the most efficient techniques within the field of law enforcement. It is also by far the most important element of counter-terrorism work. But no informant will ever deal with the police or security services unless he or she is confident that their identity will never be disclosed.

Whilst the prosecution and judicial authorities in Scotland and most other countries have ways of preserving the anonymity of informants, I would have had to name an informant if a court insisted upon it during the course of a criminal trial.

In contrast, as a United Nations appointee, I could not be summoned before any court and so if I told someone I would keep their name secret, I could guarantee to do just that.

Over the years I built up quite an extensive network of informants in countries across the world. Sometimes these were government officials but often they were people involved in, or on the fringes of, wildlife trade. Sometimes they were carrying out their business legally, sometimes not. The latter provided some of the most valuable insights into what was taking place and supplied information that I was able to pass on to national authorities, prompting investigations and seizures. Unfortunately, there were several occasions where information came to me so late, especially taking time differences into account, that I was unable to stop the smuggling.

I once, for example, received a phone call about a passenger carrying a rhino horn who was heading from Johannesburg to Ho Chi Minh City. By the time I managed to alert the authorities in Viet Nam, though, the flight had already arrived and the person had cleared customs and left the airport.

But it was not just the public who contacted me. There were many occasions when law enforcement officials, for one reason or another, preferred not to pass intelligence to their counterparts elsewhere in the world, either directly or via Interpol or World Customs Organization channels. In such cases, they would ask me to act as the communication conduit, knowing that I could absolutely promise that the identity of the source would not be disclosed.

Unfortunately, I was aware of other UN staff who did abuse their status. Sometimes this was so that they could transport wildlife souvenirs back home, like ivory carvings or ornamental big cat skins, knowing that CITES permits would not be issued because of the nature of the item. At least what amounted to smuggling in those cases was not of a commercial nature or involved live animals. But we also learned of incidents where it was or did, and these invariably involved UN peacekeeping forces.

Two illustrations come readily to mind. In the first, I was told by several sources that exotic skins, of animals such as leopard and snow leopard, were openly on sale in the markets of Kabul. This was shortly after the US-led invasion of Afghanistan. I was also informed that some of the most regular customers were military troops who were purchasing skins and other wildlife products prior to going on leave or returning home at the end of a deployment period. Some of these items were being purchased simply as souvenirs but I heard of military personnel who were buying them in such numbers that they clearly intended to sell them in due course.

In the other case, a troop of UN peacekeepers were about to board a military aircraft in West Africa to return to their home in Eastern Europe when local wildlife officers noticed that they had a live juvenile chimpanzee with them. The officials demanded its surrender but the soldiers refused. The wildlife officials called their customs colleagues and asked for their support. Unfortunately, unsure of their legal authority, the customs officers declined to act, having been swayed by the insistence of the men in blue berets that they were immune from the country's wildlife laws.

Notice of this incident did not come to Geneva for several weeks. As soon as it did, I contacted CITES authorities in the country which had provided the peacekeeping unit and asked them to investigate. But it was too late. The soldiers all denied the matter and it is not known what happened to the chimp.

Once again, the CITES Secretary-General and I tried to act. I prepared letters which he sent to the head of Peacekeeping Operations at UN headquarters in New York and to the Secretary General of NATO. I also contacted the CITES office in each of the countries that were supplying troops for operations in Afghanistan and encouraged them to check returning troops and their baggage. At the same time, I worked with my counterpart Chief in the Investigations Division of the UN's equivalent of internal affairs to warn United Nations staff that the organization would take action against anyone abusing their status and to put in place mechanisms to facilitate that.

I cannot claim that we eradicated such abuse but it seemed to reduce and at least we helped spread the word that no one is exempt from the provisions of CITES. A couple of years later, I was contacted for advice by senior officers of a military peacekeeping force who had discovered a soldier sending commercial-size quantities of ivory out of a central African country where they were trying to maintain order. The solder was sent home in disgrace and court martialled.

That was another small step forward that helped me think that I was, occasionally, making a difference.

CORRUPTING, THREATENING AND KILLING

CORRUPTION OF JUDICIAL PROCESS

In many parts of the world, those tasked with enforcing their nation's wildlife laws will be parks, forestry or game department personnel. They seldom enjoy parity with their counterparts in customs or the police. This applies not only with regard to the training they receive, the legal authority or powers that are provided to them in legislation, the equipment issued to them, the salaries they receive and the compensation available to their families should they be injured or killed on duty, but also to the status they enjoy in the community.

I have been told, on several occasions by different officials in different countries, how they have approached a suspect – in an airport, for example - and have asked to examine their luggage, only for the person simply to ignore them and walk away. Calls to customs or the police for assistance may be similarly ignored or, worse, a customs officer will lead the person away but refuse to allow the wildlife officer to accompany them. A short time later, the suspect will be seen being waved off from the customs area but still in possession of the item that attracted the wildlife officer's attention. A bribe had obviously been paid and accepted. There are, regrettably, more examples of how some law enforcement agency staff will deliberately abuse their authority to manipulate a wildlife-related incident to their own profit.

Many wildlife officials around the world have the power to arrest individuals they have discovered committing an offence but are unable to report such people for prosecution or keep them in custody until they appear in court. Instead, they must hand the suspect over to the local police. This may make sense: few wildlife departments or park headquarters have cells, for instance, while most police stations do. It may also seem prudent to have police officers, more experienced in preparing cases for court, check over the evidence and the way in which it was collected, take or review witness statements and conduct any interviews of the suspect. But it adds a link, perhaps an unnecessary one, to the judicial process chain.

During a visit to Indonesia in 1999 to examine poaching and illegal trade in tigers, and then while in the same country in 2006 to examine illegal trade in orang-utans, I heard from several forest officers that they viewed the police as the weak link in the chain. This displayed itself in various forms: the police did not take wildlife seriously and could not be bothered to write a prosecution case; they would demand to be paid to take the case forward (the few forest officials who agreed to pay were never sure whether such fees went into official police coffers or just into the local policemen's pockets); the police would subsequently advise forest officials that the evidence was insufficient and that the suspects had been released (it was acknowledged that such assessments would, from time to time, be justified); and the police would insist on the gathering of further evidence or information but in an oppressive manner (it was not clear whether this was simply to discourage forest officials from arresting suspects or to justify why a case was not prepared). Forest officials would subsequently learn from other sources that the suspects had been released and no case prepared. They would also learn that the suspect's families had bought their freedom from the police or that pressure and influence had been brought to bear to secure their release.

Trying to overcome hurdles like these was difficult, especially if it was hard to distinguish between what was a simple lack of interest and what was abuse or misuse of authority. At the time of the 2006 visit, however, the Forest Department was negotiating with the prosecution authorities to enable its staff to report cases directly.

In Africa, where wardens and game scouts had often been in the habit of reporting poaching cases directly to prosecutors' offices, another hurdle sometimes presented itself. There, a warden who had elephant poachers in custody and would be bringing them into court could approach the police and ask for details of any previous convictions the accused might have on record. The judge or magistrate would want to have that information when determining an appropriate sentence. The police would supply it.

However, if a warden was investigating poaching and was perhaps trying to corroborate intelligence that he had received, he would not encounter the same level of co-operation. If the warden approached the police and told them that John Sellar was in custody and would be appearing in court the next day, for example, he would get details of Sellar's previous convictions. But if he approached the police and told them that an informant alleged that John Sellar was controlling poaching and that he was interested to learn whether Sellar had convictions that might demonstrate the truth of the information, the details would be declined.

This appeared to be due to nothing more than the police failing to respect the warden's position as one of the nation's law enforcement officers. They saw the warden purely as someone whose job it was to react to events. They did not see him as having a proactive or investigatory remit.

Failures on the part of customs or police agencies to assist or support wildlife enforcement officials corrupts the judicial process just as effectively as if some customs or police officer takes a bribe to look the other way or let the guilty go free.

And the weak links do not always wear uniforms. Officials dressed in wigs and gowns were also regularly described to me as being responsible for allowing criminals to escape justice.

BRIBERY AND CORRUPTION

When the illegal trade in caviar from the Caspian Sea area was at its peak, in the late 1990s and early 2000s, it was noted that major quantities were entering international markets through a particular country in the Middle East. Since that country had no caviar production of its own, the shipments, sometimes involving huge quantities, were leaving the country with CITES re-export certificates. Theoretically, there need not have been anything wrong. Historically, much of the world's caviar had been re-exported from, for instance, Germany and Switzerland. However, that was because companies based in those nations had been trading in caviar and other luxury food products for decades. They, and their management and staff, were renowned around the world for being the absolute experts in selecting the finest ingredients and had built up relationships over many years, stretching back into the days of the USSR, with the fish and caviar processors. They enjoyed similar relations with the processors in the Islamic Republic of Iran.

But when I looked at the certificates being presented to importing countries, the information quoted on them about the origin of the caviar, and the countries from which it was allegedly exported, either did not make sense or it was in conflict with data I already had from those countries. As time passed, I became more and more convinced that a major laundering operation was in place. I wrote to the country in question and asked that they provide copies of every permit or certificate authorizing trade in caviar that had been issued that year. It was by then October and quite a bundle duly arrived in Geneva.

I began to work my way through the pile of paperwork and compared the documents against copies I had called for from Azerbaijan, Iran, Kazakhstan and the Russian Federation. Over the course of several days, and not a few evenings, a pattern of massive fraud began to emerge. I cannot describe the exact nature of it, as that might simply provide a how-to guide for future criminals, and what materialized helped flag up ways of preventing and detecting future crime. But if I was impressed by the scale of what was very clearly highly-organized and sophisticated deception, it was nothing compared to when I took a calculator and began to try to work out just how much money was involved.

This was not straightforward. To begin with, I tried to estimate the value of the caviar in each shipment and this had to reflect not only the species involved - beluga caviar is much more expensive than sevruga, for instance - but also the country of origin, as some countries' products attracted higher prices than others. I also had to bear in mind that, while I tapped away at the keys of a calculator and scribbled increasingly long lists of figures, forensic science was disclosing a whole new dimension to illicit trade in caviar.

The forensic laboratory of the US Fish and Wildlife Service, a facility that I had the great pleasure to visit on several occasions and which was a front runner in the development of techniques to assist wildlife law enforcement and to uncover fraud, had begun routinely to obtain samples from every caviar shipment arriving at that country's ports. It was then subjecting them to the still fairly new process - in terms of wildlife cases - of DNA profiling. This was enabling the lab's scientists to determine whether consignments declared as containing beluga caviar did actually consist of the eggs extracted from the relevant species of sturgeon. In the case of beluga caviar, it is the processed eggs of only one species, *Huso huso,* the largest and longest-living of all sturgeon and also arguably the largest freshwater fish in the world. Females do not become sexually mature, and so do not produce eggs that can be processed into caviar, until they are about 25 years old, but they can live for over 100 years. Many specimens of beluga have been recorded at over 1,000 kg in weight and over 5 metres from head to tail. It is estimated that fully-grown females can produce up to seven and a half million eggs.

Time after time, the laboratory's DNA results were demonstrating that the refrigerated freight landing at places like JFK Airport in New York had been misdeclared and, consequently, that American companies were being deliberately conned into paying for sub-standard merchandise. It also, of course, called into question whether the CITES permits accompanying the freight were genuine and if the caviar itself was legal-origin. If the permits were questionable, did this indicate fraudulent applications by traders or corruption and collusion on the part of issuing authorities?

With this in mind, I gave up trying to compute accurate estimates and just used guesstimate values instead. I really need not have worried that I might be under-estimating the scale of criminality. When I totalled everything up, I discovered that, at a minimum and at wholesale prices, the equivalent of 21 million dollars' worth of caviar had been laundered through the Middle East nation. As this was still before the price of caviar absolutely sky-rocketed, then today that figure would have to be multiplied by at least five. And if the total were converted to retail costs, it would probably need to be multiplied again by ten. I could not believe my own addition and asked a colleague to confirm my figures. He was as stunned as I had been at the huge profits that were obviously being made by whichever groups were behind this. And this was just for one ten-month period of one year.

But what the copy documents from the Gulf State did not tell me was who those groups were and, equally importantly, how they had been acquiring the CITES certificates. The certificates were not forgeries or counterfeits. They had not been stolen. They were the genuine article and they had been issued by the CITES authorities in the re-exporting country. What was not clear to me at that stage was what had led to them being issued. Whilst fraudulent and false declarations at the time of application could offer some explanation - government officials having been duped into issuing the certificates - the scale of the criminal activity made this hardly credible. What also indicated some corruption or collusion was that the same false origin details had been entered on many certificates. Surely even the most incompetent civil servant would have spotted that something was wrong? Additionally, the simplest of checks would have shown that these substantial quantities of caviar had not been cleared for import into the country. So where had they come from? They must have been smuggled in: there was no other possible answer.

At this point, I should emphasize that I did not then, and do not now, have any suspicion that anyone in a senior position in the government had any knowledge of or involvement in what was taking place. And this is why.

There are few countries in the world where wildlife trade features prominently in gross domestic product or brings substantial revenue to government coffers. Consequently, those who oversee and authorize transactions in fauna and flora are often situated within environmental ministries, parks authorities, forestry divisions, veterinary departments and the like. To find CITES matters inside a ministry of trade and industry is rare. And because CITES is, or has often been, seen as of minor importance, the number of people devoted to its administration and implementation may be very limited. I have visited several countries where the responsibility may rest with one single civil servant. Even where there are more, one often finds that overall responsibility and oversight rests with a lone mid-level manager. This may have a number of knock-on consequences.

It is not unheard of to find the individual has been in that position for many years. He or she has built up knowledge of the Convention and has a relationship with traders that no one else shares. This creates a situation where that individual may guard, very jealously, his little bit of power and knowledge. It has made him, or less commonly her, the nation's expert on CITES. If one adds to this scenario the fact that those further up the managerial or civil service tree do not usually want to hear that there are problems, then the individual may be left feeling very alone and unsupported. Indeed, I came across several cultures around the world where identifying problems is actively discouraged. That is why, several years ago, some of India's tiger reserves were gradually being emptied of their tigers by poachers but senior management in the ministries of environment and forestry in state and central Government were ignorant of the fact until it was too late. The managers of the reserves and their staff knew that a crisis was occurring but were, essentially, too scared to report it to their supervisors.

It is said that, 'power corrupts, absolute power corrupts absolutely.' This need not mean that those in charge of CITES offices inevitably become corrupt or collude in criminal behaviour, but a very few will. There can also be a total lack of action when problems begin to surface. I lost count of the number of times that we in Geneva would write to national management authorities expressing concern about a particular issue, or the general implementation of the Convention in a country, only to get no response at all or to be fobbed off with empty reassurances.

Sometimes, addressing and resolving the concern would be wholly outside the individual's power or remit. For instance, it might be that his country's legislation has been analysed by the Secretariat's lawyers and found to be inadequate with regard to implementing the Convention. Reminder after reminder would be sent but nothing would happen. The head of the national CITES office could no more introduce new legislation into parliament than I could, but he did not want to have to go to his masters and report that things were beginning to go wrong or that their nation was coming under international scrutiny or, even worse, criticism.

And, so, when I sought and received an invitation to visit the country in the Middle East through which the caviar was flowing, I discovered, as I had elsewhere, that the several faxes of concern that we had sent, over a period of many months, had gone no further than the middle manager's desk. Was that person corrupt? Was he colluding with the criminals? Was he incompetent? Was he simply unaware of what others were doing behind his back? I do not know. I have my opinions but I will keep them to myself. I do, though, know what was motivating one of his junior personnel, whose job it was to process permit and certificate applications.

I met with this man and asked him about the manner in which certificates were being issued and described the conclusions I had reached when I had reviewed all the copies. He seemed at a loss for words. I posed several questions, pointing to features on the documents that showed that everything was not above board. He remained silent. I do not know that there was anything specific that made me do what I did next. Maybe it was intuition, a detective's hunch? Call it what you will, but a realization was gradually dawning upon me.

'You've been threatened, haven't you?' I asked. His face took on a stunned expression and I knew I had hit the mark. 'You mustn't tell anyone!' he gasped. 'Please!' he implored, 'They said they'd hurt my family.'

Over the next few minutes he described how, one day, he had been approached by someone who regularly came to his office to apply for caviar re-export certificates. The applicant, as he had often done before, presented paperwork to justify the origin of the shipment. The civil servant had seen the paperwork many times and, like me, had come to realize that this was a complete scam. He began to say so and indicated that the days of his supplying certificates were over. Instead of being warned off, though, the applicant started to name the official's wife, his children and where they went to school. He also told the official what would happen to him and his family if certificates were not issued. The civil servant begged me not to tell anyone else.

He had continued to issue certificates, mainly because of the threats but also because he realized that he had repeatedly been taken in by fraudulent applications and was scared that his own colleagues and managers would not believe that he had not participated willingly and corruptly.

This reflected what I had read in the transcript of an interview which had been shared with me. In it, a person who had been prosecuted far from the Middle East had admitted how he had travelled there to view, select and purchase caviar. He had confessed to having paid, on occasion, Caucasian prostitutes to entertain CITES officials in return for re-export certificates. He had also described how, on other occasions, he had paid bribes to the same officials in order to obtain documents. Another passage of the transcript told how he had once been taken to a large refrigerated warehouse to sample caviar stored there. He had met with people of Russian origin with whom he had conducted business. He expressed amazement at the quantities of caviar in storage and had noted that men armed with AK-47s were on guard. The caviar had two prices: the first, and more expensive, came with CITES documents. If he chose the cheaper caviar, he had either to arrange for the goods to be smuggled out of the country or make his own arrangements to obtain CITES certificates.

Over the course of the following year the Secretariat worked closely and very effectively with the country, which became a shining example of effective CITES implementation. I suspect, as with illegal trade from several other countries, organized crime had identified institutional weaknesses which they manipulated, very profitably, to their own ends.

The caviar laundering? It ceased from that country but shifted somewhere else. And yet it reduced markedly and the groups behind it did not enjoy the easy passage that they had previously so effectively exploited. As far as I know, none of the people responsible for the laundering were ever identified or prosecuted.

And the office manager? I do not know what happened to him but I never saw him at another CITES event.

Sitting in an office in Geneva, it was sometimes very difficult to determine what was behind some of the apparent collusion or corruption that I witnessed. Some of it was regular and widespread but went on unnoticed a good deal of the time. Unless there were specific reasons to do so, as in the major laundering case described above, neither I nor my colleagues would routinely review the permits and certificates that national CITES authorities were issuing. We did often learn of problems, though, when we were contacted by CITES offices in importing countries.

Many countries around the world have policies under which they will not authorize an import of CITES specimens until they have seen a copy of the export permit or re-export certificate issued by the country from which the shipment will arrive. When they were troubled by features of that document, they would contact Geneva. I soon lost count of the number of times that I would examine such copies and find, for instance, that they authorized trade in captive-bred specimens, even though no such operations existed in the country in question. Alternatively, we would see quantities of birds, for example, being exported in numbers that would have required massive breeding operations that were well beyond the capacities of traders in the country. I would also see specimens authorized for export, marked as having been taken from the wild, from countries where those species did not even exist. When I wrote to the issuing countries, outlined my observations and sought their comments, some of what I got back was incredible.

I would be told that 'the permits had been issued in error'. How could officials mistake which species existed in their country and which did not? How could they issue a document declaring something as bred in captivity, knowing that there were no breeding facilities in their territory?

Another common response was that the permit was a forgery. And yet it appeared to be genuine, might have a genuine security stamp on it and bore a signature identical to that of the person who was replying to me. When I pointed that out, I would be told that they had just realized that it must be one of a batch of permits, pre-stamped and signed but left blank, that had been stolen from the office and that they apologized for not telling us about the theft sooner. It stretched my credulity beyond breaking point. However, without firm evidence to demonstrate either corruption or collusion, it was difficult for us publicly to challenge some of these statements and diplomatically inappropriate for us as UN officials to comment that we thought we were being lied to. I was often aware that importing countries, seeking our guidance, must have been very frustrated by our carefully-worded and sometimes vague responses.

Another area of concern involved countries where export quotas had been adopted for specific species, either voluntarily at the country's own instigation or on the recommendation of the CITES scientific committees. However, we would discover that some CITES offices would continue to issue permits long after the quota had been exceeded. Here, too, we would be told when we voiced our concern either that it was a mistake or that the specimens intended for export had been harvested in previous years and should be allocated to past quotas (ignoring the fact that they too had been exceeded). Sometimes we were asked to accept the explanation that birds had been sitting in a trader's premises for more than two years before they decided to export them. That does not make financial sense in the best economies of the world and certainly not in nations where the majority of the population was living on or below the poverty line.

When I first moved to Geneva I was taken aback by what I was convinced were downright lies in some of the messages that would arrive from national authorities. I soon learned that this is what operating at international levels sometimes involved. During my 14 years in the job, there were several occasions when the Secretariat was obliged to issue notifications to all the CITES signatory countries recommending that they should not accept documents from such-and-such a country without first checking with us. In the case of one country, the falsehoods and different explanations we received, while the person with whom we were dealing was sending conflicting messages to importing countries, became so tangled and extensive that we ended up simply having to say that we were not in any position to advise whether exports from that nation were legal or illegal.

A sometimes maddening thing about communicating with national authorities is that one is usually obliged to connect only with whatever office, or whichever official, has been designated by its government. This works well until trust breaks down. When that happens, you are left corresponding with an individual whom you may suspect of corruption or collusion with unscrupulous traders. And, as we've already seen, you may be writing to that person asking for specific action, or seeking an invitation to visit, knowing that he is simply sitting on those messages, denying that he is receiving them or simply destroying them.

When things got really bad, we usually opted to communicate via the Permanent Missions in Geneva, and using diplomatic channels could certainly help most of the time. Not always, though. I once wrote to diplomats in Geneva providing them with allegations of corruption against the head of their country's CITES Management Authority. I had hoped they would pass these to an appropriate investigatory agency in their capital and specifically requested them to do so. Instead, they forwarded the message to the suspect and asked him to comment. Not surprisingly, he denied everything. However, the allegations continued and I finally obtained some clear evidence. This time, the Mission took action and the individual was 'retired'.

Even when you do trust the person at the other end of the phone, fax or email, technology can let you both down. It is not unusual to hear people in Britain complain about broadband connections or speeds. I wonder how they would cope with the horrendous connections in West and Central Africa, where it can take hours to download the simplest document from the internet. I know of some CITES offices where the staff have to go to internet cafes in order to send and receive messages. Parts of Asia suffer too, but in other ways. When I was last in Kathmandu in early 2011, a government official said he was pleased if he had uninterrupted electricity supply for three hours each day.

My work for CITES shared one frustrating aspect with my work in the police: it's all very well to 'know' something, but proving it can be another matter. And, just as you cannot drag an accused criminal into court unless you have evidence that he might be guilty, you cannot go criticizing countries in front of the international community unless you are really sure of your position and can back it up.

Often the only way to resolve matters, discover the truth and make contact with someone who can make a difference is to go to the country in question. That wasn't possible every time a problem arose, and in any case I was already spending a lot of every year travelling the world. CITES badly needs to undertake more *in situ* verification and assessment work but simply does not have the financial and human resources to do so. I regret that the parties to the Convention, and its committees, sometimes have completely unreasonable and unrealistic expectations of the Secretariat.

One group of individuals whose complicity in illegal wildlife trade is generally overlooked, I think, are veterinary surgeons. Although I can think of two vets who contacted me to express their concerns about what they were encountering during their day-to-day work, there must be countless others who came across patients whose presence in a country or possession by an individual should have rung alarm bells.

And I use the word 'complicity' deliberately. Veterinarians may not be morally obliged or legally bound to report suspicious circumstances, but just as a trauma room doctor may have to report to the police a patient brought in with gunshot or knife wounds, I know of many instances where it must have been abundantly clear to vets that crimes had been committed.

One of the vets who contacted me was utterly fed up of being called to treat leopards and cheetahs owned by wealthy clients in a country where the surgeon knew very well that the animals could not possibly have been imported legally. The other was the personal vet of an individual who owned a very extensive exotic species collection, to which had been added a mammal that could not possibly have been of legal origin. Whilst the vet insisted on anonymity, I think his contacting me was commendable and probably displayed a not insignificant degree of courage. I am sure life would have become very uncomfortable for him if his employer had learned what he had done.

But others should hang their heads in shame. There were vets working, some of them full-time, in zoos and safari parks that were acquiring animals like orang-utans in numbers that displayed blatant violations of the Convention. Their conduct was even more disgraceful in those facilities where animals died during training that involved inhumane practices.

The same embarrassment should be felt by particular quarantine officers around the world, some of whom were also veterinarians, who must have regularly endorsed documents relating to shipments of animals and plants that they knew, or ought to have, known, were being transported illegally. These same officials appeared also, on occasions, to have ignored the fact that live animals were being shipped in crates and containers utterly unsuitable for the purpose and which failed to meet the well-known requirements of the International Air Transport Association. Whilst I accept that some of these officers may have been ignorant of the requirements, had not been trained adequately, were under-resourced, poorly equipped and overworked, I can see no explanation for the failings of others other than that they had accepted bribes to turn a blind eye or, alternatively, that they simply did not care.

In recent years, during the upsurge of rhino poaching in South Africa, some vets appear to have crossed the line completely and have actively and personally engaged in criminality. It seems that individuals have supplied tranquilizing chemicals to rhino poachers while others may actually have been present at poaching sites, perhaps even firing the tranquilizing darts into the animals.

Veterinary surgeons and quarantine officers, by the very nature of their profession and calling, have a duty to do their utmost to protect fauna and flora. If they deliberately fail to do so, they are as contemptible as the worst 'bent cop'.

Whilst not exactly worthy of the title 'official', I would direct the same condemnation at some members of the professional sport hunting industry in South Africa. These people were hired, often for significant fees, to lead individuals posing as hunters in fraudulent expeditions to track and kill rhinos. The horns, purportedly obtained as trophies, would then be shipped to black markets in Asia. These professional hunters know a *bona fide* client when they see one, yet I have been told of clients who not only had obviously never handled a rifle before but who did not know how to aim or fire it. It seems that some of these professionals may, not infrequently, have shot rhinos on the clients' behalf. Not only were these professional hunters and guides complicit in wildlife crime, but they appear to have milked it for all it was worth. The sums charged for rhino hunting markedly increased when the pseudo-hunting was at its peak. The only compensation is that several of these so-called professionals have found themselves in South Africa's courts and will hopefully spend many years in prison. They will have time to reflect on how they brought shame upon an activity that ought to contribute to conservation and bring important revenue to rural communities.

The military, too, were occasionally guilty of shameful behaviour. One non-commissioned officer of Zimbabwe's elite Commando force led poaching gangs in search of rhinos, using his marksmanship, his knowledge of how to move through enemy territory and his camouflage skills. This man was finally arrested when wildlife park officers responded to reports of gunshots in one of the country's national parks. The NCO, together with his accomplices, was stopped, dressed in a police uniform, as he drove out of the park. He tried to bluff his way past a roadblock by claiming that he was actually in search of the offenders but the presence of a high-powered rifle in the car and bloody rhino horns tied to the chassis did not help his case.

If I recall correctly, he was subsequently granted bail – in itself bizarre, given the seriousness of the crime and the abuse of his position – and fled the country. For the moment, I believe he remains a fugitive from justice. Readers may ponder, as I did, whether the granting of bail in those circumstances suggests yet more corruption among officials.

CORRUPTION OF LAW ENFORCEMENT PERSONNEL

When one sees the poor pay levels endured by those who work in developing countries, it should come as no surprise whatsoever that some men and women will be tempted to add to take-home wages that barely feed them and their families. Many of the countries I visited had no free education or very poor quality schools, so enforcement officials who wanted to finance their children's future had to find the money to send them to classes.

I can as a result empathize, to a degree, with the individual who is offered money to turn a blind eye to something or, for example, to facilitate smuggling by signing export forms without properly checking the cargo.

What I have less tolerance for are those law enforcement officials who seem actively to seek opportunities to acquire bribes. Unfortunately, those in positions of authority or influence are inevitably regularly presented with such opportunities. I greatly admired Michel Danet, the Secretary-General of the World Customs Organization during my early years with CITES, who did much to encourage that organization and its member countries to tackle corruption, a subject which many people will not even mention, let alone address. I have often quoted his words: 'There are few public agencies in which the classic preconditions for institutional corruption are so conveniently presented as in a customs administration.'

I have never forgotten the time the head of a wildlife agency in central Africa described to me how he had been invited to speak to a gathering of 30 customs officers, drawn from all around his nation. I asked him whether they had shown interest in his talk about wildlife laws and the important role that customs authorities have in protecting natural resources. 'Well,' he said, 'as the lecture progressed I could see that I was reaching my audience. However, what I could also see was that about half of the people in the room were thinking that, yes, this was a worthwhile area for customs officers to focus upon and that they did have a vital part to play. But I could also see that the other half were sitting thinking, 'Ah, there's money to be made here, I need to give this more attention.' I wondered, Mr Sellar, whether I was cancelling out the good at the same time as creating it.'

I had a similar experience years ago in Mozambique. Training was not a large part of my work but I was certainly keen to get involved where it was obviously badly needed, as it was in many regions. Unfortunately, those officials in specialized agencies such as forest departments or game park authorities, for whom wildlife law enforcement may be a full-time task, seldom receive the same basic training that, for example, a customs or police officer in their country might get. They might not, for instance, be taught interviewing skills, how to prepare prosecution cases, examine scenes of crime, gather evidence or handle informants. As a result, we organized several events across the globe during my time with CITES at which we tried to deliver what I would regard as elementary policing skills.

Unfortunately, it is also the case that many customs and police officers in such nations do not get anything like the level of training given to their counterparts in Europe or North America.

The training course in Mozambique was organized by the TRAFFIC non-governmental organization, which does excellent work around the world in supporting enforcement and in monitoring legal and illegal trade in wildlife. If I recall correctly, we travelled several hours from the capital of Maputo to the simple rural town of Naamacha. It was lovely countryside but one could see that it had suffered during the years of civil unrest that had plagued this beautiful country. The owner of the hotel where the training took place had many interesting tales to tell about the war years, especially as Naamacha was located close to the border with Swaziland and South Africa. Several of the major buildings in the town were abandoned and bullet-scarred. I was conscious, however, that Mozambique is in no hurry to forget its struggles for independence and democracy, particularly as its national flag bears the image of an AK-47 assault rifle.

The capacity building, delivered over several days, was quite slow, as most of those attending spoke only Portuguese, whilst the trainers spoke only English. With the help of bi-lingual participants, though, we struggled through. Listening to consecutive interpretation can be tedious but everyone showed a great thirst for knowledge and the enthusiasm and active participation was among the best I had experienced.

I recall a senior wildlife warden from the north of the country, an English speaker, who was especially helpful and who paid great attention to my enforcement-specific inputs. It was with great sadness that I learned, several months later, that he had been shot during an anti-poaching incident. My sadness deepened, however, when I discovered that he had been shot by the police. It was the warden who had been leading the poaching gang.

I have often wondered whether the training equipped him to be a better poacher. Regrettably, bad cops (whatever agency they belong to) make really good criminals. And, equally regrettably, it is far from unknown for anti-poaching personnel to turn rogue and use their skills, and government-supplied weapons and ammunition, to engage in illegal hunting.

VIOLENCE TOWARDS LAW ENFORCEMENT PERSONNEL

It is important to acknowledge that violence need not always be physical, but can encompass threats, harassment and intimidation.

Any poacher suddenly confronted by a law enforcement official may react violently in order to avoid arrest. Those who are part of organized gangs and networks, though, tend to go prepared to use violence, like the rhino gangs equipped with their rapid-fire AK-47s or the Somali gangs entering national parks in Kenya carrying rocket-propelled grenades. The mere fact that gangs are likely to be armed in this way has an incredibly powerful and perfectly understandable effect upon the motivation of anti-poaching personnel. This is even more acute if the department that employs them has no scheme to compensate either them or their family if things go horribly wrong, as they easily can.

I was constantly impressed by the way in which front-line staff displayed astonishing bravery and dedication in the face of horrendous odds. Seldom were they equipped with the same level of firepower as those they sought to detect and arrest. I remember being flown in by helicopter to spend time with a three-man patrol in the middle of a vast national park in Zimbabwe. Their food rations, and occasionally water too, were dropped from light aircraft at intervals during their 14-day shift. They were dressed in shorts and short-sleeved shirts. They each carried a camouflage jacket in their backpacks.

They had one map and one compass between them but they probably knew the area better than any cartographer. They had field dressings in case one of them was hurt in an accident or suffered a gunshot wound. They had no anti-malarial medicines and nothing to treat the dengue fever which was rife in the area. They laughed when I asked if they had insect repellant although tsetse flies were commonplace there. They slept in the open. They did have a radio but there was no reception in some areas, or they had to climb a hill to get a signal strong enough to contact their base. They each had a rifle and a small amount of ammunition but the rifles were old and only semi-automatic.

The senior game scout in charge of the team spoke good English but the others spoke the Shona language of rural residents. Times were hard in Zimbabwe. It was the late 1990s and the country was heading into a recession where the cost of a beer would soon reach millions of Zimbabwean dollars. Anti-poaching patrol work entitled them to a special allowance, over and above their salaries, but the allowance had not been paid for months.

It was approaching midday. It was open savannah. The few trees around were devoid of leaves and offered no shade from the baking sun high overhead. But they were in good spirits and had been heading towards a hill in the far-off distance where clumps of trees offered shelter and wood for that evening's small campfire. They did not always light a fire to cook on, however, since it risked giving their position away to poachers.

The senior scout was especially happy. He was just back from leave, when he had visited his home village, hundreds of miles from the park, and seen his first-born child, a son, born a few weeks before. He was as pleased and proud as any other new dad. 'What would you like your son to be when he grows up?' I asked. He looked puzzled and, thinking he hadn't understood, I was about to pose the question again, but then he spoke. 'A game scout.' And I realized that his puzzlement was because he could not imagine what finer calling a son could possibly answer and had assumed that this would be obvious to me.

Later that day, looking down over the Zambezi as the helicopter banked to land at the park headquarters, I could understand why the scout was proud to do what he did and why he would be proud for his son to follow in his footsteps. And I was more than a little ashamed to know that I would not want to do that job.

Several years later, I went on patrol with fishery protection officers in Kazakhstan. As we headed downriver towards the Caspian Sea, they proudly described how the vessel we were in, although relatively simple and open-topped, was equipped with really powerful Japanese-built outboard motors. When the throttles were opened, the bow rose up impressively and a massive wake stretched out behind us.

They explained how, until relatively recently, none of their Russian-manufactured outboards were fast enough to catch the poachers' speedboats. But the team leader went on to describe that, sometimes, catching up with poachers was not such a good idea. He related the experience he'd had one dark night the previous year, when he and his two-man crew had spotted, through binoculars, a boat, with three men hauling in a net that was clearly heavy and full of sturgeon.

The fishery protection unit slammed their vessel into as high a speed as possible and sped towards the offending craft. The poachers, alerted by the noise, let go their net and sped off. This was a scenario that the fishery officers regularly encountered. That night, however, something seemed to be different. The poachers' boat was not making nearly as good progress as might have been expected. Thanking God, or Stalin, or Lenin, or whoever Kazakh law enforcement officials thank, the team leader told his crew that luck was with them and that something must be wrong with the motor on their target vessel. Gradually, they drew close to the poachers and called upon them to heave to.

As they pulled alongside, though, the real trouble started. Just as the team leader swung a boat hook across to the other vessel a grenade dropped at his feet and rattled around the deck planking. He just had time to say whatever Kazakh law enforcement officials say in such a situation, shout a warning to his crew and then dive over the side into the freezing Caspian waters. As he did so, he saw the poachers' boat race off at the high speed it could easily have done, had its occupants not chosen to lure the fishery protection officers into an ambush.

The grenade exploded and the fishery vessel promptly sank. Fortunately, its gunwales absorbed most of the blast and the crew, with only their heads protruding from the water, escaped serious injury. As they swam to the shore, which was luckily not far off, they found that they could not communicate with each other, as they had been deafened by the noise, but the ringing in their ears lasted only a few hours.

On the opposite side of the Caspian Sea, in the Russian provincial capital of Astrakhan, another senior fishery officer told me of the night his house was firebombed and how he and his family escaped in their nightclothes and lost all their possessions. The week before, he had ignored an anonymous phone call to his house suggesting he seek alternative employment.

Perhaps one of the worst single atrocities faced by wildlife law enforcement officials also took place alongside the Caspian Sea. The full circumstances of the incident have never been made public, aside from rumours quoted in the media, but this is the version described to me. It apparently occurred in about 1996 or 1997, in the region of Dagestan, which is the southernmost province of the Russian Federation adjoining the Caspian and which borders Azerbaijan. In one of the towns or cities bordering the sea there was located a federal border guard divisional headquarters. It was a multi-storey block, with administration on the lower levels and apartments for officers and their families above.

Shortly before the incident occurred, orders had come down from Moscow for the guards to increase their anti-poaching activities. Whilst such work was not a usual priority for them, it was only they who had vessels powerful enough to pursue and catch the speedboats used by sturgeon poachers. The guard crews were all armed and each of their vessels had a large-calibre machine gun mounted on its bow.

Orders being orders, the federal border guards did as they had been instructed. A few weeks passed and then, one night, a large bomb detonated at their headquarters. It is alleged that 48 men, women and children died or were injured in the blast, which reduced large parts of the building to rubble.

I have heard it said that the bomb was actually planted by Chechen rebels. But fishery staff who described the incident to me, and several did, all maintain that it was the work of the Russian mafia.

By way of some form of corroboration, I was chatting to the captain of a federal border guard vessel one day as we travelled along the River Volga. He told me that he was soon to retire. I was astonished, as he looked to be only in his early thirties, and told him that it was hard to believe. He explained that he had only recently transferred to Astrakhan after many years of service in Dagestan. He then went on to clarify that each year of service in Dagestan counted for three years of service anywhere else in the Russian Federation. He was very much looking forward to retirement. I bet he was and I bet he had earned it. I would also been willing to bet that he did not want his son to grow up to become a Dagestan border guard.

Getting to the truth behind stories is not easy and is certainly never easy in Russia. One incident that struck very close to home remains a mystery to me. In the early 2000s, the CITES Deputy Secretary-General, the Chief of Capacity Building and I went on caviar-related missions to the Caspian region. We started in Astrakhan on the banks of the River Volga. This is an area that was no stranger to terrorism or organized crime. It came a close second to Dagestan as the capital of illegal trade in caviar. Having flown into the city from Moscow, we were shown to our hotel. There we were led to rooms far apart from each other and all on different floors. When we suggested that we be located next to each other, having noted no difference in the quality of rooms, the hotel management advised us that they were acting under instructions from the Governor's office.

When we returned to the hotel that evening, after a dinner with local dignitaries, we found a heavily-armed and uniformed guard in place at each of our room doors. They came, we subsequently discovered, from a Spetznaz (Special Forces) unit, and were apparently there to deter any kidnap attempts.

During our visit to the region, we spent a couple of nights away from the city, downriver towards the Caspian Sea. Upon our return, we overheard some conversations among other foreign visitors in the hotel about an explosion that had occurred in the centre of Astrakhan. I asked the hotel barman about this and he confirmed that a bomb had exploded downtown. But he went on to say that it was being kept very quiet (difficult in the case of a bomb, I would have thought) and he did not even know where it had happened, whether any damage had resulted or if anyone had been killed or injured.

When we asked our guides and local officials about the incident, they denied such a thing had taken place. One of our interpreters suggested - I suspect with a twisted sense of humour - that it might have been a mafia warning for the UN to get out of town. Bizarrely, though, the same interpreter told me later the same day that she had sought more information and had been assured that no explosion whatsoever had occurred.

To this day, I do not know what, if anything, happened. But I do know that when I subsequently voiced a desire to visit Dagestan, officials in Moscow agreed to make the necessary arrangements but declined to accompany me to that region. Eventually, the United Nations Security Section ruled that it was too dangerous for me to undertake the type of activities I wanted to in that area and planning for the trip was cancelled.

Anti-poaching work is undoubtedly one of the most hazardous forms of law enforcement. More often than not, criminals are armed and, what is more, they usually have a high level of marksmanship – it would be rather pointless if they did not. Encounters will usually occur far from habitation and therefore far from witnesses and from any back-up or support. The FBI in America collates statistics each year relating to deaths and injuries sustained by law enforcement officials, whatever their agency, be it federal, state, county, city or tribal. I recall one year, not so long ago, when the FBI's analysis of the figures determined that the most dangerous policing job in the United States was to be a Fish and Game Warden.

There is an area in the north of the Democratic Republic of Congo where more than 200 rangers were apparently killed on duty in the space of a decade. Their deaths seem to have gone relatively unnoticed outside that area, maybe it is because it's remote, but maybe because they were called rangers. I would be willing to bet that if 200 constables, deputy sheriffs, marshals, troopers or patrolmen were killed in just one area over the course of ten years, there would be an absolute outcry from the wider law enforcement community, from local citizens and from politicians.

In India, a more subtle approach was taken to deterring forestry officials. There, they would be subjected to formal complaints and even to litigation in the courts. Many could not afford to defend such cases and, in some states, their departments would not contribute to legal fees. The Indian court system being what it is, these cases would drag on for years and years. The criminals and illicit dealers behind these moves did not care if the case was won or not. They achieved what they wanted: the complete demotivation of the individuals concerned and also of many of their colleagues, who saw no reason to open themselves up to such actions.

But there are always two sides to every coin. In all the years that I wore a police uniform in Scotland I suppose I must have arrested more than a dozen armed poachers. On several occasions I was alone. On none of those occasions was I carrying a firearm. Not once was I threatened or did I even feel threatened. Why not? Frankly, I do not know. I suppose we are just immensely lucky in the UK that police officers are, generally speaking, still widely respected and that shooting a cop is just not the done thing. I also suppose that we cannot expect this to last forever.

Several years ago, I wrote in a report to a CITES committee that the world does not appreciate the dedication and commitment shown by wildlife law enforcers. I believe those words remain true today and I do not see many signs that the situation is changing. In many respects, society simply does not deserve what it gets from these men and women.

THE WORLDWIDE WILDLIFE WEB

Fraudulent advertising of wildlife

Although the internet is undoubtedly used as a means for illicit dealers to reach out to potential customers, I am yet to be convinced that this is as significant as some of the studies conducted on this subject would have us believe.

For one thing, I think it is too haphazard to make it a reliable, commercial and profitable means of marketing illegal-origin items on a significant scale. I believe the money transfers needed when a customer purchases something through online auction or trading sites are, at present, too traceable to make them attractive to organized crime groups.

That said, the internet does present criminal networks with many opportunities, not least of which are the problems of jurisdiction faced by investigators when trying to establish who is behind adverts. But I always encouraged agencies to look very carefully for indications that suspicious advertisements might be truly commercial and connected to other similar entries before possibly wasting time pursuing them. I used, for example, to receive fairly regular emails from members of the public or NGOs, drawing my attention to an advert on an internet site where someone was offering, for instance, an animal skin or ivory carving for sale. The price sought might be as low as 25 dollars or could reach several hundred dollars. I ignored most of these contacts and I should explain why.

Although some internet auction site companies have excellent relations with law enforcement agencies and may willingly provide seller details, not all do. If they do not, the investigator may have to apply to a court for a warrant requiring the disclosure of those details. One detail subsequently obtained will inevitably be an email address used by the seller. Will the internet service provider inform the investigator of the name and address of the person to whom that email relates? If not, it is back to court again.

I will presume that the investigator has the name and address of the seller. Does that person live within the enforcement agency's jurisdiction? Probably not, in many cases. The advert may, for example, have been viewed by someone in Glasgow but the seller might be in Shanghai. If there is an offence, where does it take place? In Glasgow, in Shanghai, or where the internet auction site company is based?

For the purposes of this description, I will presume that both the potential customer and the seller are in Glasgow. Detectives go to the seller's house. The householder agrees that the email address is his but he denies placing the advert. If a sale had taken place, the investigator could track the money transfer, but that would necessitate another court order to gain access to the seller's bank account. If it had not gone that far, and it is just placing the advert that needs to be proved, what would be the next step? The detectives will need to seize the seller's computer. Potentially, another court warrant would be needed. The detectives would then have to persuade their forensic computer expert to find time in his already busy schedule to search through the myriad of data in the hard drive to find evidence of the advert. If he does find it, how does one then prove that it was the householder who was using the computer that day? It might just as easily have been his wife, his daughter or anyone else in the home that could access the computer.

It is an absolute nightmare of an investigation. And all this for an ivory carving worth 25 dollars? It is simply not worth the cost. What is more, many of these investigations end up discovering that the item was actually legally possessed, perhaps an antique, and that no offence was being committed.

This is why the agencies which can afford them have established specialized units to focus on cyber-crime and have the software that enables them to identify commonalities in relation to adverts and website postings. Creating such units is not cheap, though, and there are areas of cyber-crime, including paedophilia, for example, which understandably get higher priority. Personally, were I still a policing manager, I would use my already stretched resources in other ways, which I believe would be more effective.

That said, there are areas of the internet, like chat rooms and specialized forums, which certainly deserve to be targeted and monitored. These have been shown to be exploited by criminals who aim at consumers seeking out very rare and highly-endangered species. Illicit trade in reptiles and plants has regularly been conducted this way.

From the mid-2000s onwards, animal and plant collectors and traders began to find themselves targeted via the internet by a new set of criminals. These were people engaged in what are known to the police as 419 frauds, so called because many of the perpetrators were located in Nigeria and 419 is the number of the section dealing with fraud in Nigeria's criminal statute.

Most of us have probably been the target of a 419 fraud. These are the emails that come to you from, allegedly, the niece of some African ruler who has died, but not before squirreling away millions of dollars, which his relative now wishes you to help her transfer out of the country. She needs your bank account details to do so. If you are stupid enough to supply them, do not be surprised if you find, next time you go to the ATM for some cash, that your account is now empty.

I do not think anyone knows what prompted it but these scammers began to home in on people who might be interested in purchasing wildlife. It seemed, in some cases, that they had probably hacked into the distribution lists associated with specialized chat rooms or accessed the email address books of *bona fide* dealers. However it came about, they began to send out messages offering, usually, animals for sale. At times, these would be carefully prepared lists of, say, lizards and geckos, but on other occasions they were practically catalogues with lengthy inventories of all manner of species. Sometimes, they were not terribly clever: one emailer claimed to be authorized to trade in all native Nigerian animals but his list included a price for tigers.

Some of these fraudsters included attachments with their emails and these were commonly copies of licences or permits, which they claimed had been issued to them by the relevant government department and which established their credentials as genuine dealers.

Some of these documents were pretty convincing, whilst others were very poor adaptations of the real thing. As time passed, more and more of these messages seem to originate from Cameroon and the attachments would be in both English and French, reflecting the bilingual status of that nation. Occasionally, rather than try and prove their trading legitimacy, senders would attach copies of documents like driving licences, incorporating their photograph, to help convince the recipient of their identity. Some of these had not been thought through properly. One potential customer in the UK opened the email attachment and saw a driving licence that was clearly fake, especially as the photograph was that of the British government's then Home Secretary.

These scams became so prevalent that we put a special warning on the CITES website homepage to discourage people from being taken in by the emails. Presumably, though, some recipients were gullible, thought they were getting a bargain, were desperate to acquire an exotic pet or were just plain stupid. They sent off their money and sat back waiting for the postman to call. They might just as well have emptied their wallets into the toilet and flushed it, because the email sender wasn't a dealer and he didn't have access to tadpoles, let alone to tigers. Eventually waking up to the fact they had been duped, I think most people probably just put it down to experience and moved on with their lives, hopefully acting more wisely in future.

Some, though, were so outraged at being conned that they took themselves off to the authorities. So, too, did others who had not yet worked out that this was a scam. Both groups often turned to a national CITES office, which could not really help, since this was criminal fraud rather than illegal trade in fauna and flora. Occasionally, I would be contacted and most of the time, I redirected them to their local police office.

There were a few cases, though, where I thought I might be able to do something. One customer in Europe had sent money via a Western Union transfer, thinking that an African grey parrot would arrive in due course. This case provided enough information to enable an effective investigation and finally resulted in a prosecution. Interestingly, though, following the money transfer records actually led to someone in Tanzania, even though the original email indicated that the dealer was based in West Africa.

Financial investment in technology

Much of the illegal trade in wildlife is clandestine in nature. It occurs under the counter or on the proverbial black market. It is not all like that, though, and will sometimes, of necessity, need to be conducted in plain sight.

The poaching of sturgeon, the stripping of their eggs and their conversion into caviar has undoubtedly gone on for centuries. When it took place at a local level, it could be done simply and cheaply. That still happens today, to a limited degree. Indeed, the fishery protection agencies in the nations bordering the Caspian Sea will, from time to time, come across people in bars or on street corners selling caviar that has been roughly salted and stuffed into jam jars or other plain containers.

But when the illicit trade in caviar was at its height, in the 1990s and early 2000s, those involved, including the Russian mafia, were not so interested in domestic sales. The real profits were to be made if the caviar could be laundered into international markets and sold to the trading companies that supplied the finest restaurants of Europe and North America. Money, too, was to be made by marketing to the catering companies supplying the world's leading airlines, where it would then find its way onto the plates of passengers in first class cabins.

These luxurious niche markets could not be supplied using jam jars containing a foul-smelling product whose shelf life was clearly over. The criminals needed the sturgeon eggs to be properly processed into merchandise that would pass the scrutiny of connoisseurs and gastronomes and rank alongside the finest of caviars which would have been the food of tsars. Once processed, and depending upon the final market, it would certainly require refrigerating and, in some cases, pasteurizing. It had to be packed into tins that bore counterfeit labels identical to those of the legitimate producers.

It then had to cross borders to reach consumers in the international markets. In the early days, some of these export deals took place behind closed doors and involved unscrupulous purchasers who did not care where their caviar came from, as long as it passed muster with the final customer. However, as the price of caviar spiralled and the numbers of wild sturgeon plummeted with every passing year, it became more and more attractive and profitable to be able to pass off illicit caviar openly as the real thing. That required forged CITES documents, security stamps and container labels, or the corrupt purchase of genuine documents.

Illicit caviar was certainly smuggled across land and sea borders in small quantities, often hidden in vehicles' boots, in passengers' suitcases, in airline crew's luggage and, in one case, strapped to the undercarriage of a sleeper train, yet tonnes of contraband products also flew thousands of miles in the refrigerated holds of cargo planes, openly declared and transparently headed for those niche markets.

None of this came cheap but the rewards were worth it. And no simple ex-Soviet country fish poacher could possibly enter the sophisticated arena of this type of crime. Criminal groups needed to invest at every stage, from harvesting to marketing. Some, though, as we'll see, simply took over existing processing facilities. This really was organized crime by any definition of the phrase.

SPOT THE GANGSTER

Whilst the activities of some organized crime groups were subtle and conducted behind the scenes, there were also times when it was not hard to detect the involvement of people who could justifiably be described as professional criminals.

PREVIOUS CONVICTIONS FOR OTHER TYPES OF CRIME

Having considered possible links between wildlife crime and organized crime, it should not come as a surprise that people arrested for, or suspected of being involved in, such crimes are often found to have previous convictions for other forms of crime. And it is worryingly common for those convictions to include crimes of violence.

I was often frustrated, though, by a failure to run checks on people who came to notice.

During my early days with CITES we introduced a computerized system on which we hoped to record details of wildlife crime around the world and, importantly, the details of those involved. It was not long before we ran into problems. Firstly, the submission of information from countries was so haphazard and incomplete that it became almost meaningless, especially if one tried to analyse the data. For most of its operational life, for instance, the system would have told you that Austria had the highest levels of illegal wildlife trade anywhere in the world. This, of course, was utter nonsense. What the data, in reality, showed was that Austria was the only country which systematically and routinely provided details of each and every seizure that its customs authorities were making.

As time went on, the data became more and more skewed and we seriously questioned whether it was worth the effort of inputting it.

Since it was neither practical nor feasible for us to allow countries to input seizure data and other intelligence remotely, it fell to me and one other colleague to do so. However, we simply did not have time alongside our other duties and terrible backlogs built up. From time to time I would engage in a purge of data insertion and once benefited from the services of an intern. Her work, together with that of a consultant for several weeks, cleared some of the worst of the outstanding data but it was not long before we were back to square one. Finally, we had to give up. To this day, there is no database anywhere that has a balanced and truly accurate picture of the nature, spread or levels of wildlife crime. We simply do not know how much is taking place each year, where it is happening, what it costs, or who is involved. While Interpol and the WCO are making a better job of collating data than the CITES Secretariat did, they suffer from the same major problem: not all their member countries report, and few report everything.

I would have loved to maintain the CITES database, but I cannot imagine that it will be resurrected unless the human and financial resources in Geneva are increased and I do not see that happening anytime soon. It is especially frustrating because we seemed to attract information that did not go to other international bodies. This was demonstrated by an exercise we conducted where we arranged for the data held in CITES, Interpol and WCO computers to be compared. Fascinatingly, there was very little duplication, so it is clear that each organization has its own, distinct sources of information.

I have described this background because it links into my observation regarding the failure to run checks. On more than one occasion, I found myself entering someone's name only to find that it was already in the system. I once came across the same individual who had been dealt with in five different countries on three different continents. His home nation, though, only knew about three of the incidents. Perhaps I can best illustrate what can go wrong with a story about someone we will call John Green.

The story emerged when I was looking at reports about ivory seizures, an area on which most countries were good at reporting. I think this was because elephant poaching and illegal trade in ivory were such high-profile subjects and considerable effort was made to encourage data submission. Many of these reports passed across my desk. While I did not have time to study them in detail, I did try to at least glance at them all. One in particular caught my eye, as the report form had been used to provide information not about ivory, but about rhino horn.

One day in 2008, Mr Green had been driving his Ford car through an African country, accompanied by his girlfriend. I will call the country Blueland. They were on their way home to Purpleland and they were coming from Redland. The border control officers in Blueland stopped Mr Green and he seemed nervous when they spoke to him. Their suspicions mounting, they decided to search the car. Hidden amongst clothing on the back seat, they found eight rhino horns. Mr Green and his girlfriend were arrested. When questioned, Green admitted that he had acquired the horns in Redland but refused to divulge how or from whom. Since I am regularly referring to colours, I might also add that Mr Green was a citizen of Purpleland but he was a white African.

The two appeared in court next day, charged with illegal possession of the horns. Green plead guilty and the prosecutor accepted the girlfriend's plea of not guilty. The Blueland judge fined John Green the equivalent of $1,500 and the horns were confiscated and forfeited. John paid the fine and he and his girlfriend drove off back to Purpleland.

Although, in 2008, illegal trade in rhino horn and poaching of these animals had still to reach its peak, it struck me that Mr Green had got off relatively lightly for smuggling a not insignificant number of horns. What also struck me was the fact that he had been able, so quickly, to pay the fine. A white African did not strike me as your average mule. I decided to look into this more closely.

Firstly, I contacted Blueland and confirmed all the particulars of the case. I also got fuller details of Mr Green, such as his date of birth and passport and national identity numbers.

Then I contacted Redland. They had never heard of Mr Green and had not been told about the incident, even though the horns were understood to have come from their country. Consequently, they were none the wiser regarding a significant smuggling incident involving their nation, which presumably would also have been linked to poaching of their rhinos. What is more, being completely unaware of John Green, his girlfriend, his car registration number, passport number or any other official details, they had been given no chance to keep a lookout for Green in the future or perhaps make enquiries about his trip to Redland. They might, for instance, have been able to track down where he had stayed, who he had met, where he had visited and so on. They thanked me for passing on the information.

Next on my call list was Purpleland. Its authorities had not been told about the incident either. But they certainly knew John Green. In 2005, they had caught Mr Green selling rhino horns to a Vietnamese citizen who was visiting Purpleland. John had been fined the equivalent of $3,600 for that offence, with the alternative of two years' imprisonment if he failed to pay. At the time of his arrest, he had been found in possession of seven counterfeit Purpleland passports. They thanked me for passing on the information.

But I wasn't finished; Interpol was next. It had not been told about the incident in Blueland or the previous incident in Purpleland, but it did know John Green. That was because he was in their criminal record system as a drug trafficker. Mr Green had spent three years in jail in Yellowland, in Europe, on a drugs-related charge.

So Mr Green was, at the very least, an international smuggler of significant contraband involving different types of crime. He was also, most likely, a contraband dealer. He operated intercontinentally. He had access to counterfeit travel documents. He had contacts in the criminal world in at least three African nations and on three different continents.

If the Blueland judge had known about John's previous convictions, would his sentencing have been different? I would certainly hope so. John and his girlfriend must have laughed all the way to the Blueland/Purpleland border on their way home from the court.

Until I stuck my nose in, Blueland border control officers were congratulating themselves on their capture. However, what they had actually done, to all intents and purposes, was let a major criminal slip through their grasp. I was left feeling very frustrated.

Although the finger deserves to point most forcibly towards the border control officers, it should also swing towards their supervisors and, importantly, the Blueland prosecutor along with, to a lesser degree, the Blueland judge. I would hope a Scottish judge, faced with a foreign offender in the dock, would ask whether appropriate enquiries had been made with the authorities in his homeland.

Blueland border control should have checked with Purpleland and Interpol before they brought Green to court. They should, subsequently, have informed Redland, Purpleland and Interpol about the conviction. Purpleland should have previously told Interpol about the first rhino-related conviction.

Fortunately, we managed to salvage something from this near fiasco when Interpol subsequently made John Green the subject of one of its notices to all member countries about criminals likely to be operating across international borders.

INVIOLABILITY OF THOSE INVOLVED

The illegal trade in caviar provides one of the best examples of inviolability in wildlife crime.

I visited the Caspian Sea region on several occasions. These missions invariably led me to encounters with many, if not most, of the major legitimate caviar producers. One such producer then occupied what had been one of the USSR's most significant fishery operations. Adjoining a river, it had large quays where fish of various varieties would have been brought ashore from the river- and sea-going vessels. A short distance away, across a tarmac compound, stood a massive grey concrete factory where good communist men and women had no doubt slaved for decades. Inside was a series of high-ceilinged rooms where the fish would have been gutted, filleted and had their eggs extracted. Alongside were smoking houses and other processing and packing areas.

Whilst the factory had huge refrigerated storage facilities, each the size of a large warehouse, the whole place was unheated. Neither was there any air conditioning. Like most fish-processing facilities, I imagine it was freezing in the winter and stifling in the summer months, which can be really hot in that part of the world.

What really caught my attention, though, was an old railway carriage, a goods wagon, which sat on its own in a far corner of the huge compound. My interest grew as we were led by the factory management towards it. Its coat of red paint - very appropriate for a Soviet facility, I thought - was beginning to flake badly. Intrigued, I noticed a refrigeration unit had been mounted high up on one of the carriage's end walls and was humming away noisily. The factory foreman unlocked a padlock securing the two doors of the carriage and slid them apart. I was waved in.

The carriage had been fitted with shelves and its internal temperature was just a few degrees above zero. Each shelf was packed, from floor to roof, with tins of caviar. There were literally millions and millions of roubles' worth of caviar in there. Having admired the contents, I was then led back towards the factory, the visit over.

I had noticed that there did not seem to be a burglar alarm fitted to the carriage. There was no external lighting on it or near it. As mentioned, it was in a corner of the compound, close to the edge of the river, with no apparent security whatsoever other than a simple padlock. I asked the management whether they ever had problems with attempted thefts or if there was any history of anyone trying to break into the carriage. 'No,' came the simple and stark reply. And yet this was in a region of the world infamous for its high levels of criminality and corruption. It just did not make any sense.

A few days later, in the country's capital, I described what I had seen to a senior official of the State Security Service. He asked whether I had formed any impressions or come to any conclusions. I told him that I believed there were only two possible explanations to account for what I had seen. Either, that the management of the factory paid protection money to the mafia or that the whole place was actually mafia-owned and operated. Either way, it was abundantly clear that no one dared even think of trying to rip off caviar from that facility.

The KGB officer smiled and said, 'Mr Sellar, you and I share the same understandings when it comes to organized crime.' In the years since, I have often thought that his wry smile, somewhat weary in nature, also communicated what he could not voice: that he was probably powerless to do anything about it.

Mind you, the same officer had actually laughed out loud when I had also recounted how the commander of the uniformed police in the region had assured me that his area contained no organized crime groups or networks.

PAYMENTS TO ORGANIZED CRIME GROUPS

There is a fairly regular illicit traffic of endangered species between the far east of Russia and China, its immediate neighbour to the south. This involves tiger skins and bones, leopard skins, including those of the terribly endangered Amur leopard, of which there may be fewer than forty left in the wild, and bears, which feature prominently in this trafficking. Juvenile bears are smuggled into China where they may be used in illegal bear farms; there are also rumours that they are transported to government-approved farms, to be laundered into the breeding stock to improve the genetic variety. But bear parts, especially paws, are regularly smuggled as they are viewed by some Chinese consumers as a delicacy.

Over the years, I spent many hours in the company of Inspection Tiger Brigade personnel of the Russian Federation, either in the areas they patrol around Vladivostok or when Brigade members participated in training courses which I organized in Hong Kong and India. They told me that they were not aware of the Russian mafia being actively involved in wildlife crime but that anyone who was involved had to pay the mafia in order to operate within their area of control. This very much reflects the situation elsewhere in the world, where the organized crime group which is uppermost in a city, state or province will expect a percentage of the profits made by lesser groups further down the chain.

I was told that this particularly applied to wildlife smuggling conducted over the Russian-Chinese border. If, for instance, one wanted to move bear paws across, then some form of payment had to be made to the mafia groups that controlled these stretches of the Primorsky and Khabarovsky provinces. The money had to be paid whether one arranged the smuggling oneself or chose to use any influence that the mafia might have with customs and other border control officials.

However, it seems likely, and intelligence certainly suggests, that organized crime groups are increasingly involved in, and controlling, wildlife crime. This is perfectly understandable, given the huge profits that are available in some regions and in relation to some species. It would not make sense for mafia groups to allow others below them in the criminal pecking order to exceed the returns they themselves were making.

ORGANIZED CRIME'S OWNERSHIP OF WILDLIFE

When I was a policeman in Scotland, I was struck by the fact that it was not at all unusual to see minor criminals, especially those who fancied themselves as hard men, strutting down the street with a vicious dog like a pit bull terrier or Rottweiler on the end of a leash. I suppose they thought it added to their macho image.

It should not have come as any surprise, therefore, when a police colleague from home called me in Geneva one day. She was on a short-term secondment with the United Nations in Kosovo. The UN civilian police unit was trying to help combat organized crime there. Its staff had noticed that several of the crime bosses and warlords were in possession of dangerous animals. Bears seemed to be a popular pet but since these were native to that part of the world, their ownership might not be illegal. What was more difficult to account for, however, was the possession, by several heads of organized crime groups, of tigers.

She realized that illicit ownership of an exotic animal probably was not going to result in any of these men getting jail time but she was adopting an age-old and sometimes very effective police approach: 'There must be something we can pick these criminals up for.'

To her disappointment, I explained that governments in that part of eastern Europe had not yet acceded to the CITES Convention and, consequently, it was unlikely that they could use the treaty to show illegal import. In any case, the tigers were more likely to have been captive-bred somewhere in the region, as opposed to having been smuggled from their natural habitats in Asia. I told her simply to hope that the beasts turned on their owners one day and wished her luck in finding some other way of bringing them to book.

When I think 'organized crime' and 'exotic species', the name Pablo Escobar springs to mind. Often described as a drug lord and narco-terrorist, Escobar was head of the Colombian Medellin drug cartel. He is thought to have been responsible for, or to have ordered, hundreds of assassinations of law enforcement officials, politicians and rival drug dealers and traffickers. He is also believed to have funded left-wing guerrilla groups and encouraged one of them to storm Colombia's Supreme Court in an attack that left half the judges of the court dead.

Escobar owned a massive hacienda and in its grounds he had a private species collection of nearly zoo-like proportions. It included animals such as giraffes, elephants and hippopotamuses. At the time of his death in 1993, when he was shot dead during gunfire exchanges with the Colombian National Police, the collection was so large that the local government found it impossible to cope with. Indeed, the hippos escaped and have gone feral in a number of lakes in that part of the country.

In a more up to date case, I recall being told of a surveillance operation conducted by the anti-mafia units of the Caribinieri, Italy's national military police, in the early 2000s. During it, they were observing a social function at the luxurious home of a mafia family head, to which several very senior figures from other crime families had been invited. The Caribinieri officers were impressed by the spread of food and drink that had been laid out for guests to enjoy but were astonished to see several large silver salvers being carried in by waiters. The salvers were laden down by piles of caviar, and this at a time when CITES restrictions meant that there was no legal supply of caviar into international markets.

HUGE PROFITS

It seems logical to end a discussion on organized crime indicators with this heading, since the very *raison d'être* of organized crime is to make money. That is why anti-money laundering and asset recovery work has been so successful in combating some criminal networks in recent years, as it hits them where it hurts most: in their pockets. Regrettably, hardly any such efforts have been brought to bear against wildlife criminals.

One of the most common questions put to me by enforcement agencies around the world was 'What's the price of..?' They would explain that a case involving a skin, a horn, a tusk, some caviar, an orchid or a quantity of timber was coming to court and that the prosecutor wanted to be able to tell the judge the value of the commodity, since this would undoubtedly influence sentencing. It was one of the hardest questions for me to answer.

For a start, so much depended upon just where in the world and, consequently, at what point in the chain of criminality the item had come into the possession of an enforcement agency. An elephant tusk handed to a dealer or poaching organizer in the country where the animal was killed, for example, gives a much smaller return than it does when, perhaps many months later, it is delivered into the hands of a trader in Asia.

Some people argue that the value ascribed to an item, regardless of the point in the chain at which it was intercepted, should be what it would have been worth at the final point of sale. But that may not be simple to estimate, because we may not be able to predict how it would have been used. A piece of raw ivory, for instance, might be used to produce several 'hanko' name seals, which could make the seller several hundred dollars. On the other hand, that piece of raw ivory, if passed to a skilled craftsman and converted into an intricate carving, could take on a value of many thousands of dollars.

Much, too, will depend on the quality of the tusk and its origin. Forest elephants have tusks that are of a thicker consistency than those of their savannah counterparts. Asian elephant ivory also tends to be harder than that of African elephants. Historically, the elite among ivory carvers and craftsmen have favoured the hardest ivory to work with. Having seen hundreds of confiscated elephant tusks, I find that no two are alike unless they are a pair from the one elephant, and even then they will differ. Ivory degrades if not stored under the right conditions. I have held tusks that have become so weathered and brittle that they are utterly worthless. I have handled tusks so small that any processor would be very limited in what he might use them for. I have also struggled to lift tusks so massive, so heavy and in such beautiful condition that even the layman would recognize their beauty and potential value.

I have noted the very same with tiger and leopard skins. Some were clearly removed from mangy old animals, were badly damaged as a result of the poaching, had not been preserved properly or had been treated by someone who was no more skilled in taxidermy than I am, whilst others, stunning in appearance, made it easy to understand why someone might wish to possess them.

There seemed to be more or less general agreement in the wildlife law enforcement community that we should not comment publicly on the possible maximum prices of illicitly-traded fauna and flora. The traditionally- and historically-held view was that to do so risked encouraging speculative poaching or dealing. I abided by this approach prior to retirement, although I must say that I found this unrealistic for various reasons. For one thing, the media and NGO community did not adopt that approach. Reading newspapers, watching television documentaries or simply browsing the internet would soon throw up some so-called expert's opinion on the current price for any given species or its body parts.

I also thought that it was unlikely to motivate crime. What exactly did we in the enforcement community think would happen? If I were some unemployed individual, living in rural poverty, desperately seeking money to put food on the family table and clothes on my children's backs, and I saw in my local paper that a tiger skin was selling for x amount of dollars, I might be envious of those who were making that profit, but what could I do? If I were fortunate enough to live in tiger habitat, how would I set about poaching one? The likelihood of my having the tracking and hunting skills to do so is surely remote. And even if I struck lucky and managed to bag myself a tiger, how many of us could, without prior experience, make a half-decent job of skinning and dismembering a rabbit, let alone one of the world's largest land mammals? Imagine, though, that I did have beginner's luck and got myself an intact and preserved skin, together with the skeleton (ignoring for the moment how I got rid of the meat, muscle, sinew and so on) – what next? How do I set about either finding an unscrupulous dealer or introducing myself to the local organized crime network? And do all this without coming to the attention of a law enforcement agency? To my mind, it all seems rather unlikely.

I would not wish to be misunderstood, though. I had been in policing long enough to know that desperate times can sometimes call for desperate measures and that individuals certainly turn to crime on occasions, seeing it as the only way out of their predicament. It is why people who have previously led law-abiding lives turn to shoplifting, burglaries, muggings or drug smuggling and dealing. However, I have little sympathy for, and do not believe, the American and European men and women who regularly profess innocence having been caught with narcotics in their luggage as they return home from holidays in parts of Asia. Pleas of 'I didn't know it was in my suitcase' or 'Someone asked me to take this package back for them but I didn't know that it was heroin' fall on very deaf ears where I am concerned. I firmly believe that these people saw an opportunity for an easy score and it went terribly wrong. If they end up spending 30 years in the Bangkok Hilton then they have only themselves to blame.

I've described how the caviar business can bring the money rolling in, but it's not alone. In the mid-2000s, I was told by a government official in the Middle East of a sheikh who had paid $200,000 for a single falcon. This was obviously an extreme case but it does illustrate the very top of the scale. Personally, I think some of the prices paid on the falcon black market in the Gulf States are just plain silly and may in fact reflect how some individuals there have 'More money than sense!', as my mother would have said. In a case in Switzerland, embroidered *shahtoosh* (Tibetan antelope wool) shawls were on sale in a ski resort boutique for the equivalent of 35,000 dollars each, although I have bargained with traders in Bangkok, Kathmandu and New Delhi who would have sold me one for less than 2,000 dollars. In early 2013, a kilo of rhino horn could apparently fetch up to 70,000 dollars. By way of comparison, a kilo of ivory seemed to go for no more than 8,000 dollars. A tiger skin might cost the equivalent of 15,000 dollars. One might have to pay many hundreds of dollars for a live parrot from the Amazon or the equivalent in euros for one from Africa. A poison-arrow frog from South America will cost between 200 and 300 euros. And organized crime isn't involved in wildlife crime? Don't make me laugh.

WILDLIFE CRIME AND TERRORISM

When hijacked planes hit the twin towers of the World Trade Center in New York and the Pentagon building in Washington D.C., the world changed forever. And so did the law enforcement community.

When I started work with CITES in 1997, wildlife crime was slowly but steadily appearing on the law enforcement agenda and was beginning to be recognized as serious law breaking involving organized networks. But then 9/11 happened and I honestly believe our cause was put on hold for more or less the decade to come. It is only since the late 2000s that the theft of natural resources, together with other forms of environmental crime, have begun to receive the political attention they deserve. I believe, however, that they have yet to receive the full attention of the law enforcement community.

I have already outlined the way in which I had to justify, for want of a better word, a serious focus on wildlife crime and how I was often called upon to demonstrate the involvement of organized groups. Post-9/11, more and more people began to question whether there was any link at all between terrorism and wildlife crime. I felt we'd come full circle. It seemed not to matter that wildlife crime was bringing several of the world's most endangered species close to the brink of extinction, was providing organized criminal networks with substantial profits, involved the exploitation of rural communities often living well below the poverty line and was regularly resulting in the deaths of anti-poaching personnel. Or it seemed not to matter enough, anyway. It looked as if, once again, we were being presented with hoops through which we would have to jump if we were to attract support and resources.

My patience was beginning to run out. I was prompted to think of the time when I was a village policeman in Scotland. As my workload was not excessive, I took the opportunity to attend college and obtain a formal vocational qualification in police studies. Criminology was one of the subjects in which I was obliged to obtain a pass grade. I recalled the lecturer who had taught us how various theories had emerged as criminology developed. He had explained that the first academic researchers of this topic, who came to be designated criminologists, had postulated that crime was 'the work of the devil', and went on to say that some people still believed this.

I am not sure I would subscribe to that explanation any more now than I did when I first heard it. I do not know that my college studies, or my many years in law enforcement, have made it any clearer why people commit crimes. What I do know, though, is that law enforcement is not rocket science.

I sincerely believe that, as with links to organized crime, we do not have to look too far to see the connection between wildlife crime and terrorism. But not all wildlife crime involves organized crime and not all wildlife crime involves terrorism. Once again, quoting statistics or citing hard evidence is not straightforward. Nevertheless, in my opinion, it is not difficult to demonstrate connections between the two.

We have seen how some rebel groups have poached and traded wildlife to help fund their activities. This brings us to an age-old problem: where some will see a rebel or terrorist, others will see a freedom fighter.

The Lord's Resistance Army, thought to be engaged in elephant poaching and illegal trade in ivory is, deservedly, currently viewed as a terrorist group or militant movement. It has been accused of, among other atrocities, murder, the mutilation of prisoners, rape, abduction, slavery, child sex and the forcible recruitment of child soldiers. Interestingly, in an age when there is perhaps a tendency to associate terrorism with Islamic fundamentalism, the Lord's Resistance Army may be driven by the complete opposite. Some explain its motives, while not justifying or excusing them, as rooted in Christian fundamentalism. They believe that its members may be engaged in legitimate armed struggle against oppressive governments and seeking to combat ethnic abuse of their tribal origins.

I have written about the way in which Angolan rebels traded in ivory to help fund their activities. Whilst the Angolan civil war resulted in over 500,000 deaths and led to over a million displaced citizens, it might be viewed as part of the country's violent struggle for independence and eventual democratic government. Was what happened there 'terrorism'? I suspect the acts of subjugation conducted by colonial powers such as Belgium, Britain and France in centuries past might be seen, by those who experienced them, as a form of terrorism.

Much more recently, and perhaps even more difficult to define, is what happened in the mid-2000s in Nepal. There, Maoist rebels fought against the existing and long-standing monarchist rule. It is alleged, probably accurately, that some Maoist groups poached elephants, tigers and rhinos in the national parks and traded their tusks, skins, bones and horns to help subsidize their struggle. The Maoists appear, on occasions, to have engaged in atrocities.

What is undisputable is that the poaching of endangered species in Nepal's parks dramatically reduced, and even completely disappeared in some places, once the monarchy's influence dissipated and the existing government and Maoists reached an accord. Were the Maoists terrorists? I don't care to comment but I do know that, perhaps bizarrely, given what had gone before, Maoist politicians were subsequently appointed to senior positions, including in some cases ministerial posts, in departments dealing with wildlife, forests and the environment.

It can be too easy to get utterly bogged down in trying to distinguish between the terrorist and the liberator. I think it is simpler, and probably better, to examine what might prompt links between terrorism and wildlife crime. And, as with the links to organized crime, it is money that keeps those links in place.

Terrorism, like any other activity, needs to be funded. Al-Qaeda benefited, and continues to benefit, from some people inclined to Islamic fundamentalism. Osama bin Laden brought his own, not insignificant, personal wealth to bear in establishing al-Qaeda and convinced others to support the movement financially. There appear to be good grounds to suspect that a number of Muslim-related terrorist activities have been state sponsored.

Closer to home, or at least to my home, we have the example of NORAID, the Irish Northern Aid Committee. Established in the late 1960s, its aim was to support processes that would lead to the creation of a united Ireland. NORAID was particularly active in raising funds among the Irish-American communities of the United States and it is thought that millions of dollars were donated. This money was to be used, among other things, to ease the suffering of families caught up in what were described as 'the Troubles'. However, it is alleged that significant sums from donations were diverted to purchase weapons for the Provisional Irish Republican Army.

History has shown us that relatively few terrorist or freedom-fighting groups could rely solely upon donations from like-minded individuals. Almost without exception, such groups have had to turn to crime to raise the money needed for weapons, ammunition, explosives, to bribe officials or just to feed and clothe members of their units and cells. And, in turning to crime, they have had to use whatever opportunities presented themselves.

- Action Directe in France and Baader Meinhof in Germany carried out bank robberies and kidnapping

- Colombian rebel groups, such as FARC, also engaged in kidnapping to extract ransom payments from relatives but are alleged to have engaged in drug dealing too. Indeed, a National Police report in 2008 estimated that 78% of the funds of the Revolutionary Armed Forces of Colombia resulted from narco-trafficking

- The Provisional Irish Republican Army undertook a range of criminal activities to pay for weapons and explosives. This included the extortion of protection payments from businesses but also exploited what was on its doorstep. It engaged, for instance, in considerable fraud in relation to the discounted diesel fuel that was widely available across the large agricultural communities of Northern Ireland

- Somali pirates have made huge profits from ransoming the ships, cargo, crews and passengers that they have captured in the waters off northeast Africa. Their claims to be motivated in their struggle by the plunder of their territorial waters by foreign fishing vessels, and a desire to aid the communities based along the Somali coast, do not stand up to scrutiny today. While that may have been the initial intention of some of the groups - and it was a worthy goal given the manner in which fish resources had been exhausted - it seems that financial gain is now the primary motive. This appears to be corroborated by the fact that several international law enforcement bodies have noted that some property developments in Nairobi, in neighbouring Kenya, seem to be financed by money coming from people believed to be the leaders of the piracy movements. Some of these investments bear all the hallmarks of money laundering

It has been noted repeatedly that terrorist groups, and especially their leaders and senior figures, have often succumbed to diverting profits from crime to their own personal ends and that some of these people enjoy lives of luxury wholly inconsistent with their professed aims.

These examples illustrate that when terrorist organizations, groups, units and cells engage in crime to bolster their coffers, they invariably focus upon what can be exploited or targeted within their areas of operation. For simple reasons of geography, Baader Meinhof could not engage in piracy any more than Somali pirates could become bank robbers.

It surely makes sense, therefore, that if locally-sourced fauna and flora offer a source of income, terrorist groups may harvest and trade them illicitly. Since several terrorist groups are located in areas of high biodiversity, it follows that they will be involved in wildlife crime.

As I said, it is not rocket science. One does not need a PhD in criminology to see the potential. And if we wait for the data to be collected, the hard evidence to be gathered or the research papers to be peer reviewed, as some people did in relation to the involvement of organized crime, it will be too late, far too late, for some endangered species.

Personally, I believe people who break the law ought to be brought to justice. Whether those individuals are, or have been, terrorists or are, or have been, freedom fighters, should not matter.

It seems, however, that progress is being made. In late 2012, the United Nations Security Council called for an investigation into reports that the Lord's Resistance Army was engaged in elephant poaching and trade in ivory as a means of funding its other activities. As I write this, I do not know whether anyone is answering that call or exactly how such an investigation will be conducted. Equally importantly, what will result from such an investigation?

Shortly before the Security Council initiative, the then soon-to-retire US Secretary of State Hilary Clinton, while making a speech highlighting the seriousness of wildlife crime, said she was 'asking the intelligence community to produce an assessment of the impact of large-scale wildlife trafficking on our security interests so we can fully understand what we're up against.' I hope the intelligence community responds; it would be the first time, to my knowledge, that such work will be undertaken.

It was marvellous to see someone at Hilary Clinton's level acknowledging that wildlife crime deserves much greater attention. I think, though, that I would have been more confident that the words might lead to action had the speech come from the US Attorney General or the head of the Central Intelligence Agency.

THE CAVIAR CRIMINALS

There can be few species listed in the appendices of CITES which come with such an extensive history of criminality as sturgeon. The family of fish known as *Acipenseriformes* includes sturgeon and paddlefish. It is the unfertilized roe of these fish that are processed into the luxury product called caviar. All 27 species of sturgeon and paddlefish came under the regulation of CITES on 1 April 1998. It was perhaps ironic, given what was to come, that April Fool's Day should have been the date when the Convention started to do its best to safeguard the future of these fish. What very quickly became clear was that the criminal groups who were controlling a very lucrative illicit trade had a huge head start on the law enforcement community. If I am honest, I do not think we ever caught up. Indeed, it was the ever-decreasing wild sturgeon populations which ended up significantly reducing illegal commerce in caviar: poachers simply couldn't catch enough, or certainly not enough to justify the processing and smuggling effort and the expense of paying off relevant officials, vital if they wished to continue laundering their products onto international markets.

With hindsight, I think many people would now agree that several geographical populations of sturgeon were commercially extinct by the time these species were proposed for CITES regulation. In fact, several conservationists and organizations were saying just that back in 1998. This term has been used more and more often in recent years to describe a species that, while still present in the wild, and perhaps present in reasonably large numbers, has fallen to a point where business-related sustainable harvests are no longer possible. It is actually quite hard to completely eradicate a species, especially a marine species which exists in an environment into which man can reach only so far. The same applies, for instance, to Asian big cats like the tiger, leopard and snow leopard. They lead such secretive lives, often in remote areas and in habitats hostile to humans, that, try as they might, poachers are relatively unlikely to track down and kill the very last one. Instead, the point comes when nature itself steps in. Impacts such as a lack of genetic diversity or unfavourable breeding conditions mean that populations reach a tipping point, becoming so small that they simply cannot recover.

Over recent decades, despite the warnings provided by, for example, the utter collapse of commercial cod harvests in parts of the world, several governments and fishery industries chose, and continue to choose, to ignore what marine survey statistics were telling them. In many respects, *Homo sapiens* has been driving fish in our rivers, lochs, seas and oceans closer and closer to, or beyond, that tipping point for quite some time now. I am no mathematician but it does not seem to need arithmetic skills to work out that, when it comes to humans and fish, there are too many of us and not enough of them.

And since the very basis of the CITES Convention is that any trade which takes place must be sustainable, those very same governments and industries have done their utmost to resist efforts to list more fish species in the CITES appendices. As someone who spent years as a uniformed police officer and later a detective in the major fishing ports of northeast Scotland, I do not need to be told how important that industry is to local economies. I can recall the days when my birthplace of Aberdeen played host to the largest fish market in Europe. However, it is oil industry supply vessels, not trawlers, which sail in and out of Aberdeen harbour these days. You can only go so far down the road to extinction before there is no turning back. I got really fed up hearing that CITES was not the appropriate regulatory mechanism for fishing and that this was much better left to existing regional fishery management organizations (RFMO). While it is certainly true that CITES has some way to go in evolving its controls to cope with large-scale marine harvesting, it strikes me that several RFMOs do not have a terribly good track record in ensuring sustainable harvests.

I am afraid these debates - and one encounters very similar arguments from those who resist the listing of timber species - are awash with oceans of hypocrisy. Governments and industry mainly want to keep CITES at arm's length because they know that, to a significant extent, the Convention works. It is far from perfect, as you might have gathered by now, but it is not the treaty which is at fault: it is the people who administer and enforce it. Governments know that if trade comes within CITES regulation then, somewhere down the line, those national officials whose job it is to implement it may be called upon to prove that the harvesting is both legal and sustainable. And they know, or certainly fear, that demonstrating this will be problematic.

What frustrated me most when listening to some of the debates was the way in which what I saw as the greatest strength of the Convention was ignored and, I suspect, conveniently and deliberately ignored. Although CITES benefits from the fact that it is not some feel-good gathering of like-minded people who only act once consensus has been reached, and that it is not an organization which relies totally on voluntary implementation of its recommendations and decisions, its real power lies in the often-overlooked reality that the Convention is international law. Its reach, then, is truly global and, very importantly, enforceable. If a policeman walks into a shop in London and finds a tiger skin on sale, he is empowered to investigate its origin because tigers are listed in the appendices of CITES. If a patrolman in New York finds elephant ivory on sale in a Fifth Avenue store, he can do likewise. If a customs officer in Panama City observes an Amazonian parrot being sold, he too can act. But if any of those officials come across fish or timber on offer, and they are species not listed by CITES, there is every chance that they will have to walk on by. Easy as CITES is to ridicule, the fact that it provides a legal basis upon which law enforcement officers in 179 states can work puts it head and shoulders above any other mechanism. It is high time that that this was more widely appreciated and implemented.

It is vital, therefore, that species are listed appropriately and in good time so that the provisions of CITES have a meaningful chance to make a difference. I believe that the sturgeon offers us an important lesson.

I understand that sturgeon have been around since prehistoric times. They are primarily bottom feeders and can be large, lumbering creatures that one can certainly imagine fitting right in alongside dinosaurs. Once relatively widespread, their wild populations are now much more restricted in distribution and are only found in a limited numbers of rivers, coasts and seas.

The best known of these, and the one that holds the sturgeon that are thought to produce the best caviar, is the Caspian Sea. Surrounded by Azerbaijan, the Russian Federation, Kazakhstan, Turkmenistan and the Islamic Republic of Iran, this vast inland stretch of salt water has seen millions of sturgeon harvested over the centuries for their eggs and meat. Sometimes referred to as 'black gold', caviar has been an important source of revenue for the people living on the shores of the Caspian, and along the rivers that feed into it, as well as its governments, particularly that of the USSR.

Historically, caviar in Western Europe was seen as the food of tsars, kings, aristocrats and the weathly. By comparison, the caviar extracted from sturgeon and paddlefish in North America was, at one time, so common that bowls of it could be found on the counters of bars in New York, where it was offered free like peanuts. As with peanuts, its salt content helped encourage the drinking of more beer.

The Caspian Sea and the countries which border it are host to a huge range of habitats and temperatures. At different times of the year, the coastal lands may be lush or desert-like. They can be baking hot or covered in ice and snow. Several of the rivers in the north freeze over for months at a time. Sturgeon exist across these habitats but escape to warmer southern waters, closer to Turkmenistan and Iran, over the winter.

The Caspian is also home to the most prized of the 27 sub-species of sturgeon and paddlefish. Its scientific name is *Huso huso* but it is better known as beluga, which is also the name for the caviar produced from it. Beluga caviar is the most expensive in the world, with wholesale prices of several thousand dollars per kilo. As the female beluga sturgeon takes so long to reach sexual maturity, it is highly vulnerable to over-exploitation and its populations will take correspondingly longer to recover from over-harvesting. Of all sturgeon species, it is this one that certainly seemed to fall appropriately within the description of being commercially extinct. Some conservationists suggested that *Huso huso* met the criteria indicating that it should have gone straight into Appendix I of CITES in 1998. That, however, would have been unacceptable to those countries in whose waters beluga still swam.

Although some amount of poaching will inevitably have taken place over time, the fact that these creatures inhabited waters governed by countries such as the USSR and Iran meant they had a degree of protection often not available to fauna and flora elsewhere in the world. Sturgeon poaching was not a good career path for Soviet citizens. This did not, though, protect them from overfishing and degradation of their habitat, particularly due to oil extraction developments in the northern Caspian and the generally increasing pollution of rivers caused by greater use of agricultural chemicals and the disposal of industrial waste. The damming of rivers and increased water extraction were also interrupting access to traditional spawning grounds. As we approached the turn of the century, the future for the sturgeon of the Caspian was looking increasingly bleak.

As if the general conservation problems facing many animals and plants were not enough, the break-up of the Soviet Union created major socio-economic problems for the Russian Federation and for most of its communist state counterparts. In many of the ex-USSR countries that I visited over the years, I found a very mixed attitude towards *perestroika* and the fall of communism. The younger generation was almost inevitably optimistic, enjoying living through a new dawn of freedom and looking forward to increasing levels of democracy, although still nothing like those in western Europe.

In stark contrast, I spoke with several middle-aged and elderly people who, while glad to see the passing of many of the worst aspects of communism, nonetheless seemed almost bewildered by the new state of affairs. Many had suddenly found themselves unemployed, with little if any social welfare provision. Veterans of World War Two, in particular, who had enjoyed a significant level of status in the community and good pensions - in terms of the socialist states - found their incomes drastically reduced and faced a future perhaps as bleak as that of the sturgeon.

The situation had particularly harsh effects on people living along the coast of the Caspian and its tributary rivers. Time and again I saw fish processing factories and fishing fleets that would once have employed many hundreds of men and women but which were now operating at vastly reduced levels. They had turned - almost overnight, in many cases - from state corporations into private enterprises where staffing numbers and every other aspects of business were dictated by profits.

It was easy to see how hard it must have been to go from a situation of 'jobs for all' to one of not knowing where your next rouble was coming from. Subsistence poaching was widespread and alongside it, in some areas in particular, organized crime groups had moved in and taken control of potentially profitable ex-state companies. The same groups also seemed to be taking increasing control of local councils, government agencies and other bodies that would once have been arms of the state.

This change was reflected in some of the new owners and managers of fisheries. Several had been employees of state-owned enterprises, some of them very substantial operations with fishing flotillas, large factory premises, processing and refrigeration facilities and marketing operations, but they had apparently been able to purchase these former government monopolies outright. Had some of these individuals, presumably used to receiving salaries from a communist public sector employer and with limited opportunities to build up personal wealth portfolios, been financed by organized crime groups? It was very difficult not to ponder that question. The fact that one or two of these individuals looked as if they had just walked off the set of *The Godfather* did little to dispel such suspicions. One man in particular appeared to get up in the morning and dress himself so that he could pass as a *capo* or 'made man' in a New York crime family, right down to keeping his shirt unbuttoned to mid-chest so that his large gold medallion was displayed to best effect. I had a fascinating opportunity one day to view this man in what I believe were his true colours.

My colleagues and I had been transported downriver and were well offshore on the Caspian Sea. We were on board a fishing company's large vessel and had been invited to watch a 'scientific' harvest of sturgeon. Years before, the USSR and Iran had agreed that commercial fishing for sturgeon should be restricted to the rivers into which they swam to reach their spawning grounds. This was intended to improve the regulation of harvests but also to ensure that eggs in gravid females would be nearing maturity and thus produce the highest quality caviar. This policy had continued after the break-up of the Soviet Union.

'Scientific catch', though, was permitted out in the open waters of the Caspian Sea. The riparian states of the Caspian had agreed among themselves a quota for this activity, limiting the quantity (total weight) of fish that could be taken in this way each year. Not being an ichthyologist, I never fully understood why these catches had to take place in open waters but I presume it was something to do with population surveys and also with monitoring the dispersal of sturgeon around the Caspian. Whatever the reasoning, some of this work was conducted by government research boats but a good deal of it was undertaken by the commercial fishing companies on behalf of the research facilities. They willingly agreed to this arrangement as they were allowed to retain most of what was caught once fish had been measured, sampled and so on. The fish they kept could be processed for their meat and some would also contain eggs that could be processed into caviar. What was happening in these waters reminded me of what happens in relation to whaling. Japan engages in the 'scientific' harvesting of whales but much of the meat obtained - what might be described as the by-catch of these operations - is subsequently sold. It occurred to me that some of the people who regularly question whether such 'whale research' is not just a cynical cover for a commercial activity were likely to be similarly troubled by what I was witnessing in this mass of water dividing Europe and Asia.

The vessel we were on was sailing around scientific harvest sites in which fixed hang nets had been placed. As their name suggests, these nets hang down from buoys anchored in the water and are set at depths at which sturgeon are likely to be swimming. Hang nets can be devastatingly effective and their use is strictly controlled, or even outlawed, in some fisheries. One of the rules associated with the use of these nets for scientific purposes in the Caspian Sea was that any fish which were found still to be alive had to be released once they had been measured. And it was in just such circumstances that I encountered the mobster medallion man.

My colleagues were at the bow of the boat, engrossed in discussions with sturgeon scientists, caviar and fishing industry representatives and government officials. I had wandered off, as I regularly did, to have a nicotine injection. I did not deliberately exploit these occasions – well, not usually - but they were a very handy chance for me to saunter away on my own for several minutes. People soon got used to my habit and instead of wondering where I had got to, would think to themselves, 'Oh, John's just off for a fag again.' I found myself amidships while three fishermen, supervised by a foreman, heaved a net over the starboard gunwales. Quite a large number of fish were entangled in the net and it was taking considerable strength and effort on their part to bring it on board. As the fishermen struggled with the net, the foreman began to unravel the fish caught up in it. I noticed him catch sight of me out of the corner of his eye. He had unwrapped quite a number of sturgeon of differing species and sizes when, with great grunts of exertion, his colleagues brought a large and beautiful beluga over the side. It began to thrash about wildly on the deck planking and worked its own way free of the mesh. The foreman stepped forward and, with the help of one of the fishermen, weighed and measured it. They then moved to the side of the boat and dropped it overboard. This was when a howl of rage came from around the side of the nearby wheelhouse. I did not need an interpreter to tell me what was being shouted.

'Medallion man' rushed forward and, with clenched fists, grabbed the lapels of the fore-man's jacket, shaking and berating the poor fellow. Terrified, the foreman started to gesticulate desperately with his eyes and nods of his head in my direction. By now really concerned for his wellbeing, I made my way across the deck and, as I did so, the company boss finally be-came aware of my presence and looked around. Releasing his underling, he stormed back to-wards the bow but not without first throwing me a look of utter hatred. If I had not been there, I am sure the foreman would have followed the beluga into the dark waters of the Caspian Sea. If my colleagues had not been there, I suspect I might have too. Of course, if I really had not been there, there is absolutely no way the beluga would ever have been released. I could not help thinking of the often-quoted phrase from *The Godfather* about how one of its characters ends up 'sleeping with the fishes', following his assassination by a rival mob.

My smoke break finished, I joined my colleagues. The gangster avoided me and no mention was made of what had just happened. It had obviously gone unnoticed by everyone else. However, I had a fascinating tale to recount to my companions once we were alone together that evening. As it happens, my suspicions and assessment of this company owner were more than confirmed in the years to come as I came across fraud involving CITES documents bearing his firm's details. I do not suppose he was ever brought to justice, as precious few of those engaged in and controlling illegal caviar trade from the Caspian ever seemed to be, but that man certainly deserved to feel handcuffs click around his wrists. It was one of those occasions, not uncommon during my years with CITES, when I sincerely wished that I could wave a magic wand and transport the scene and its actors to Scotland, to the moment when he would realise that I was not just a UN official but a police officer and could make him face the consequences of his actions.

However, during my visits to the Caspian region I was to see that law enforcement seemed to be targeting and picking off the subsistence poachers, while the more organized crime groups appeared, in some parts, to operate freely. Indeed, I heard from more than one source that organized crime was encouraging and bribing enforcement agencies to remove the small poachers who were interfering in their large-scale operations.

EXAMINING CASPIAN CRIME RESPONSES

In the early 2000s, I carried out several enforcement assessment missions to Caspian Sea countries. The aim was to gain an understanding of how they were enforcing their fishery legislation with regards to the harvesting of sturgeon and the production of caviar. I was accompanied on most of these by law enforcement officials from various countries, selected because of the support they gave to the implementation of CITES, providing them with an opportunity to see for themselves what was happening elsewhere in the world. Their presence also offered me a degree of security and corroboration which can sometimes be handy in the high crime areas of the former USSR.

It was a commissioner of the Belgian Federal Police who accompanied me to Kazakhstan. Kazakhstan was of special interest to me as it was at the time an important source of illicit caviar. It was particularly worrying that shipments of Kazakh caviar arriving in Europe and North America were regularly accompanied by documents that appeared to be either counterfeit, or altered versions of the genuine article. There were also suspicions that genuine documents were probably being issued corruptly. In the United States, which had started to sample all caviar shipments declared for import and then subject them to DNA profiling, it was also being found that caviar was being misdeclared with regards to its species of origin. By using fish species of lesser quality, but declaring the caviar as top quality, traders were fraudulently making huge extra profits. Beluga caviar was the highest priced, but some traders were actually using eggs from the Sevruga sturgeon.

One of the things that the commissioner and I had learned during a day spent visiting caviar processors was that all genuine and legal shipments of caviar exported from Kazakhstan should have been accompanied by CITES documents issued in Atyrau, the Caspian area's major Kazakh city. I knew, however, because copies of them were regularly sent to me, that many of the permits being shown to customs officers in airports like Schipol or New York had apparently been issued in Almaty, the former capital of the country, from where the shipments were flown abroad.

It was clear that criminals were replacing not only the documents issued in Atyrau but also the caviar that had been inspected by local officials there and determined to be *bona fide*. What we could not establish was whether the crooks were acting alone in this or if they were in cahoots with CITES officials in the capital. Frankly, I suspected the latter. I had received highly unsatisfactory and sometimes downright misleading or dishonest answers to requests for information that I had sent from Geneva to Almaty.

I had taken with me a copy of a permit that had accompanied a large quantity of caviar which had been flown into a major airport in Europe a few weeks previously and I showed it to customs and fishery officers in Atyrau. The shipment had been detained when it arrived in Europe. The Kazakh officials spotted two things as soon as they looked at it. Firstly, the name of the exporting company that was recorded on the document was a complete fabrication; no such company existed, or at least no such company was authorized to trade in caviar. Secondly, the permit showed that the shipment had been inspected and cleared by customs from Almaty airport. The signature of the customs officer was also false; there was no such official by that name.

These were hardly earth-shattering discoveries, but they illustrate the importance of getting on the ground. Without being able to speak to officials on the frontline, it is next to impossible to understand how trade is managed in practice. It was opportunities like that which allowed me to design strategies to combat illegal trade. It also, importantly, enabled me to give accurate guidance to CITES enforcement officers in importing countries as to whether or not cargo should be allowed entry.

The officials in Atyrau told me that it was vital for a copy of the permit to be sent to the CITES office in the capital. I said that one had already been sent, weeks ago. The officials spoke together in a huddle. I could not understand what they were saying but I could see they were annoyed and frustrated. 'What's the problem?' I asked our interpreter. 'They're talking about how they've never heard of the shipment being detained and how they've never been consulted by government officials in the capital.' Here was yet another reason to suspect corruption.

I later sent details of the shipment to the Interpol office in Kazakhstan and asked for a police investigation into how it was able to leave the country and the circumstances of its export clearance. I never heard (I often did not) the result of any investigation. What I did notice, though, was that one of the Kazakh officials who had regularly attended CITES meetings in Geneva and elsewhere, and who seemed to be responsible for permit issuance, never again appeared at such meetings.

Another day during the mission saw us making the long journey by road from Atyrau to one of Kazakhstan's land borders with the Russian Federation. As we approached it, we passed huge queues of articulated lorries and other commercial vehicles all waiting to be processed through the border checkpoint. The queue must have been at least a kilometre long. Most of the trucks bore Russian number plates and many were from Moscow. The majority were apparently simply in transit through Kazakhstan, having started journeys in the various 'stans to the east of the Caspian, including countries such as Turkmenistan and even Afghanistan. Perhaps some were even en route home from China.

The border point was populated by officials from a large range of agencies: the Militia (police), customs, Border Guard Service, Federal Security Service (KGB) and fishery protection officers. We were impressed that several of the agencies, each with their own suite of offices, had computers with access to databases. The militia, for example, were able to access details of stolen vehicles.

We saw that every vehicle was stopped and documents examined. Some drivers were being asked to open the back doors of their articulated lorries, to show what cargo they were carrying. Although we noted that no vehicles seemed to be thoroughly searched or have their cargo unloaded, the border control seemed, on the face of it, to be efficient, although anyone crossing there would have a considerable wait before driving onto the soil of Mother Russia.

The senior officers of each agency were brought together in a group so that we could talk with them. 'What', I asked through the interpreter, 'is the most common form of contraband seized here?' The officers listened to the question but then looked at each other with puzzled faces. A customs officer responded, apparently speaking for everyone. 'Nothing', translated the interpreter. Presuming that I had not made myself clear, I rephrased my question. The same answer came back, 'Nothing is seized here.'

The commissioner and I looked at each other in disbelief. This could not be right. Here we were, not only at an important crossing between two major trading nations but on the main route linking Russia, one of the most powerful countries in the world, with its neighbours to the east. Many of those neighbours had been members of the Soviet Union and so had decades-long, if not centuries-long, links with the motherland. Thousands upon thousands of tonnes of cargo must have crossed the border each day, accompanied by the drivers and passengers on board the hundreds of trucks, buses and cars. It simply did not make sense that no smuggling was taking place. Today, it is probably also a route regularly taken by terrorists and militant religious fundamentalists.

I tried again. 'Maybe I'm not being understood,' I told the interpreter, and outlined my observation about the volumes of traffic. 'People must be trying to smuggle things across here. Drugs, firearms, counterfeit DVDs, humans. The agencies here are bound, even if purely by chance, to discover contraband of some form and subsequently seize it.' I could see that the interpreter understood the point I was making and he said that he, too, was now puzzled by the replies. He spoke to the officials again, this time at some length.

The conversation became intense, bordering upon heated, as the interpreter obviously expressed incredulity at the responses which were coming back to him. Eventually he turned back to me. 'They're adamant that nothing is ever seized here. They say that no one would dare to try and smuggle anything across this border and past them.' The expression on his face told me that he thought this as incredible as I did. It was clearly pointless to pursue this and after some exchanges of a more general nature, we headed off.

Some weeks later, I described this incident to a colleague and friend in the World Customs Organization. I was taken aback, and very disheartened, when he expressed no surprise whatsoever at what I had seen and heard. He explained that the same scenario might be encountered at a number of border points around the world. Customs officials, and their counterparts from other government agencies, had had next to no training in risk assessment, profiling or targeting. They had not been trained to search vehicles or effectively screen documents, whether driving licences, passports or cargo manifests. What was worse, they were simply part of a massive bureaucratic system and spent their days going through the motions, with little incentive or motivation and with scant understanding or appreciation of what their goal ought to be.

It also, however, reflected the fact that many customs officers in developing countries saw themselves, and still do, primarily as gatherers of revenue rather than as law enforcement officers. It also had to be recognized that if violations were stumbled across or deliberately uncovered, they would often be viewed as a chance to extract personal revenue in the way of bribes. This was, and still is, the way in which some enforcement officials are practically obliged to supplement the meagre wages that their country pays them.

I should stress that the picture painted above comes from a decade ago and I presume people cannot move around with such impunity in that region today. It must have been a smuggler's paradise back then.

Over the course of several years, and with the exception of Iran, I visited every country surrounding the Caspian Sea during enforcement-specific missions or as part of small teams of CITES Secretariat staff examining the general sturgeon trade situation. We regularly found ourselves bewildered by what we were told, faced by utterly conflicting information from one country to another and left struggling to understand the true situation.

In our early dealings with officials from Azerbaijan, Kazakhstan and the Russian Federation, the CITES Secretariat was assured that, as a conservation measure, all the caviar produced through legal harvesting was destined for export. In those days, the early 2000s, none of those countries produced caviar from fish raised in aquaculture operations, although there was some very limited experimentation in this. Similarly - although again there were some ongoing trials - there was no extraction of eggs from live fish. The vast majority of sturgeon caught were removed quickly to a fishing station, knocked on the head with a lump of wood resembling a small baseball bat, had their stomachs slit open and the membrane sac which held the precious eggs cut out. Given the length of time that all sturgeon, not just beluga, take to reach sexual maturity, this seemed terribly wasteful.

We discovered, however, that the assurance that production was limited to the international markets was given to help convince us of the sustainability of the export quotas which the countries were setting. In fact, some of it was utter nonsense. The domestic demand in almost every country around the Caspian was massive. Caviar was a traditional foodstuff, regularly enjoyed. Although it had, centuries before, been somewhat restricted to the tsars and the aristocracy, it was nonetheless a standard ingredient at, for example, every wedding and in meals served on high days and holidays. Tins of caviar were available in every supermarket and it was on the menu in almost every restaurant. This applied not just in the towns along the shores of the Caspian and of the rivers that ran into it, but also in the major cities and capitals of each country, even though these could be thousands of miles away.

The Deputy Secretary-General of CITES and I visited a nightclub in Moscow one evening and were intrigued to see portions of caviar mentioned on the menu, alongside other snacks and cocktails. We asked the waiter if it would be possible to see the container of the caviar on offer. He brought us an unopened tin, on which we immediately recognized the trademark. It belonged to a company whose owner, only days before in Astrakhan, had sworn to us that he was earmarking its products solely for export.

We began to quiz the waiter about the popularity of caviar in the establishment and the quantities being sold. However, before we could get many answers the manager appeared, accompanied by one of the club's massive bouncers. The tin was taken from us and we were advised to change the subject if we wanted to remain on the premises. Had I still been a cop, I would have been willing to risk a confrontation with the doorman, but discretion seemed the better part of valour for a UN official.

In the major supermarket in a city in a Caspian Sea country (not within the Russian Federation) we found tin upon tin of caviar, although interestingly all were apparently of Russian origin. The labels and images on the tins seemed to be of poor quality. While they purported to be the products of a Russian company with which I was well acquainted, I was unconvinced and suspected that the tins were counterfeits, quite possibly containing locally-poached and illicitly-produced caviar. When I told them what I had seen, local officials claimed that this was the first they had ever heard of such items being on sale. Given that they and their wives were likely to shop in this store on a regular basis, it seemed hard to believe.

One of our most bizarre interactions with the caviar industry took place in the same country. At the time of this particular visit, sturgeon fishing and caviar production were in the hands of a state company, which held a total monopoly over every aspect of the trade. The company had allocated one of its fishery inspectors to transport us to an open-air market located on the outskirts of the city. The market was an extensive collection of simple stalls, selling a large range of fresh goods and other products. Whether you wanted a nail or a refrigerator, a beef steak or a cabbage, you would get it there. As with any similar enterprises around the world, the various stallholders shut up shop at the end of the day, loaded unsold items and their trestle tables into their vans and headed for home, leaving behind a vacant lot with no evidence of the major trading that had taken place.

Before our arrival in the country, we had been told by informants that there were several stallholders at the market who specialized in caviar and sturgeon meat, which is why we had specifically asked to visit it. The inspector drove us to the market and led us into its myriad corridors of stalls. We arrived at an area where there were many stalls selling fish and tins of fish roe, but neither sturgeon nor caviar. There were, though, several wooden tables in the same part of the market that were wet and slimy, although no fish was in evidence. We asked our interpreter to find out from nearby stallholders why these tables were bare. 'The sturgeon sellers packed up their stock and left about 15 minutes ago,' came the reply. A coincidence? I think not.

Driving back to the state company's head office, we passed through the centre of the city. We spotted a shop, obviously a fish shop, which had a sign above its doorway bearing the logo of the monopoly. We asked the driver to pull over and made our way into the place. The inspector, somewhat reluctantly, followed us. Inside, we found a large variety of fish on display, including sturgeon meat. More importantly and interestingly, there was an extensive display of caviar in tins of all sizes. They all bore the logo of the state company. After a chat, via the interpreter, with the shop assistants about prices and demand, we continued our journey back to the monopoly's offices.

There we described to its deputy managing director what we had just seen. He flatly denied that the company owned such a shop and insisted that all its caviar production was devoted to export and international markets. When we expressed incredulity, he sent for the inspector who had accompanied us. When he entered his boss's office, the poor man was subjected (although we could not understand what was being said) to what was obviously a tirade of abuse. He was then clearly told to get out. It would not surprise me to learn that he was also told never to come back.

The deputy director then explained, through the interpreter, that the inspector had made a mistake and repeated that the shop did not belong to the company.

Later, on the way to our hotel, I tried to get the interpreter to tell me what had passed between the boss and his underling. He said that he had not been able to follow the conversation. His face, though, like that of several interpreters I worked with over the years, said, 'You fly out of here in a few days. I have to spend the rest of my life here.'

During the same trip, we went one evening for a drink in the city's newest and most luxurious hotel. To avoid any embarrassment, I will not name it but it was part of a chain that has properties in almost every major city around the world. It was with no great surprise that we saw caviar on the menu.

Hoping to avoid a repeat of our Moscow nightclub confrontation, I left my two colleagues and quietly made my way towards the kitchens. It being early evening, I had no problem in locating the head chef there. He turned out to be a German, who had recently been moved to this hotel by the chain's management from a position as assistant head chef in one of their other hotels. I gave him one of my business cards, with its UN logo, explained who I was and why I was in the country. Reassuring him that whatever he told me would not be passed to local officials and that I would never identify my source, I asked to see the hotel's stock of caviar. He led me to the kitchen's refrigerated store where, amongst chilled sides of beef and all the usual culinary stores, were many tins of caviar.

None of them, though, bore any identifying marks of the producer and there was certainly no sign of the state monopoly's logo. 'Who do you buy these from?' I asked. There then followed a conversation like very many I had had as a detective, during which I had to convince him that he could trust me not to disclose where I had got my information. Finally satisfied, he said, 'The mafia.' As I was not aware of any formal mafia in that country, I asked him what he meant.

He told me that, once a week, a man would come to see him and would ask how much caviar the hotel needed. The required amount and quality would be delivered the next day. He said he had started dealing with the mafia because their caviar was of a better quality than that supplied by the state company. He also preferred the mafia supplier, since the man was always happy to provide receipts that could be used for the hotel's accounts and records. In contrast, the state company salesmen were always reluctant to issue receipts and he got the impression that any deals he had conducted with them were taking place under the table and that such sales had probably never appeared in the company's books. I remember wondering who were the bigger crooks: the mafia or the apparently legitimate supplier.

The state company really had it all sewn up. Not only did it regulate all the harvesting by licensing or employing sturgeon fishermen, control all the processing and export and act as the country's CITES management authority for trade in sturgeon, but it also employed the inspection force which was authorized to enforce the nation's fishery legislation. It was also the country's focal point with officials and consultants from a number of major aid and development agencies which, at that time, were spending millions of euros and dollars trying to assist the country to ensure its fishery operations (for all species, not just sturgeon) were being conducted sustainably. These agencies, along with a range of conservation and research bodies, had observed that fish stocks in the Caspian Sea were diminishing rapidly. There were also growing concerns that the oil industry around the Caspian could have dramatically negative impacts upon the health of the sea.

We were astonished and dismayed to find that few of these consultants and advisers had ever been allowed to visit any of the fishing stations located on the country's rivers and coast. We met one consultant who was highly experienced and very knowledgeable about fishery matters but who had spent three years of his contract in the nation's capital and had never actually seen sturgeon harvesting taking place. Equally importantly, he had never visited any of the state company's hatchery operations, which were intended to farm juvenile fish intended for release into the sea to enhance wild stocks. This was despite that fact that the agency employing him, and other international bodies and individual western governments, were being asked to fund the construction of new aquaculture operations.

The hatchery facilities were of the utmost importance and were, in essence, similar to those operated by many fishing authorities around the world. I am by no means an expert in fisheries or in fish reproduction but, as I understand it, only a very small percentage of the eggs that are laid during natural fish spawning will ever survive to adulthood. All manner of things impact upon those eggs and prevent their development. Other fish species and other animals will eat some of the eggs. Tides and currents will sweep some downstream to destruction. Weather, especially freezing winters, will kill them off. In recent times, factors like dams and commercial fishing in estuaries have combined to reduce, or in some cases completely preclude, access to historical spawning beds. In many parts of the world, in relation to many fish species, overfishing prevents sufficient sustainable natural reproduction.

As a result, some fishing authorities remove eggs deposited by fish in spawning grounds and place them in hatcheries, so as to help radically improve the number that will mature. An alternative is to catch gravid females as they head towards the spawning grounds (especially important if those grounds no longer exist or cannot be accessed) and transport them to aquaculture facilities. When the eggs develop into fish of a stage described as fingerlings or hatchlings, they are returned to the river or sea in the hope that they will reach maturity in the wild.

These techniques are used by commercial fisheries but are also widespread in the management of recreational species such as salmon and trout.

This artificial reproduction has become, in recent decades, especially important for sturgeon populations in the Caspian Sea. It was started in the Soviet era and has continued ever since. So important is it that harvesting quotas are partly determined by the amount of aquaculture that each country undertakes. The USSR introduced hatcheries in all its relevant territories because it recognized that overfishing was preventing sufficient natural reproduction. If one examines catch data during the latter part of the Soviet period, numbers of wild-caught sturgeon were dropping year on year.

The state company of the country I am talking about had, in simple terms, got away for years with denying access by outsiders to any of its operations. The aid agencies were largely obliged to accept, or had decided to accept, without any means of challenge, whatever that nation and other Caspian Sea countries chose to tell them. But the same applied to the countries themselves. Whilst the riparian states of the Caspian agreed between themselves their annual catch and export quotas, they made no effort to visit each other's aquaculture operations to see whether the statistics presented at their meetings were accurate. I regularly heard them say that such inspections would be useful and that they would welcome their foreign colleagues should they choose to drop in, but no one ever actually seemed to. In reality, I suspect they each knew that their operations might not stand up to scrutiny and that there was an unwritten and unspoken pact of 'I'll accept the figures you present, if you accept mine.' However, the state company now faced a quandary. Like those in its neighbouring countries, it had to abide by the terms of the CITES Convention if it wanted to access international markets, which meant satisfying the CITES community, via the CITES Secretariat, that its caviar trade was not detrimental to the survival of sturgeon in the wild.

Consequently, the CITES Secretariat obtained previously unknown and unparalleled access to sturgeon harvesting and caviar producing facilities around the Caspian Sea. Alongside missions to determine conservation and management issues, the staff in Geneva were also tasked with examining enforcement-related matters. That was where I came in.

The Azerbaijan capital of Baku that I first visited was a depressing city. Its architecture was wholly Soviet-style and, on its southern side, it was awash with drilling rigs extracting oil. These were the rocking rigs like the ones in the movies set in places like the Texas oilfields, and nothing like the platforms operated in the North Sea off my home city of Aberdeen. The land and coastline bordering Baku was stained black by oil. There was one area at the edge of the city where the ground was literally on fire; escaping natural gas burned in fissures in rocks and the soil. Watching the Eurovision Song contest broadcast from the Azerbaijan capital in 2012, I could not recognize it as the same place I had visited a decade or so before.

The countryside south of Baku was another world in the 2000s. The further one travelled from the city, the lusher the landscape became. There were also many business facilities, factories, industrial and agricultural premises that seemed to be descending into ruins, though. Our government guides explained that Azerbaijan had been one of the first countries to seek independence following the break-up of the USSR. The political leaders in Moscow had apparently acquiesced but had, at the same time, cancelled all trade arrangements. Once the bread basket for much of the Soviet Union, with its huge areas of highly-productive agricultural land, Azerbaijan found itself with no market for its produce. Its economy seems much better today, but it clearly went through many years of hardship.

We were first taken to a sturgeon fishing station at Neftçala. This threw up the first of many puzzles.

The fishing post at Neftçala was located close to the mouth of the River Kura, which is where sturgeon returning to the site of their birth in Azerbaijan historically had their spawning grounds. The river, like those elsewhere in the Caspian region, had been affected over recent decades by dams and water extraction, so that accessing spawning grounds was becoming increasingly difficult for fish. The station, though, was actually on the coast, which surprised us. We had been told that Azerbaijan, as well as Kazakhstan and the Russian Federation, prohibited the catching of sturgeon in the Caspian Sea.

Before we could ask about this apparent conflict, we were taken down to the beach and into rowing boats. We then rowed out about a hundred metres, towards lines of hang nets positioned in the sea offshore. This really seemed to be contrary to what we had heard about fishing methods. We observed fishermen checking these nets but they were empty.

Back on shore, we explained our confusion. The manager of the post hurried to assure us that all was above board and told us that any sturgeon caught in the hang nets were brought ashore alive and transferred to Azerbaijan's hatchery. On a subsequent visit I was able to see for myself the beginning of such a transfer, which involved lowering the fish into the container behind the cab of a vehicle that had originally been built as a petrol tanker. Commercial fishing - and the manager was adamant about this - was solely conducted on the river. Given that access to spawning grounds was apparently reducing with each passing year, my first thought was that the hang nets seemed ideally placed to intercept fish heading for the river and would surely be the most productive way to carry out harvesting, whatever the purpose. However, it is not for me to say that we were lied to.

We lunched at the fishing station and were introduced to a very elderly-looking man who was the person responsible for processing eggs into caviar. His skill was apparently legendary and it was the way in which he cleaned the eggs and treated them with just the right amount of salt that determined how fine they would taste. This man told us, with great pride, that it was he who had produced caviar for Winston Churchill.

Before returning to Baku, we visited a hatchery. It was a large facility, with several ponds designed to hold fish of differing stages of maturity. It certainly appeared to be generally fit for purpose but also had a general look of dilapidation. We were provided with a tour of the premises and an explanation of its workings. Something of an anti-climax was reached, though, when we ended up beside the largest of the hatchery's ponds. 'Oh, if only you'd been here two weeks ago,' said the manager. He explained that we had missed seeing the millions of fingerlings that had been in the pond, immediately before being transported to the sea and released.

The trouble was that the pond had a small tree growing out of it, its surface was cracked in many places and weeds were dotted about its concrete base. I am no expert in either aquaculture or horticulture but it struck me that the pond had not held a large quantity of water for months, if not years, and that it certainly could not have been a holding area for small fish. On the other hand, everything else about the large operation had the appearance of being in relatively good order. It was yet another occasion where one's credulity was really put to the test. I came away puzzled.

That was how I felt on the occasion when I met the country's Water Police. With staff stationed along rivers and at each of the major towns on Azerbaijan's Caspian Sea coastline, they were able to describe the number of poachers they had caught in the past year and the number of nets they had seized. The numbers were quite impressive. Especially impressive in light of the fact that, in answering one of my questions, they revealed that they had no boats. They apparently used to, but none of them were serviceable at that time and they did not have the funds to replace them. Mind you, the fishery protection agency did not have any serviceable vessels either.

We were told that Azerbaijan's Border Guard Service had some operational vessels. We also heard that, the year before, they had intercepted a large commercial vessel, registered in Turkmenistan, fishing for sturgeon in Azeri waters. We never, unfortunately, met with this service. I asked what action had been taken regarding this major poaching incident and was told that the fish had been seized and the vessel's captain told to sail home and not come back. It was not clear why anything more punitive had not been done.

I later expressed my surprise at that to the head of Azerbaijan's criminal prosecution agency. He said he had never been informed of the incident. I do not know but I suspect that any prosecution might possibly have faced legal difficulties over jurisdiction. At that time, and maybe still today, the five countries of the Caspian had not, as I understood it, formally agreed on just where each of their territorial waters' boundaries were. If that was the case, then it would undoubtedly have been awkward to prove that the Turkmenistan vessel was not entitled to fish where it had been.

What was impressive in Azerbaijan was its customs service. It was an active member of the World Customs Organization, hosted a regional training establishment and appeared to use highly effective risk-assessment and intelligence-gathering techniques. And its staff seemed to be imaginative in their targeting, and using informants effectively. On one occasion, they were told of a caviar shipment that was to be smuggled out of the country by light aircraft. Unfortunately, when the plane was ordered to land, its occupants were able to dump three tonnes of caviar before it was searched. In another incident, customs had set up a roadblock and were waiting to intercept a truck that was heading out of the country laden with caviar. The officers waited for hour after hour but it never appeared. Finally, word reached them that the truck had broken down. Even more frustrating for them was that the police had stumbled across the broken-down vehicle, had chanced upon the caviar and were taking the credit for a major seizure and important arrest.

Many, if not all, of our missions resulted in our being able to make suggestions for improvement. Sometimes these were in reports that contained formal recommendations, but several of my enforcement-specific report had to be of a restricted distribution and were never made public. They sometimes described serious shortcomings that could have been exploited by criminals had they become widely known, although I was pretty confident that criminals were already exploiting weaknesses in many cases. The reports also contained passages relating to organized crime matters that we believed made them inappropriate and unsuitable for wide distribution, but there was sometimes a chance to influence policy-makers in an informal way.

At the end of one visit to a Caspian Sea country, my colleagues and I were taken out to dinner by a very senior political figure who had recently been appointed to head the ministry responsible for fisheries. Educated abroad, fluent in English, clearly highly intelligent, he was also obviously daunted by what lay ahead of him. He admitted he had next to no knowledge of fisheries and acknowledged that his country faced major problems with crime and corruption, but was determined to try and do his best. 'If you were in my position,' he pondered, 'where would you start?'

In that country, at that time, fishing and caviar production rested in the hands of one company which enjoyed a total monopoly. It was state owned, a scenario that was found, at different times, in each of the Caspian Sea states. The three CITES Secretariat staff at the dinner table looked at one another and wondered where on earth to begin. I decided to jump in.

'If I were you, Minister, I'd send accountants in to examine the monopoly's books.' I suppose he had expected a response about conservation or trade control matters because his face showed utter puzzlement. 'Why that?' he asked. I replied 'Because here is a company that has had total control over caviar production for decades. Probably since before you were born. Throughout that time it has been exporting a luxury product, one of the world's most expensive food items. It paid Soviet wages for most of its existence and probably still only pays the equivalent today. But its profits must have been enormous.' I could see the Minister still did not understand. 'Have you been to any of the monopoly's facilities?' I asked. He had not. 'Well you need to. You'll see for yourself how run down they all are. There's been no reinvestment in company logistics, equipment or infrastructure for years and years. But look in the managing director's office, where plenty of money seems to have been spent. And I'll bet that the revenue handed over to the State Treasury hasn't increased in line with the way that caviar prices have multiplied year on year recently.'

The Minister did not answer but sat mulling over what I had said. I do not know if he ever did get the books examined but I do know that, when I returned to the country the following year, the State monopoly had been disbanded. Unfortunately, several of its management staff had been re-employed in the private enterprises that had replaced it.

As an aside, this apparent grip by people in positions of authority or management in CITES-related matters was something I was to see repeatedly across a range of species and countries. I can think of several individuals who were widely spoken of as being corrupt or who abused their status, yet who clung fiercely to their posts and seemed able to resist efforts to displace them. Such people, especially in countries where the commercial exploitation of natural resources is highly profitable, have very considerable power and their control over licensing, for example, must present them with regular opportunities to extract bribes or other favours.

There would have been a time, for example, when being in charge of a ministry of environment might have been regarded as a relatively insignificant government post. However, since almost every commercial activity - especially any new development - now requires some form of environmental impact assessment, these post holders have acquired very considerable influence. I know of one environment minister in an African nation who has served for years and years in that post, well beyond the time one would normally have expected. Whenever I have expressed surprise at his political longevity, nods and winks would come in my direction, signalling that he would much rather stay in what some might regard as a junior government post because of its extra benefits. This seemed to be corroborated by the fact that, whenever the minister and I met together, his focus always seemed to be upon revenue gathering rather than on conservation or enforcement.

Another department head, whom I met many times, was regularly alleged to be corruptly allocating hunting licences in his nation's parks and reserves. When I questioned his survivability, the response was 'He knows where the bodies are buried.' I should, of course, acknowledge that my own profession was not free from characters who might abuse their position. One has only to think of the head of a certain major US-based enforcement agency who, years ago, was alleged to have files on everyone in government and who was said to be not unwilling to refer to them when he wanted to bring his influence to bear. Thankfully, however, I do not believe anyone ever alleged that he was motivated by a desire to benefit financially.

Although anti-corruption work was not really one of my prime duties, I do take some satisfaction from the knowledge that my activities in this field resulted in the removal, or early retirement, of a number of senior national CITES officials.

CONTROLLING CAVIAR COMMERCE

The five countries of the Caspian - Azerbaijan, Kazakhstan, Iran, Russia and Turkmenistan - had formed a Bio-Resources Commission where they discussed, and sometimes reached consensus on, catch and export quotas for fish species. Reaching consensus seemed to be most difficult when it came to sturgeon. This had not always been the case. In the days of the USSR, its government seemed to work well with its opposite numbers in Iran when it came to dividing the natural resource spoils of the Caspian Sea. Perhaps, though, those were just the days when no international scrutiny was placed upon the use of such resources and so both nations could do what they liked.

However, when CITES began to regulate the caviar trade, things changed dramatically. It used to amuse me to watch the delegations of the former Soviet countries at international meetings. During the day, they would bicker and haggle but, at night, they would disappear into the bar *en masse* and sit drinking vodka and speaking Russian together. After all, many of these individuals had trained and studied together and would have spent weeks and weeks in each other's company in Astrakhan, where most research and fishery management was conducted in Soviet times. The Iranians, of course, were excluded from such alcohol-fuelled collaboration. One of the quota-related issues with which we struggled was the fact that, prior to CITES involvement, the countries had not taken any account of illegal fishing and they challenged suggestions that they ought to. However, when we pointed out that their own research documents and scientific papers estimated that, for every sturgeon harvested legally through government-licensed fishery operations, anything from five to twelve sturgeon were being caught by poachers, they finally agreed to make allowance for this in their quota-setting calculations.

Each of the five countries took turns to chair the Commission and host its meetings. We regularly heard complaints that meetings would be called by the current chair country with such short notice that at least some delegations would have too little time to get visas to attend.

During the 2000s, the CITES Secretariat devoted significant hours of staff time towards bringing the countries together and aiming to ensure that quotas were established in a sustainable and scientific manner. At times, we seemed to be making considerable progress. At others, we felt we were banging our heads against a brick wall. Deadlines we set for the receipt of information would be missed by weeks or, more often, months. There were years when we were unable to publish any quotas at all and, consequently, none of the countries were able to access - legally - international markets.

As time passed, more and more of the international demand for caviar was met by aquaculture operations that were being established in Europe and North America. Sturgeon 'farms' even sprung up in what, to the layman, seemed bizarre locations, such as Ecuador and Israel. Companies in these countries would import thousands of live fingerlings from, in particular, the Russian Federation and then rear them to a point at which they could be slaughtered for their eggs and meat. As these facilities became more established, they no longer needed to import live fish from the Caspian and simply set aside some of their stock to reproduce fingerlings in-house.

I recall an occasion, in the mid-2000s, when word reached me that a company based in Saudi Arabia was intending to enter the caviar trade. 'Someone's really taking the mickey now', I thought. 'How can you possibly have a fish farm in the desert?' Well, fact can truly be stranger than fiction because before I left CITES I stood inside its warehouse, not far from the border crossing to Bahrain. Although it had not reached the stage of regular caviar production, its ponds were full of apparently healthy sturgeon of various species and various ages. And there weren't any trees growing out of its ponds.

These farms could, in fact, benefit from a hot climate. Just like other fish, sturgeon can be raised more quickly with the help of water warmer than that of their natural environment and extra feed. I believe chemicals may also be used to quicken maturation. In normal circumstances, sturgeon aquaculture is not immediately commercially attractive as it can take females, depending on the species, anywhere from 8 to 25 years before they become sexually active. Fish farming techniques can drastically reduce this.

But it was no surprise to me that fish farms could also be exploited to launder illicit-origin caviar and I regularly warned countries with such operations to watch out for this. Although some fraud was uncovered, and continues to be so, I think much more might be waiting to be discovered. A major problem for CITES and law enforcement authorities in the countries in question is that they seldom have national scientists or other suitable experts with enough knowledge to spot when, to paraphrase an old saying, something fishy is going on.

One of the most fascinating missions I conducted in the Caspian area was to Turkmenistan. This massive country, with Kazakhstan to the north and Iran to the south, was not a CITES party. It also, we were assured, did not engage in any fishing for sturgeon. This dated back to the days of the USSR, when Turkmenistan had been prohibited from engaging in sturgeon harvests for, from what I could gather, three reasons. Firstly, Turkmenistan primarily consists of desert. I think, at one time, it may have had rivers that flowed into the Caspian Sea but those days were long gone. As a result, sturgeon were unable to enter any part of Turkmen territory to spawn. The Soviet government ruling was that sturgeon could only be fished for commercially in fresh water and there was nowhere in Turkmenistan that this could happen. Secondly, it was suggested to me that, even should fishing in the Caspian itself be allowed, it would not be right for that to happen off Turkmenistan's coast. This, seemingly, was because many, perhaps all, of the Caspian Sea's sturgeon populations over-winter offshore from Turkmenistan's seaboard and commercial fishing conducted there risked becoming unsustainable. This second explanation also took account of the fact that when sturgeon were in Turkmen waters they would not be gravid, i.e. the females had yet to begin developing eggs. Without eggs, it was pointless to harvest sturgeon for caviar production. The third and last reason was apparently that sturgeon spend their over-wintering period at depths of between 200 and 300 metres in waters 20–30 miles offshore, which meant fishing was problematic.

I visited Turkmenistan briefly in 2001, when it was still led by the man who had ruled since its independence from the Soviet Union, President for Life Saparmurat Niyazov. President Niyazov, depending upon whom you spoke to, was a totalitarian dictator, a man who loved his people or a raving loony. Despite the fact that my mission to the country was to assess fishing-related enforcement matters, the entry visa issued to me on arrival at the airport was restricted to the capital city of Ashgabat. When I queried this, I was told it would be pointless for me to visit Turkmenistan's coast, since no sturgeon harvest occurred there. This meant that I had no opportunity to see what anti-poaching or fishery control measures the country had in place. After all, Turkmenistan did have a fishing industry, even if it purportedly targeted only species other than sturgeon.

Ashgabat was one of the most bizarre cities I ever visited. It was relatively new, the original city having been destroyed in an earthquake in 1948 that unofficial sources estimate killed over 170,000 of its inhabitants (the Soviet media reported the figure as 40,000). Since an even earlier capital had been levelled by earthquake in the first century B.C., one wonders why they kept rebuilding in the same spot. The city was crossed by massive roads and, although its population was comparatively small and certainly not outwardly wealthy, there were buildings more grandiose than I had ever seen. Each of them was lavish in a manner utterly out of keeping with a town situated in what was essentially a desert. As I was not going to the coast, officials occupied my time one afternoon by taking me to a national museum on the outskirts of the city. It had one of the most imposing driveways I had ever encountered and the museum itself was housed in a splendid and imposing structure that left one wondering what it must have cost. Once inside, each room was dazzling and the finest marble covered the floors. There did not seem to be a great deal on display, however, although the ostentatiousness of the place kept one constantly fascinated, if also somewhat bemused. One thing I did notice was an almost complete lack of fellow visitors and a UN local employee, who was acting as my interpreter, explained that Turkmens were not encouraged to visit. It all seemed to be opulence for opulence's sake. Even the city's street lamps were crazily sumptuous. But the best was yet to come.

In the city's centre, not far from a parliament building the size and grandeur of which would have been more appropriate in one of the world's largest capital cities (although even there it would have been regarded as utterly over-the-top), stood a 250-foot tower. Atop the tower rested a 50-foot statue, in gold, of President Niyazov. There he stood, arms outstretched, with the sun's rays illuminating him in gleaming splendour. And to make sure the rays did shine constantly on the President for Life, a mechanism inside the tower rotated the statue to ensure it always faced directly into the sun.

But beneath all the opulence, Ashgabat reminded me strongly of the USSR I had visited with my wife in the early 1980s. Locals spoke proudly of the wealth of their nation's natural resources, especially oil and gas, which meant that no one paid anything for the power that lit and heated their homes. An internal return flight between Ashgabat and the coast, or other cities in a country larger than California, cost the equivalent of a dollar. Locals, though, became very quiet if you asked about the President for Life. I was told that, for every one Turkmen citizen, there were two policemen; clearly an exaggeration but a telling comment on personal freedom. Most ex-Soviet countries, by early 2000, had either disbanded, re-named or allocated criminal law enforcement to their KGB. Whilst the KGB in Turkmenistan had been renamed the NCB, it apparently remained wholly an organ of political and state control.

As in all missions of this nature, I was taken to meet senior customs officials. I had often experienced some reticence on these occasions. The officers were clearly rather wary that I was on some form of inspection or assessment of their work; I would have been, too, had a UN official been ushered into my police station in Scotland. What's more, I invariably found that the more law enforcement was under political control in a country, the greater the caginess and restraint displayed by its managers. This meeting was like nothing I had ever had to deal with and was like pulling teeth. I asked what form of contraband Turkmen customs most commonly came across. A silence filled the room and stretched on and on. One officer finally indicated that the smuggling of arms and narcotics through Turkmenistan was a major problem, although he received serious scowls from his colleagues for this admission. When I asked for further details, none were forthcoming, but the officers said they did not have any because customs had no investigative powers and simply controlled the movement of goods. They also went on to tell me that any contraband which was seized by customs had to be passed immediately into the control of either the NCB or the Militia (police). I was never taken to meet either the NCB or Militia, it being explained that neither had anything to do with fishery controls. If I had been of a suspicious nature, I might have found myself wondering whether they were trying to restrict my access to information.

Coming from a policing system that has historically both enjoyed and fiercely guarded its independence from political control, it is really frustrating when I find that absent elsewhere, not just because I object strongly on grounds of principle but because it invariably leads to incredible inefficiency. Law enforcement is determined and directed by people who have no relevant experience or training whatsoever. It goes a long way towards explaining why many,

many countries around the world have yet to adopt modern practices such as intelligence-led and pro-active policing. Furthermore, because it encourages parochialism, it leads to an unwillingness among agencies to collaborate and communicate, both nationally and with counterparts abroad. Because the governments or rulers of these nations lack confidence in themselves, they view the police as firstly an organ of the state to control the public and suppress any revolt or dissent. Their insecurity, though, makes them distrust the police too, which is why they create KGBs or other similar bodies. And then they start to mistrust the KGB, at which point it becomes a really vicious circle.

I am convinced this political interference has been a high hurdle in making progress in the fight against illegal trade in caviar around the Caspian. When you then combine it with corruption, law enforcement is going nowhere fast.

During a meeting with another branch of government, I met up with an ex-Turkmen customs officer. When he discovered that my job incorporated species other than sturgeon, he told me that he was very concerned about illegal wildlife trade, especially in falcons, which was affecting Turkmenistan. He described how he had previously been stationed at Ashgabat's airport and said that it was not unknown for calls to be made to the staff there, from customs headquarters in the city, in which they would be advised of flights arriving from the Middle East. They would be instructed that no inspection was to be conducted of the passengers or cargo on the aircraft. These flights would bring in large hunting parties of falconers and their birds. No checks, including animal health quarantine checks, were carried out. Subsequent flights taking these hunting groups back to their countries of origin would, he told me, always seemed to involve the loading of more falcons than had been on the incoming plane. He said he thought that some of what happened was on the instruction of people in government more senior than his customs managers, as he understood that hunting was illegal and that for foreigners to by-pass passport controls must have been approved at very high levels. There were rumours, he said, that senior customs officers received bribes when such movements took place but he had never seen such payments and he had never received money.

He had seen one form of payment, though. He related how he had been on duty one night when an aircraft with Middle Eastern registration markings arrived. It was the size of a cargo plane and a model similar to those used by the military, but it had no airline or air force livery. The rear cargo door lowered and a brand new and latest-model Mercedes was driven out, over the edge of the runway and across to the terminal buildings area. Since such luxury-class cars were relatively few and far between in Turkmenistan, he went closer to admire it. He tried to engage the driver in conversation but he only spoke Arabic and the customs officer only spoke Russian and Turkmen. A few minutes later, a car with a local registration appeared, a man got out, and the car drove away. The man, who the customs officer saw was carrying a large cardboard box, made his way to the driver of the Mercedes and presented the box to him. Really puzzled by now, the Customs official strained to look in as the driver removed the lid of the box, obviously wishing to check the contents. He could hear noises coming from within and realized there was something alive in there. In the glow coming from the terminal buildings he could just make out what seemed to be chicks, perhaps as many as a dozen.

Apparently satisfied, the driver handed the keys of the Mercedes to the deliveryman and walked back into the aircraft, cradling the cardboard carton. The cargo door closed, the aircraft engines roared and it disappeared back into the night sky. Completely bewildered by now, the customs officer held up his hand in a signal to stop as the deliveryman lowered himself into the driving seat of the Mercedes and started the engine. 'Were those really chickens?' he asked. 'Don't be stupid,' came the reply. 'They're baby falcons.' The ex-customs officer told me how he had watched the man drive away and that he had thought to himself, 'I'm in the wrong line of work.'

Fascinated and entertained as I had been by the tale, falcons were not my reason for being in Turkmenistan. I was keen to find out what happened to Turkmenistan's compensatory share of the sturgeon fishing and caviar production which was carried out by its ex-Soviet neighbours. During USSR rule, Turkmenistan having been prohibited to undertake any sturgeon harvest, it was compensated by receiving a percentage of the quota agreed among the then Soviet States of Azerbaijan, Kazakhstan and Russia. This came partly in a financial payment and partly in actual caviar. After independence, this continued, but only from Kazakhstan and the Russian Federation.

I asked what happened to the money and caviar at that time, in 2001, and was told that the funds were allocated to the fishing industry's budget while the caviar went to the 'office of the President'. I was further informed that domestic sale of caviar was forbidden. This seemed to be corroborated when I was taken to visit a shop in the capital that was owned and operated by the state fishing monopoly company. No sturgeon meat or caviar was on sale.

What did not make sense, though, was that in every restaurant I was taken to during my few days in Ashgabat, and in the hotel in which I stayed, sturgeon and caviar featured on the menu. I ordered smoked sturgeon meat in one restaurant but it was very poor quality and did not appear fresh. I asked fishery officials about this apparent anomaly and was told that meat and caviar were imported from one country in the Middle East. It came as no surprise to me when they named the country that I was investigating as being the base of a massive laundering operation for illegal-origin caviar. What was surprising, though, was that whilst examining all the re-export certificates issued by that Gulf State I had seen none which related to shipments to Turkmenistan. I asked fishery officials if I could see copies of any documents relating to caviar imports to Turkmenistan and was told that I would be supplied with them. However, they did not appear and I was later told that they were kept by customs and could not be released. This was to remain yet another of life's great mysteries.

Over drinks in my hotel bar one evening, a local person told me that drug abuse was becoming a significant social issue in Turkmenistan, particularly among young people. The man held a senior post in the oil industry, was able to travel abroad regularly and so had a better than average overall insight into world affairs. The media in Turkmenistan at that time had not evolved from Soviet days. He said that opium and heroin arrived from Afghanistan and Pakistan and moved through Turkmenistan, via Kazakhstan, to Russia. He said it was also rumoured that illicit arms shipments frequently moved eastwards through his homeland. Given the country's extensive border with Afghanistan, this needed no explanation. He went on to tell me that the fierce grip of the NCB seemed to have prevented the emergence of any significant home-grown organized crime and that arms and narcotics trafficking was said to be controlled by criminal networks based outside Turkmenistan. He did not elaborate or explain the remark, but I clearly recall his statement, 'The Kazakh mafia is much worse than the Russian mafia.'

While conceding that the man did seem to be absolutely bonkers, he mentioned that one of the President for Life's policies with which all citizens agreed was that Turkmenistan should remain neutral and divorced from what was being conducted next door by the Taliban and al-Qaeda. Given that Turkmenistan is traditionally, historically and culturally a Muslim country, it might theoretically have been possible for it to be drawn into conflicts. However, I had already noticed that, unlike some Muslim countries I had visited, work was not interrupted for prayer, alcohol was freely available (and consumed in quantities matching its ex-USSR neighbours) and I had seen no women wearing veils. The oilman told me that he and his family were deeply troubled, however, by foreign media reports that action was about to take place in Afghanistan. I left Turkmenistan on 5 October. On 7 October, the US-led invasion of Afghanistan began.

By 2013, Turkmenistan still had not acceded to CITES and it had not designated any authority to administer CITES-related trade. Consequently, no CITES-listed specimens should be leaving or entering the country.

I have mentioned how, after the end of the Cold War, several ex-Soviet state security agencies took on different roles, but that it was hard for them to dispel the image which had built up around them over decades. I came across one example of this in Russia.

While making arrangements for a strictly enforcement-related mission to the Russian Federation, I read in the media one day that President Putin had instructed the Federal Security Service, by then known by the initials FSB instead of KGB, to tackle organized crime involvement in the caviar trade. My interest aroused, I was determined to meet with the FSB. Our CITES focal point for sturgeon issues in the Russian Federation was the State Committee for Fisheries. I got in touch with my contact there and asked him to arrange an appointment with the Federal Security Service. He was not pleased by the request. 'John,' he explained 'you have to appreciate that although it's now referred to as the FSB, we all still think of it as the KGB. You just don't phone up the KGB and ask for an appointment. The average Russian, and that includes me, has spent decades avoiding any contact whatsoever with the KGB. Please don't ask me to do this.' I said that I understood the point he was making but stressed that I really wanted a meeting. When I was subsequently provided with a draft programme for my visit to Moscow and the Russian area of the Caspian, there was no mention of a meeting with the FSB. When I queried this, I was told it was still 'under consideration.'

A New Zealand law enforcement colleague whom I had invited to join me for the mission duly arrived in Moscow and we flew directly to the Caspian area for several days. Every so often I would ask whether the FSB appointment had been made to coincide with the time we would spend in Moscow before leaving Russia. My contact informed me that he had, finally and very reluctantly, called the FSB and explained what I wanted. He said it was a phone call that he had never in his wildest imagination ever envisaged making. The FSB were, in their turn, seemingly mulling over whether they wanted to meet me. However, the day before we flew back to Moscow, word came through that an appointment had been made. I was very pleased. The only disappointment was that the FSB did not want me to come to them but that they would come to me. I had quietly hoped that a meeting would provide me with an opportunity to visit the KGB's famous headquarters, the Lubyanka. Silly, really, but in law enforcement circles, as well as in movies and novels, Moscow's Lubyanka is as well-known as London's New Scotland Yard or New York's 1 Police Plaza. It was explained that our meeting would, instead, take place in the offices of the State Committee for Fisheries.

Back in Moscow, I and my colleague found ourselves shown to a very opulent room within the Committee's offices, where I suspect board meetings were usually held. The walls were panelled in wood and hung with impressive portraits, while ornate chandeliers lit the chamber. We were shown to chairs on one side and towards one end of a massive wooden table. An interpreter sat next to us. The fishery officials sat around the other end, not very subtly concealing their desire to remain as far from the FSB as possible. About six people occupied a space which could have coped with many times more and waited patiently for the arrival of the Russian Federation's State Security Service representative.

A very ordinary, if well-dressed man was shown into the room and sat down opposite us. This was the FSB in person. Whilst he did seem to have a certain air of authority, he certainly would not have stood out in a crowd as an official of one of the most feared enforcement bodies of the world. Neither, though, did he appear over-friendly and I got the impression that he was not especially pleased to be there. I began by giving a brief overview of my, and my colleague's, law enforcement backgrounds, our current positions and the purpose of our visit to his country. He listened as the interpreter converted my remarks into Russian but did not react at all and looked uninterested. I pressed on regardless and explained that in our meetings with a variety of agencies so far we had opened by suggesting that they describe their position in either the governmental or judicial systems of the Russian Federation and the role they played in either regulating fisheries or combating crime. I said that we had found this a successful tactic which had invariably been very enlightening for my colleague and me. I asked whether he would care to follow this approach.

I didn't need the interpreter to explain the FSB officer's response of 'nyet'. However, the interpreter went on to explain that the FSB officer suggested, instead, that I pose questions and that he might, or might not, be in a position to answer them. There then began a period of some 15—20 minutes of very strained and awkward communication, drawing forth very short and blunt replies. We seemed to be getting nowhere. I decided upon a different tack. I asked the interpreter to convey to the FSB representative that I would describe some of what my colleague and I had seen during our visit to the Caspian area and the conclusions we had drawn. This produced a nod of agreement. Immediately the whole tone of our encounter changed. From a position where he was obviously reluctant to (and perhaps under orders not to) volunteer information or opinions, the FSB officer seemed happy to confirm that our conclusions were accurate, expand upon them, suggest modifications or provide additional insight. It evolved into a fascinating encounter but much of what was said cannot be described here. After an hour or so we began to run out of topics for discussion and I asked the interpreter to convey to the officer our very grateful thanks for having taken the time to meet us.

However, before the interpreter could begin to speak, the FSB official rose from his seat. He headed towards me, his palm outstretched, and grasped my hand firmly and warmly. 'It has been a pleasure for me to meet you, Mr Sellar. Your organization and the Federal Security Service clearly share some common goals and I sincerely hope that our two agencies can work together in the future.' The FSB man spoke perfect English. He shook my colleague's hand, turned and left the room, leaving behind a very startled interpreter. Regrettably, it was to be my one and only encounter with one of the world's most famous, or infamous, enforcement bodies.

I like to believe that the efforts of the CITES Secretariat, and law enforcement agencies based far from the Caspian Sea, considerably reduced the amount of poached caviar that entered international markets. It was a real learning experience for many of us. Most of the wildlife law enforcement officials who were, at a stroke on 1 April 1998, suddenly confronted with combating illegal commerce in a luxury food product, had no previous experience of this field and were much more used to focussing on tusks, horns, skins, bones or live animals. Some, like the US Fish and Wildlife Service and the US Department of Justice, did a tremendous job. Some others, I'm afraid, just could not get their heads round it and there were parts of the world, in Asia for example, where some relatively small but troubling active trade spots did not get the attention they deserved. For instance, caviar featured on the menus of many of the world's finest hotels and restaurants but I very seldom saw any sign of their stocks being checked. There were times during the late 1990s and early 2000s when it was next-to-impossible to obtain legal-origin caviar. Your average cop, though, isn't used to inspecting five-star hotels or airline and cruise ship caterers. The very same thing explains why I was regularly able to uncover Tibetan antelope wool shawls in high-class hotel boutiques, which no one from law enforcement seemed to be doing anything about. And, speaking of worlds apart, I very clearly remember the utter astonishment and bewilderment expressed by students when I described the illegal caviar trade during a training course held for officers from east Africa.

In the late 1990s and early 2000s I could have easily spent my entire working week focussing on nothing but illegal trade in caviar. Although it sometimes felt like I actually was, the reality was that many other species deserved attention too. Frustratingly, the flow of intelligence between myself and the Caspian Sea States tended to be very one-way. I seldom learned the results of investigations based on information I supplied. I presumed investigations did take place but it was very rare to hear of any major seizures or prosecutions happening in that part of the world. Maybe, though, that was just some throwback to Soviet times and, as the old Scottish saying has it, they didn't wash their dirty linen in public. I believe, too, that the still-present Soviet communication style was also very largely to blame for failures to get the public behind efforts to save sturgeon in the Caspian. There did not seem to be much attempt to make consumers aware that the species was in dire straits and that a reduction in demand would have to play a part in its recovery. Instead, both lawful and illicit dealers kept feeding that demand and one could find caviar almost everywhere, with apparently little being done to regulate the domestic market. Maybe, just as with the downplaying of the numbers killed in the Ashgabat earthquake, ex-Soviet States were unwilling to admit to their citizens that things were not going well and that their governments' conservation and anti-poaching activities were not stopping sturgeon swimming towards extinction. I suspect, too, that some officials were being so well paid by organized crime, both in the Caspian region and further inland, that it simply was not in their own interests to try and clean up what was happening. Those suspicions seemed to be confirmed by the number of really good people I met in countries around the Caspian Sea who invariably ended discussions with a look of resignation and a shrug of hopelessness. It was hard not to wonder whether politics wasn't constantly getting in the way too and that, try as we might, bringing the countries together seemed harder and harder. I also acknowledge that the countries must have viewed some of what CITES was trying to do as interference in their sovereign right to make their own decisions about their own resources. This could take us down the road of discussing whether fauna and flora 'belong' to any one nation, which is a subject for a whole book in itself.

What I found very irritating, though, was reluctance among several of the Caspian Sea states to review traditional and historical approaches to conservation and fishery practices. I recall being present when one fishery scientist was asked what percentage of the fingerlings released from hatchery operations into the sea were believed to go on to mature and, subsequently, return to spawn in national rivers. I cannot recall the figure that he gave but I do remember the follow-up question, posed by a colleague, who sought details of the research or study methods by which these return rates had been calculated. The scientist explained that this was determined by work done by one of the Soviet Union's most famous sturgeon specialists. The fact that this was a study conducted in 1947 did not seem to faze the present-day scientist in the slightest. Whilst I accepted that these findings might still be relevant, it did strike me that one might have been inclined to review them using, for example, the satellite, tagging or other tracking technology available today. Perhaps that was happening, but no one mentioned it, if so.

I was also bemused by the contradictory information we were sometimes given. For instance, we were told in one national hatchery operation that sturgeon bred in captivity could be readily identified, in adulthood, by the presence of a particular morphological characteristic which developed near the end of their bodies. Several days later, another aquaculture scientist, in the neighbouring country, ridiculed this information and was adamant that no such distinguishing feature existed.

Confusion, or a lack of transparency, in relation to aquaculture had important repercussions for enforcement. For instance, it was acknowledged that some of the hatchery operations surrounding the Caspian Sea had, over the years, experimented with the cross-breeding of fish. Although this had involved the various sub-species of sturgeon found in the Caspian itself, it had also incorporated sub-species from elsewhere. There are, for example, sturgeon in other parts of what used to be the USSR, such as in the Amur River in the far east of Russia. Government representatives were utterly adamant that no such hybrids had ever, either deliberately or accidentally, been released into the wild waters of the Caspian. However, DNA profiling being conducted on some caviar shipments, declared as originating from Caspian states, was showing the presence of a sub-species known as Siberian sturgeon, sometimes alongside Caspian sub-species. What we could not establish was whether this indicated criminality, i.e. caviar processed from sturgeon poached from the Amur River being mixed with that poached in the Caspian, or simply that some legally-harvested sturgeon were no longer truly distinct examples of the sub-species historically present there. I suspect a number of caviar shipments ended up being treated as fraudulent, and were seized, when actually they contained caviar processed from legitimately-caught fish, accompanied by genuine CITES documentation, issued in good faith by national civil servants.

In the end, it seemed to be ever-declining wild sturgeon numbers that inevitably led to a noticeable decline in criminality too. Crime, corruption and a lack of political will have perhaps created bigger obstacles to sturgeon recovery than any physical obstructions which prevent fish accessing their traditional spawning grounds. By the end of the 2000s, very little information passed across my desk about illicit trade in caviar. The relatively low level of illegal activity seemed more related to fraud in relation to the mislabelling of products emerging from aquaculture facilities. And it was those facilities which also filled the gaps in international markets as fewer and fewer caviar exports (legal and illegal) left the Caspian region. The locations of the largest sturgeon farms and major caviar producers were in France, Germany, Italy and the United States. Why didn't Caspian Sea states move into commercial aquaculture in a bigger way? I do not know. They had been farming sturgeon for decades but always with restocking in mind. They undoubtedly had released millions of fingerlings over time, despite what some of my observations in some places might suggest, but it was odd that the industry there had not moved into using more of their captive-bred fish for commercial caviar production.

If you were cynical and suspicious, you might think the fact that they did not corroborates my belief that organized crime was heavily involved in some of what purported to be legal caviar trade. Organized crime is seldom interested in investment; it wants to get in, get the money and then get out. Some people might look at parts of the Caspian caviar industry and think that was exactly what happened.

The caviar industry elsewhere is not without shame too, however. Whilst outwardly bemoaning what was happening to wild sturgeon populations, many parts of that business reaped greater and greater rewards as the price of caviar in Europe and North America sky-rocketed. I saw precious little sign of any of that money being ploughed back into conservation efforts or to support anti-poaching operations. There were also traders based in Europe and North America, several of them citizens of Caspian Sea countries, who were undoubtedly just the foreign representatives of Caspian-based organized crime networks and groups. There were, likewise, many caviar-trading companies which clearly chose not to ask too many questions about the source of their products. To be fair, there were companies which had been around for decades whose management became so sick of what was taking place that they closed down. There were also individuals who battled on trying to keep the trade clean. They, though, were few and far between and it reached a stage where one wondered whether anyone connected with dealing in caviar could be trusted. I knew we were approaching rock bottom when I had reason to become suspicious of someone that I had dealt with over many years and whom I had previously thought to have kept himself above the rest.

Those who know and understand the fishing industry tell me that fish can be remarkably resilient and that populations can bounce back. Historical survey statistics have shown that sturgeon populations in the Caspian Sea have gone through peaks and troughs. One can only hope that the 1990s and 2000s were a trough out of which they will swim up one of these days. But, as I said to delegates at one of the last sturgeon-related events I attended, my fear would be that the Caspian Sea states have excluded themselves so drastically from international caviar markets in recent years that re-entering those markets may not be practical or commercially viable for them. I trust my fears are unfounded.

Caspian hospitality

Working with caviar was rarely dull.

I had previously experienced the high alcohol intake of customs and police in ex-Soviet nations, but I was not prepared for what was to occur one night in Atyrau, on the shores of the Caspian Sea. It followed a busy day spent visiting caviar processors with a commissioner of the Federal Police of Belgium.

The Commissioner and I agreed that it had been a very successful day and were delighted when the local officer in charge of the arrangements for our visit told us that he would be taking us out for dinner that night. He was the head of fishery protection for Kazakhstan's territorial area of the Caspian Sea and of the rivers, such as the Ural, where sturgeon go to spawn. Although our conversation with this man had been somewhat limited, as he spoke little English and conversation took place through an interpreter, we had both been struck by his air of authority. He looked like someone who meant business, he appeared to be well-known and highly regarded among government officials and he seemed to have a knowledge of general law enforcement beyond what I would normally expect of a fishery official.

As we drove back to our hotel to get ready for the evening to come, I mentioned my observations to our interpreter. 'No wonder,' came his reply, 'He's a Colonel in the KGB who's been transferred to fishery duties.' Now I understood why he was held in such respect everywhere we went.

The commissioner and I changed into more casual clothes and were duly collected at our hotel. The KGB colonel was driving and indicated that we should join him. He was alone. As we set off, I whispered to the Commissioner my hope that an interpreter would join us, or else a night of one-sided conversation lay ahead of us. We drove into the centre of Atyrau and pulled into a large car park behind what seemed to be a substantial government building. Two men were standing there, apparently waiting for us. We found one to be the head of the Interpol bureau in Kazakhstan, while the other was the chief of the environmental police. I was reassured to find that the Interpol officer spoke good English. 'Are you hungry?' he asked, and started to walk across the car park. We followed. I presumed we were heading for some nearby city centre restaurant.

But, no, we were led to the rear of the government edifice and, upon entering, were taken down into the basement. We found ourselves in a long and fairly dingy corridor and followed the KGB colonel along it. 'What an odd place to bring us,' I thought. About halfway along, the Colonel stopped and opened a door to his left. He gestured that we should look in. Before us was a large, rather bare room but with a table laden with one of the most impressive cold buffets I had ever seen. Large platters were laden with cold meats and smoked fish, while bowls of salad, bread and other accompaniments also awaited us. There were, too, I noticed, several ice buckets, in which were resting many bottles of beer, vodka and what looked like the Georgian champagne that is favoured in that part of the world when entertaining special guests. Simple wooden benches were on either side of the table. 'Well,' I thought, 'the surroundings may be somewhat spartan but it looks like we're in for a good time.'

But there were more surprises to come. Apparently satisfied that we had liked what we had seen, our KGB host closed the door and beckoned us further down the corridor. At the far end, he opened another door and we followed him through it. Now I really was puzzled. We had entered what was clearly a locker and changing room of the type one would expect to find beside a gym or swimming pool. I became ever more puzzled as the KGB colonel and the Interpol and environmental police chiefs began to undress. The Belgian Commissioner and I exchanged glances that needed no interpretation.

With gestures, the colonel indicated that we should follow suit. 'OK,' I thought, 'When in Rome, do as the Romans do.' The commissioner and I began to take our clothes off too. As we did so, I began desperately looking around for some alternative form of clothing that we might be changing into. Tracksuits or shorts, perhaps? There was nothing in sight other than a pile of towels sitting on a table. As the Kazakhs reached a state of nature equivalent to the day of their births, they each grabbed a towel and stood waiting for my Belgian friend and me to finish undressing. We followed their example but were now exchanging increasingly concerned looks as we were led back out to the corridor. We headed back towards the room with the food and drink. My mind was working overtime, trying to make sense of all this. Why on earth did we have to take our clothes off for a buffet, even if it was to be washed down with vodka?

But we did not turn right into the dining room. The KGB officer instead opened yet another door, opposite it. We were, by now, well used to this game of follow-the-leader. Even before I arrived at the doorway, I could feel heat coming from within.

The first thing I saw as I crossed the threshold was a deep pool of water. This was obviously some form of tiled plunge pool which, I was to discover, was absolutely freezing. Off to the side was the typical pine door that I immediately recognized as a leading to a sauna. I like saunas and can usually stand hot ones better than most, but this place was hotter and steamier than any I had ever experienced. The five of us sat down and began to sweat. Really sweat.

Ten minutes passed before the colonel led us out and into the plunge pool. It was a relief, although a really shocking one, from the near-boiling atmosphere of the sauna cabin. Sufficiently chilled, we crocodile-filed across the corridor and began to replace fluids with bottles of beer and shot glasses of vodka. The marvellous spread of food also countered any potential weight loss from the sauna.

After twenty minutes or so, the colonel, by now well into the vodka, guided us all back to the sauna and plunge pool once more. And in so doing, he set the ground rules for how the evening was to be conducted. The five of us entered upon a seemingly never-ending round of food, alcohol, blistering heat, freezing cold, food and alcohol. Any inhibitions of sitting naked alongside people who had been perfect strangers an hour or so before soon disappeared. As the hours passed, though, I began to see a glint appear in the veteran KGB man's eye. A determined glint. And I realized that there was a bit more to this than just hospitality. A degree of sportsmanship and competition was beginning to emerge. Appropriately naked, like gladiators, Spartans or Olympians centuries before, this was clearly to be a vodka and sauna battle to the death (or unconsciousness, as the case may be).

By midnight, the five original entrants were still in the game, although each experiencing differing rates of exhaustion. But by 1 a.m. the environmental police chief and Belgian commissioner had fallen by the wayside. By 1.30, the Interpol boss was also unable to rise from the bench and head for the sauna.

And so it fell to me to try and outlast what I saw was a tried and tested gold medal winner in such conflicts. It was well after two in the morning when I found myself, again in the sauna, facing a man who, judging by his age and rank, must have been a product of Soviet KGB training. I could not begin to imagine what he had seen and done over the years and what it must have been like to have been a law enforcement officer in a communist nation. Indeed, I suspected that it might not have been all that different from the Kazakhstan of the early 2000s. It also crossed my mind that while it must be odd for him now to be running anti-poaching operations, I predicted he would be as ruthless with caviar criminals as he would have been with any other enemy of the state.

Finally, just as it was time for another ice-cold dip, the veteran of the Federal Security Service reached out his hand towards the veteran of the Scottish Police Service and we shook to acknowledge that an honourable draw had been reached. 'Thank goodness', I thought, 'I really couldn't have taken much more of this.' I do not suppose he will ever read this, but if he does, I can reveal that if only he had stuck it out just a very little longer, he would have emerged the victor.

It was with very sore heads, delicate stomachs and very clean pores that the commissioner and I resumed our work later that same morning.

It was not only Kazakhstan that presented odd dining and drinking experiences. One of my visits to the Astrakhan region of the Russian Federation incorporated a trip down the River Volga to see a sturgeon fishing station. On this occasion I was accompanied by a colleague from New Zealand, an ex-policeman who had also spent time as a fishery inspection official and who was to go on to become Interpol's first full-time wildlife crime officer.

It was late in the sturgeon harvesting season and most fishermen had left the lower regions of the vast Volga delta where it enters the Caspian Sea. One or two of the major fishing structures had yet to be taken upriver, however. A federal border guard vessel dropped us for the night at one of these. It was massive, constructed of wood, and had several decks. If it had had a large multi-panelled wheel at its stern, it would have looked just like some Mississippi paddle steamer of old. Instead, it had to be towed into position by a tug-like boat and was currently partly-moored, partly-dragged onshore.

The deck at water level contained net stockrooms, fish processing areas and storage spaces. The upper decks contained a kitchen and canteen, more storage areas and huge dormitories where fishermen would spend weeks at a time before getting leave to return to their homes in the towns and villages between the sea and the city of Astrakhan. The sleeping areas were very basic, with simple wooden beds and rough blankets to ward off the cold nights. The windows had no glass but simply plain wood panels. They offered little in the way of a barrier between the men and the cold or, as the season dictated, the heat, the humidity and the insects. These dormitories would not have looked out of place on the set of some prisoner-of-war movie.

However, the vessel was empty of the dozens of fishermen and fish and caviar processors that would have packed it just a few weeks before. The only people on board were me, my Kiwi colleague, two fishery protection officials acting as our guides and the station's captain. It was decided that we would dine at the captain's table that evening. It was soon apparent that one did not dress for dinner with this gentleman. We four visitors sat on stools around a simple wooden table in the middle of what was the captain's cabin on the first deck. The captain, meantime, sat fixed in a comfortable armchair in one corner.

Dinner consisted of dried and salted fish. From what we could gather, it was 'vobla', or at least that is what seemed to be said. It is apparently some type of roach. I think there was also some cucumber and tomato but the only other accompaniment was the black bread of which Russians seem so fond. Caviar was noticeable by its absence. As ever, beer and vodka were present with which to wash it all down. We all engaged in considerable washing down that night.

I remember little of the evening, other than finally stumbling up flights of wooden stairs to reach one of the large dormitories on the upper decks. With a sweep of his arm, one of the fishery protection officers gestured that we should pick a bed for the night. If memory serves me right, there were three or four rows of at least twenty beds each. There were no lights in this enormous cabin and only moonlight, coming through the open and unshuttered windows, gave us light to see. Past caring, I flopped down onto a bed and covered myself with a blanket. No warning had been provided that we were not returning to Astrakhan that night and so my colleague and I had brought no change of clothes, night attire or toiletries.

In the middle of the night I was woken by a call of nature. With it still almost pitch dark both inside and out, I felt my way down the stairs and towards the stern. A plank of wood led from the gunwale down to the riverbank. Not knowing where the nearest toilet was, and not particularly caring, as I suspected it would not be pleasant to enter, I simply urinated onto the grass. I found my friend from Down Under doing the same. 'John', he said, 'the next time you feel prompted to ask me to go on mission with you, think of someone else.' I knew he didn't really mean it.

When daylight broke, and I saw the state of the blanket, mattress and pillow on the bed I had occupied, I was grateful not to be spending the following hours scratching bites.

Breakfast was served in the captain's cabin. The cucumbers and tomatoes had all been consumed but there was still vobla. And black bread. And vodka. I think I had some black bread. The captain was clearly bored with us by then. He ignored us and sat watching a porn film. And to think that were probably hundreds of local fishermen whose dream in life was to reach the exalted status that would allow them to occupy that cabin.

It was decided we should go fishing to pass the time waiting for the federal border guards to collect us for the return journey to Astrakhan. Getting into a small fishing boat, probably usually used to drag nets across the river to intercept sturgeon as they headed for traditional spawning grounds, we set off downstream.

We moored and dangled simple metal lures on hand lines over the side of the boat. About half an hour later, with no bites on our lines, one of the fishery officers announced, 'I know what's wrong. Not enough vodka!' He then reached over the side and pulled up two bottles that had been cooling in the river, attached to a length of string.

Fortunately, as he unscrewed the top of one bottle, we heard the powerful engines of the border guard jet boat as it headed toward us. It is not widely appreciated but the federal border guard service is part of the federal security service. I don't imagine the sight of KGB officers has often prompted gratitude among people over the decades but as I climbed on board their jet boat I could not help thinking of Martin Luther King in his most famous speech: 'Free at last! Free at last!'

ELEPHANTS AND IVORY

CITES and the signatory governments to the Convention have wrestled for decades with the question of whether or not trade in ivory should be allowed.

Throughout the 14 years I served with the CITES Secretariat, I was just about as closely involved in monitoring trade in ivory, legal and illegal, as one could be. Starting in the late 1990s, a regular part of my work was to conduct audits of government ivory stockpiles and to assess the domestic trade controls of those countries where sale of raw (i.e. unworked tusks and pieces of tusks) or carved ivory is permitted. These duties, like most other species-specific activities, also threw up bizarre experiences from time to time.

Every police officer comes across a huge variety of excuses during the course of his or her career. These seek to explain, for example, why a driver was speeding or why it was necessary to park on double yellow lines. The excuse can, occasionally, be provided by someone other than the person apparently at fault. A colleague of mine stopped a motorist one night who had been speeding. However, the driver in question had not been going fast enough to warrant being booked and a warning was going to be issued. As he was administering the warning to the male driver through the open car window, the female front seat passenger leaned over and said, 'You'll have to forgive my husband, officer, we've been to a party this evening and he's had a little too much to drink.' Too late, the awful impact of her words occurred to her. A breathalyser test showed she was right: her husband had indeed had too much to drink.

I thought I had heard my fair share of excuses during my police career, but I was to hear a real cracker while visiting a national parks department one day.

On two separate occasions during my time with CITES it was agreed by its Conference of the Parties that legal trade in raw ivory could take place, under specific circumstances and closely monitored by the Secretariat. The first of these was described as an 'experimental' trade and involved stocks held by Botswana, Namibia and Zimbabwe. The ivory could be sold to only one importing nation, Japan, and it subsequently imported almost 50 tonnes. The second occurrence, described as a 'one-off' sale, involved the original three exporting countries but South Africa was also authorized to sell its stocks. On this second occasion, China was added as an approved trading partner and was able to import ivory alongside Japan. Between them, China and Japan imported over 100 tonnes.

The first, 'experimental' sale took place in 1999, a decade after CITES had imposed a complete ban on the international trading of raw ivory, and was intended to test the procedures agreed. One of these was to audit the stocks of elephant ivory tusks gathered by governments in southern Africa as a result of natural mortality and problem animal control. The audit also needed to ensure that ivory taken into government control through confiscations, for example from poachers or during border control, was being stored separately from what was regarded as legal-origin ivory, and that ivory of illegal origin would not be entered into trade.

The second sale, in 2008, was described as 'one-off' to make plain that it did not indicate a reopening of general or regular trade in raw ivory. Personally, I think both phrases risked causing confusion and I doubt whether anyone who had not been involved in the discussions that led to the agreements for these two sales would have readily understood just what was intended or what had really been agreed. I certainly saw many comments in the media, before, during and after the sales, which showed that there was considerable misunderstanding. I believe that the pro-trade and anti-trade camps could also be fairly criticized for engaging at times in what struck me as a deliberate spread of misinformation. Lastly, we were really not helped by the fact that several countries which had participated in trade discussions, and which had formed part of the consensus on how to proceed, subsequently maintained that they had misunderstood what had been agreed or that the manner in which the agreement was recorded did not reflect what had been agreed.

Since the countries of southern Africa had accumulated many tonnes of ivory, and the potential profit from any sales would run into many millions of dollars, a great deal rested upon a satisfactory audit.

In the late 1990s, I found myself in the ivory store of a country in Africa that had probably better remain nameless. It had a huge quantity of ivory and I could immediately see that an audit would be a massive task, although all the ivory seemed, thank goodness, to have been logically stored and properly marked. It was also reassuring to learn that the government's records had all been computerized. A colleague and I set about checking tusks against the computer records and associated paperwork.

It was not long, however, before we realized that the number of tusks, stacked high on shelf above shelf in the warehouse, grossly exceeded the number of entries in the computer spread sheets. Many hundreds of tusks were unaccounted for. We asked the two officials who were responsible for the store to confirm that all records had been computerized and were assured that they had been. 'So why is there such a massive gap in the data?' we asked.

The two men looked very sheepish and embarrassed and went off into a corner where there was a hurried conversation. On returning, the senior of the two announced that they had worked out what had happened. 'A couple of weeks ago, a ditch was being dug in the road outside the store. We've just remembered that the workmen severed a cable. We now realize that some of the information in the computer must have drained out before the cable was repaired.'

We never did discover where the data had gone and the country was excluded from ivory sales until a fresh data input was conducted and a second audit carried out. But the straight-faced manner with which this excuse was delivered had us laughing fit to burst when we got back to our hotel that night.

The basic issue with which CITES has grappled over the years, in relation to several species and not just to elephants, is whether or not legal trade stimulates, or can act as a cover for, illegal trade. It undoubtedly can, but the 64,000 dollar question is whether the risks are so significant that no trade whatsoever should be allowed. And I use that cliché deliberately:

the American game show with the huge top prize was embroiled in scandal, subterfuge and the alleged manipulation of answers, just like the discussions on trade in ivory.

THERE'S NO PLEASING EVERYONE

While my colleagues and I spent many days examining government stocks of ivory in southern Africa, I also often took the lead in assessing the controls that China and Japan had put in place to regulate their domestic trade in ivory. Whether such controls were adequate or not was also highly contentious and work in this realm brought considerable criticism my way. Since I was very well aware of the diametrically-opposed views on this subject, I realized that, whatever conclusions I reached, I was bound to be attacked from one side or the other. But some of what was said was hard to ignore, especially when it became very personal or suggested that I had some prejudiced interest on whether trade took place or not. There was even an occasion when the head of CITES in a country opposed to trade alleged to the media that I had drafted the proposal for another country which intended to seek authorization to trade its stocks. This was utterly ridiculous, as Secretariat staff would never get involved in such a biased activity, and I never discovered just where he had got that idea from. Some critics ignored, or deliberately chose to ignore, that it was not for me to decide whether or not trade took place. My job, and that of the whole of the CITES Secretariat, was to carry out the instructions of the parties and simply assess whether or not the criteria they had set were fulfilled.

What made such assessments problematic, particularly in respect of domestic trade regulations and control mechanisms, was that we initially had to examine these in advance of any trade occurring and so were unable to test their practical implementation. This is why the first sales in 1999 were termed 'experimental' and, in that case, Japan's internal controls were later adjusted following an assessment after ivory had been imported and processed. In the case of China, the controls it had set in place went further than those of Japan and were, to my mind, perhaps unnecessarily far-reaching and impractical in relation to items such as 'chops', name seals used in place of signatures and called 'hankos' in Japan. I believed that they more than met what was required, though, as did both a highly-experienced customs officer (at that time a WCO Secretariat official) and a staff member of TRAFFIC, who probably has more experience of monitoring the ivory trade than anyone in the world. Both these officers accompanied me on my assessment mission but the subsequent decision that legal trade should be permitted to China attracted, and continues to attract, extensive criticism.

Did I ignore the fact that China was the destination for considerable illegal trade in ivory? No, of course I didn't and neither did anyone else. That was part of the reasoning when the CITES community tried to answer that 64,000 dollar question. China and Japan each have a centuries-long practice of using ivory. The two countries have craftsmen that engage in some of the most intricate and skilled art that I have ever seen, sometimes devoting a few years to just one carved piece. The results of their labours can be stunningly beautiful and, to my mind, match anything in the field of painting or sculpture. Personally, I believe the loss of such consummate skill would be very regrettable. What's more, that centuries-long culture and tradition are not going to go away any time soon. Indeed, if ivory trading is outlawed, I predict that it will simply go underground in the way that, for instance, the trade in tiger bone has. I believe it was right for the CITES community to decide - and it did so without having to vote on the issue - to try and meet the existing demand by supplying it with the legal-origin ivory stockpiled in Botswana, Namibia, South Africa and Zimbabwe. I would also like to dispel one myth that seems to be widespread. Those countries in southern Africa did not slaughter elephants in order to collect ivory. During my time with CITES there were no culls of elephants in those nations. The very purpose of my audits, and no one ever challenged their objectiveness or accuracy, was to ensure that any tusks that would be traded came from animals which had keeled over through natural mortality or had been shot during problem animal control. There was never any indication during our audits that elephants were being killed so as to extract their tusks for revenue-gathering purposes.

Countries such as Botswana, which had over 130,000 elephants, did not need to cull any of them. Elephants, like every other creature on earth, reach the end of their biological life some day and those southern Africa park departments have wildlife management programmes that include collecting the tusks and treating them as a natural resource.

With regard to internal ivory control systems, all I could do was assess them and then leave others to determine whether or not the trade should go ahead. However, some obviously did not see it that way and did not shy away from saying so. Here, for example, is an extract from a 2008 article posted online in which the author quotes someone who has devoted a large part of his life to studying the ivory trade:

> We do know that one particular person is letting us down, his name is John Sellars (sic) and nobody can understand what the hell he is doing. A one-man show, John is the only person who travels around the world for CITES examining their controls. Of course he always calls ahead giving everyone time to clean up their acts. For someone in law enforcement it's not exactly sensible is it? It's time for John to retire! My personal opinion is that he has become a liability for wildlife.

Since writing a book presents the opportunity to state one's own case, I will do exactly that. I will not dignify the individual by naming him. And I certainly will not apologize that it took slightly more than three years for me to comply with his demand that I retire. As it happens, the individual is someone for whom I had, and still have, considerable respect. He is a very committed and dedicated person who has made a not inconsiderable contribution to ivory trade research over several decades. However, it seems that he was so focussed on aspects of the trade that the reality of being an international civil servant working for a treaty secretariat, the nature of such work and its restrictions utterly eluded him.

'A one-man show' is, to a large extent, accurate, but definitely through no choice of mine. And not, for most of the time, the choice of the CITES Secretariat either. It simply reflected the lack of resources, human and financial, that existed for the 14 years of my service. But, as described above, the assessment conducted in China was not a one-man show and if the individual concerned was not aware of that then he really did lead a blinkered existence.

And yes, I always did call ahead, although it is not clear from the written quote whether I am being accused of doing so with the deliberate intent that everyone 'clean up their acts' or if that was some form of inadvertent by-product. So as to maintain the respect and courtesy for him that I have, a respect and courtesy which he did not show to me, I will not take his words to mean that I was acting in some premeditated and corrupt manner. And, to be even fairer to him, he was repeating a criticism and reproach that I regularly heard from others. So, in order to enlighten him and those like him who I am sure simply do not understand the niceties of being a United Nations official, allow me to explain.

While the title 'Chief of Enforcement' may sound very grand, I was not some form of international detective, swooping down to investigate wrongdoings wherever they occurred across the globe. I had no intercontinental authorization to conduct inspections anywhere I liked or to arrest offenders and bring them to justice. Neither do the officials who work for Interpol, the UN Office on Drugs and Crime or the World Customs Organization. Indeed, secretariat staff of these three bodies conduct considerably less *in situ* assessment and verification work than does the CITES Secretariat. In this field, the CITES Secretariat benefits from wording in the text of the Convention itself that provides it with significant oversight activities. The Conference of the Parties and the various committees of the Convention have also, over time, allocated very considerable responsibility to the Secretariat to assess implementation and to engage in enforcement-related activities. Although the Secretariat is often described as being the servant of the parties, I believe it can equally be regarded as the guardian of the Convention.

That aside, any UN official who wishes to conduct a mission to a country must first seek an invitation to do so. He or she will also need, with relatively few exceptions, to apply for an entry visa. This is despite the fact that official travel should be conducted not with one's own national passport but with the blue United Nations 'passport' known as a *laissez passer*. One cannot just drop in and wander wherever one chooses. My practice, when conducting assessment or verification missions, was to advise countries in advance of what I wished to achieve, the type of places I wanted to visit and inspect and the various agencies with which I wished to meet. I invariably asked that they prepare a draft programme which I could comment upon before it was agreed between us. However, I almost always also indicated in advance that I wished time set aside in the programme where I could, on a last-minute basis, decide locations where spot check visits or inspections could be conducted. Was this ideal? No, but it was the best that could be achieved given the restrictions with which any international inter-governmental organization must comply.

Let me put the boot on a different foot for a moment. How many NGO staff members and individual trade experts have entered foreign countries to conduct market surveys over the years? Dozens and dozens, I imagine. How many entered those countries on tourist visas? The majority, I imagine. If they had applied for any other form of visa and had explained the true purpose of their visit, how many of those applications would have been successful? I leave readers to speculate on that for themselves. I am not saying that what might be regarded, in some quarters, as subterfuge on those researchers' part was not justified. I am just saying, 'Let he who is without sin cast the first stone.'

Was I conscious that governments might be tempted or inclined only to take me to see what was favourable or known to be compliant? Yes, of course I was. If critics honestly believed that, after 24 years in the Scottish police service, together with over a decade working at international level, I could not work out the negative aspects of providing prior warning of one's arrival, then they had gone beyond naivety and were being ludicrous. Did the same critics seriously imagine that I was not equally frustrated when I saw, time after time, unprofessional and inadequate responses to wildlife crime? Of course I was. One of the most frustrating things about my role was that I had to sit in Geneva and see interceptions, seizures and detections inadequately exploited or poorly followed up. Maybe I was deluding myself but I regularly wished that I could get on a plane, head for the country in question, take control of the investigation and lock up those responsible, because I thought I could probably do the job better. That was not what I was employed to do, though. It would not have been appropriate and, being a one-man show, I could not drop everything and take off whenever I liked. When you had been a detective as long as I had, you learned at an early stage to live with the frustrations such as 'knowing' who committed a crime but being unable to prove it. And I had to adopt a similar tolerance or forbearance when working with CITES and finding myself restricted to offering advice or guidance.

However, I remained convinced that being able to gets one's feet on the ground in the immediate aftermath of a significant seizure or other wildlife crime might be an excellent way of supporting countries, with the proviso, of course, that they remained in charge. I mentioned this to my successor, especially as I was by then aware that the enforcement staffing in Geneva was to be increased. I was delighted, therefore, to see that parties to CITES decided when they met in March 2013 to create Wildlife Incident Support Teams, which will offer exactly the support and assistance that may sometimes be needed. I do not claim any credit whatsoever for the concept - just a little credit for the teams' title - and it is one that has been employed very successfully in a variety of law enforcement scenarios. Interpol, for example, has used this model fruitfully for many years to aid its member countries in times of major incidents or natural disasters.

To answer their charge that the 'call ahead' approach described above made my mission results meaningless or questionable, I recommend that detractors speak with the national government officials who organized the programmes and who accompanied me during those visits. I am confident that they would find few who, at one time or another, were not caused some embarrassment or concern when I came across shortcomings in implementation or enforcement or discovered fauna and flora on sale illicitly. I recall one day in Yokohama, for instance, where shop after shop, chosen by me at random, was displaying ivory products without being a registered retailer. The group of four Japanese government officials who were accompanying me and a colleague became, as the day wore on, more and more depressed but equally more and more puzzled. My colleague, who had recently joined the CITES Secretariat, was similarly baffled, I think. Eventually, to their relief, the day came to a close and we headed back to our hotel in Tokyo. One of the Japanese environment ministry representatives leaned across to my colleague as we sat in the train and said, 'We've decided that Sellar-san can smell ivory.' While I like to think that I have a nose for sniffing out criminals, that might have been exaggerating my olfactory powers.

I prided myself, wherever possible, on not allowing myself to become too focussed on one particular issue and also on always trying to think like a cop. One of my many visits to China had illegal trade in Asian big cats as its theme. I criss-crossed the country visiting eight cities, one of which was Xi'an in Shaanxi Province. In recent times, this city has become

Above: *Although wildlife is often thought of as meaning animals, it includes flora too. In this case, it is Agarwood chips on sale in Riyadh. This type of timber has a scent highly-prized for incense and some of the world's most expensive perfumes and colognes.*

Below: *A huge range of animal body parts are used in traditional Asian medicine or as talismans and charms. A trader had set up his stall on the roadside in Mandalay, Myanmar, where his wares are being inspected by a CITES technical mission team.*

Right: *Legal wildlife markets, like this for birds in Jakarta, Indonesia, are often the location for illegal sales too. Traders here offered to sell the author gibbons, monkeys and orang-utans.*

Below: *This monkey spent its days tethered near a stall in the Jakarta bird market. The stallholder hoped it would attract clients keen to purchase rarer primates.*

Opposite page, top: *This orang-utan, smuggled into Cambodia, is destined to spend its life in what is called a zoo, but which is actually just an entertainment park attached to a casino resort complex. Several of these young great apes have died as a result of being over-shocked by trainers using electric cattle prods.*

Opposite page, bottom: *These are just a few of the almost 1,000 orang-utans in rescue centres in Indonesia in 2006. Several had been kept as pets by corrupt government, military or police officials. Deforestation, often through illegal logging, means there is not enough jungle left for these youngsters to ever be returned to the wild.*

ការប្រើឧបករណ៍ត្រើិងផ្ទុះ និង ឧបករណ៍អគ្គីសនីជាអំពើខុសច្បាប់ អំពើទាំងនេះបណ្ដាលអោយគ្រោះថ្នាក់ដល់ជីវៈចំរុះរបស់យើង

ប្រសិនបើលោកអ្នកជួបប្រទះនេះសូមជួយផ្ដល់ពត៌មាន ដល់លោកហេង សុណ្ណារ៉ា លេខទូរស័ព្ទ (០១២ ៥២៤ ៥៥៥) (០៩៣ ២១៧ ២០៤) រឺ ឈ្មោក លីន ថាត (មន្ត្រីជលផលស្រុកព្រៃអំបិល)

Top of page: *A billboard in Southeast Asia, warning fishermen not to use electricity or explosives.*

Above: *The author with the Forest Security Bureau Chief whilst visiting patrols in the Kekexili National Park, situated on the 'Roof of the World' at over 5,000m.*

Left: *A huge mound of antelope skins seized by Forest Security Bureau anti-poaching patrols on the Tibetan Plateau, who face the harshest environment of any wildlife law enforcement officials.*

Top of page: *A floating house in the Amazon region of Brazil, home to the type of individual whose poverty may be exploited by criminals seeking to acquire rare parrots, plants or reptiles.*

Above: *The daily commute facing rural residents in parts of Asia. This river crossing in Cambodia was one of several that the author had to cross in 2007 order to reach the border with Thailand, the scene of significant wildlife smuggling.*

Left: *Criminals use a huge variety of means to conceal the contraband they smuggle across borders. Here, the screen is displaying images of car wheels that are being X-rayed by Customs officers at the border between two Middle Eastern countries.*

Top of page: *In order to screen cargo, border control officials need much larger X-ray equipment. This van houses mobile X-ray machines used by Customs in Macau.*

Right: *Forensic science can be of considerable support to wildlife law enforcers but it is all too seldom used. Here, a veterinary pathologist examines an animal carcass.*

Above: *This vehicle was stopped at a check-point by Nepalese Forest officials as it was being used to smuggle timber from India to China. James Bond-style, it had been fitted with rotating numbers plates. This shows one of the plates, faked to look like a diplomatic registration.*

Above: *Some workplaces for wildlife law enforcement officials can be very basic. This raised wooden hut is the base for Indonesian Forest Department staff to check traffic coming downriver in the jungles of Kalimantan.*

Left: *Sometimes the more dangerous an animal, the more attractive it becomes for some people as a pet. This cobra's bite is much worse than its bark.*

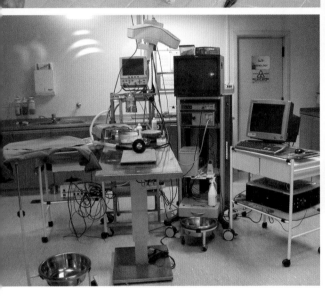

Top left: *In several parts of the world, snakes and other reptiles are farmed so that they can be slaughtered in adulthood and their skins used for leather products. These young snakes are being force-fed in a Vietnamese farm.*

Bottom left: *In the Middle East, falconry has existed for centuries and high prices are paid for birds smuggled from North America, Europe and Central Asia. This operating theatre in a falcon hospital in the United Arab Emirates shows how seriously falconers treat their birds.*

Right: *Animal skins are often found for sale to tourists as souvenirs. These snake and leopard skins were on open display in an arts and crafts market in Abuja, capital city of Nigeria, even though such trade is illegal.*

Above: *In the days of the USSR, this cold store in a caviar processing factory would have been absolutely full. In the early 2000s, the bare floor space reflected the rapid decline in sturgeon numbers.*

Left: *Wildlife traders seldom like their pictures taken. This shopkeeper in Nigeria, showing off an ivory carving, was photographed covertly.*

Below: *KGB officers agreed with the author that storing millions of roubles worth of caviar in an old railway carriage like this indicated security being provided by the Mafia.*

Top of page: *A high-powered vessel of the Russian Federal Border Guard returns at sunset to its berth in Astrakhan. It was the crew of one of these boats who rescued the author from a diet of dried fish and vodka.*

Above: *Although initially sceptical, the author had to believe it when he saw for himself sturgeons being farmed in a facility in the Saudi Arabian desert.*

Right: *The author engaged in auditing ivory stockpiles in southern Africa. These tusks were collected through natural mortality and problem animal control. They were destined for sale to China or Japan.*

Left: *This carver in a Guangzhou factory in southern China is producing one of the famous 'balls', which contain concentric circles of ivory, that require astonishing skill, learned over years studying under a carving master, to produce.*

Middle: *This ivory carver is producing figures from Chinese history, which have made such pieces so highly-desired in recent years as China's economy has boomed.*

Below: *This massive ivory carving, illustrating Chinese tales and legends will have taken master craftsmen and women several years to construct. Worth the equivalent of 2 million US dollars, it may end up adorning the foyer of a major company in a city like Beijing or Shanghai.*

Above: *This stall in Panjiayuan Market, Beijing, is openly selling high-quality ivory items. Unlicensed sales like this are totally illegal and yet the stallholder does not appear at all concerned.*

Left: *Another stall in Panjiayuan Market, which appears to be well-stocked with ivory products, but none of them are genuine. Bone, horn and Mammoth tusk items are often claimed to be elephant ivory and it may be difficult for untrained enforcement officers to tell the difference; a reason why some officials are reluctant to get involved.*

Opposite page, top: *The Paro Taktsang Monastery in Bhutan. Situated on a cliff at over 3,000m, it is also known as the Tiger's Nest or Lair. Legend has it that a monk flew on the back of a tigress to this spot from neighbouring Tibet.*

Opposite page, bottom: *The species that features most prominently in religions, art, literature and legend, the tiger is also, today, one of those closest to extinction. Almost every part of its body is sought-after for medicinal or other use.*

Above: *This young elephant, photographed in Zimbabwe in 2011, may not be alive today. Whole families of elephants have been slaughtered there during 2013, some of them when they drank at water holes poisoned with cyanide.*

Right: *The missing piece in the jigsaw explaining an increase in illegal big cat skin trade. A traditional 'Chuba' jacket on sale in Lhasa, Tibet, decorated with leopard skin panels.*

Above: *Prime Minister (as he was then) Putin at the unprecedented Heads of State tiger conservation forum in St Petersburg. But will it be enough to save the species?*

Below: *The traditional highest-quality daggers worn by males in Yemen would previously have had a handle carved from rhino horn. Here, a carver in the old souk of Sana'a prepares to fit the blade into a new dagger.*

Moments after he clicked the shutter, this rhino charged at the author.
Fortunately, it was a 'bluff' and he lived to tell the tale (and write this book).

an absolute tourist magnet because it is from here that visitors travel to see the renowned terracotta warriors that were uncovered near the Emperor Qin Shi Huang's mausoleum. Driving into the city from the airport, I asked one of the local CITES enforcement officials whether there was any significant sale of ivory in the town. He looked confused by the question and told me that there was no noteworthy history of ivory carving or trading in that part of China. An official from Beijing, who was accompanying me throughout the trip and with whom I had often worked in the past, was obviously mystified by my question too and asked what had prompted it. I explained that Xi'an had become a major visitor centre, attracting many thousands of foreign visitors. It struck me that some of them, especially those from certain Asian nations, would be potential purchasers of ivory products and so sellers would also be attracted to the area. It had also occurred to me, although I did not voice this view at the time, that since this part of the country had been home to China's emperors and that they, and their courtesans, had been avid collectors of some of the best ivory carvings, it seemed logical that ivory would be found here.

As it happened, we subsequently took time to visit outlets selling high-quality souvenirs and did indeed find ivory carvings on sale, some of them of very high quality. The local officials took the appropriate action. The mission was a tremendous learning experience for me and I like to think that, in some small part, I was able to return the favour to my hosts.

MAKING SENSE OF ILLEGAL TRADE IN IVORY

Ivory was constantly on my radar and, alongside work on the legal trade, I undertook visits to places where unregulated trade was taking place, to assess whether national agencies were doing enough to eradicate it.

As a consequence, I have visited licensed retailers and manufacturers in cities such as Shanghai in China and Kyoto in Japan but have also inspected markets and stalls in far-flung locations like Lhasa in Tibet and Kano in northern Nigeria. I have seen highly sophisticated computerized systems that should allow authorities to monitor the flow of ivory from its import to wholesalers and manufacturers, and its processing into carved objects that will end up in the display cabinets of high-class shopping malls and specialized outlets. I have also witnessed whole elephant tusks and crudely- fashioned items on open display in tourist markets in several countries in Africa where trade in ivory is, in theory, totally prohibited. One of the most blatant examples I ever saw was about a hundred metres from the police headquarters of a nation's capital, yet nothing was being done about it.

Given that the highest quality ivory carvings can sell for the equivalent of a few million US dollars, it may appear obvious why people might choose to engage in elephant poaching, the smuggling of tusks and their eventual delivery to customers on the other side of the globe. Or, of course, recruit and pay others to do that. However, I do not believe it is that simple.

During my time as a police detective, I investigated almost every crime on the statute books. I have a qualification in criminology. I like to think I understand criminals, how they operate and what motivates them. But from the day I focused on international wildlife crime, until the day I said goodbye to my UN colleagues in Geneva, I have never been able to understand some of what is happening in relation to ivory.

If a criminal breaks into your house tonight and steals your DVD, he will do his utmost to get rid of it quickly, maybe in a sale to some receiver of stolen goods. If a mugger relieves you of your iPhone, he will soon be in some bar trying to sell it to one of his friends or to some guy who wants a cheap deal. The burglar and the robber both want - and these days often need, because of drug addiction - a fast return on their investment. And they get it, because there are plenty of people out there who want a DVD or iPhone but who cannot afford to buy one on the high street.

The more sophisticated and organized criminals, those who are perhaps trafficking in narcotics, firearms or even humans, also want the same quick return. They get it, because they too are connected to a ready marketplace. It is probably located further from those of the burglar and robber; the Colombian drug cartels need, of course, to ship their product to other continents, while the human trafficker has to transport women intended for prostitution across many borders. They may have to process the product en route, turning opium into heroin, for example. They may have to acquire false visas and work permits or pay off corrupt border officials. But they have the same thing in common: once the goods hit the streets, there is a large and reliable consumer base waiting.

In financial terms, too, most criminals operate on a level playing field. To a significant extent, albeit with occasional fluctuations, they know what their return is going to be. Most cops or customs officers can tell you the street price of a deal of crack cocaine or a .45 semi-automatic pistol. Knowing, or estimating with relative accuracy, what the return will be, the narcotic, firearm or human trafficker engages in the activity with a fair degree of confidence. There is always a certain gamble involved: the smuggler may be caught and the cocaine confiscated. But it is not a lottery. Organized crime groups and networks know their trade. The gamble they take is that of the professional casino high-roller who knows how to count the cards in blackjack, rather than the gamble of putting a coin into a slot machine.

The same level of confidence is not there if one deals in illegal ivory, though. To begin with, tusks come in a large range of sizes and quality. Elephants living in forests have harder tusks than their savannah counterparts, which makes them more attractive and more suitable for high-quality carvings. Old bull elephants have long tusks that, understandably, lend themselves to large intricate carvings. Asian elephant ivory is more highly prized than African. I have heard some people liken this to narcotic trafficking, in which the purity of cocaine or heroin will determine its price. Personally, I think they are comparing apples and oranges. The drug dealer determines the grade of his product, but the ivory trader has little control over what the poacher brings back from a hunt.

It is at the consumption end of the chain where the major differences begin to show. A kilo of cocaine is a kilo of cocaine. However, a kilogramme of ivory can produce several of the name seals ('chops' or 'hankos') used in China and Japan in place of written signatures. I have visited many retail outlets for name seals in both of those countries. In Japan, they are often sold in stationery shops alongside hankos made of plastic, bone, resin and the like, as well as pens and other writing materials. The managers of such shops have told me that they will sell maybe one or two ivory hankos per month. Hardly a booming trade, then, nor a significant one financially, either, given that most hankos will sell for under a hundred dollars.

I remember, during one of my on spec. visits, selecting a shop at random from the list of registered Japanese retailers. This led us into a rural area of the country and to a small town where a stationery firm was based. The impressive shop and showroom seemed out of place in what might better have been described as a village. However, the firm was a major stationery supplier and many high-class writing materials and other office products were on display. One small cabinet had drawers containing hankos. Only two of the drawers had hankos made of ivory. The manager commented that the days when sales of ivory hankos had been profitable were long gone. I asked whether he had ever been approached and offered ivory whose origin might have been suspicious. The shop owner seemed reluctant to answer and glanced nervously at the government officials accompanying me. One of them gestured, encouraging him to respond. The manager described how, about two years previously, someone had called at the shop and asked whether he was interested in purchasing raw ivory. The manager said he had declined, not just because he was immediately suspicious but also because he was not a manufacturer and had no means of processing raw ivory. He added that he had not actually been shown any ivory; the caller had simply wanted to negotiate. I wondered what had made him suspicious and the interpreter asked on my behalf. The shopkeeper then provided me with an accurate description of his visitor. What had rung the alarm bells most loudly for him was the fact that the prospective seller had been an Indian. I could not help smiling when it suddenly struck me that the full description of the man was that of an NGO activist that I had known for years and who regularly attended CITES meetings. The manager had not encountered a criminal but a researcher, engaged in a not terribly subtle survey.

A kilogramme of ivory does not, however, have to be used for hankos. It could equally well be carved into a beautiful piece worth several thousands of dollars. I once saw a massive carving in the showroom of an ivory factory in Guangzhou that cost the equivalent of two million dollars. Such products will clearly have a smaller consumer base than the hanko or chop. If readers wonder (as I did) just who might purchase such an object, I was told that they are popular among some of China's most successful private enterprises. They apparently tend to display them either in the lobby of their corporate headquarters or in the office of their CEO, to demonstrate how financially successful the company has been and how highly the company and its management regard China's history and culture. The most intricate carvings, and consequently the most expensive, commonly depict scenes and figures from Chinese antiquity.

Japan used to be the most significant destination for illegal trade in ivory. This was demonstrated by the number of contraband shipments that were intercepted en route there. However, not long after my arrival in Geneva, but of course not related to it, I began to see that more and more seizures of ivory intercepted while heading from Africa to Asia appeared to have China as the final destination. It was not until the very late 1990s, however, that this was generally acknowledged, especially through data collected for the Elephant Trade Information System (ETIS). ETIS has developed from a simple database of ivory seizures taking place around the world into a sophisticated analytical system which helps the CITES community understand the nature of illegal trade, its geographical characteristics, enforcement impacts (or enforcement shortcomings) and some of the factors driving this criminality. I went through a period, during my first couple of years with CITES, when I would voice the view that Japan was no longer the major endpoint. I would see people look at me as if I were mad. I could read in their faces that they thought the new boy was taking time to settle in and that he would soon wake up to reality. However, as I describe elsewhere, I was in the fortunate position of being notified of major seizures as they occurred and had the 'helicopter view' that simply was not available to others. I was also sometimes provided with copies of documents relating to the shipments, which offered a greater insight into places of origin and intended destinations. Even better, I sometimes received feedback from subsequent investigations and the interview of suspects, some of which I instigated. I was, though, unable to share these details with anyone outside the law enforcement community, which sometimes led to misunderstandings or misconceptions. I am thinking, for example, of one very significant shipment of ivory that was discovered in a sea-going cargo container in a port in southeast Asia. To this day, the contraband is generally regarded as having been destined for Japan. I am convinced that it was not but I cannot publicly say why. Although illegal trade still occurs in Japan, its place in the league table has been overtaken, and overtaken big time, by China.

As China's economy has grown, many of its citizens have acquired disposable incomes unimagined even a decade ago. This had led to an interest in possessing examples of cultural or traditional artefacts and artworks and, as a result, prices have sky-rocketed. And it is not just ivory; silk ware, lacquer, porcelain and jade *objets d'art* and antiques have all markedly increased in value, both in China and at auction houses around the world. (The same has happened for rhinoceros horn objects.) Shortly before I retired, I had a fascinating appointment with the head of the legal unit of the world-renowned Sotheby's auction house in New York. An ex-federal prosecutor, this lady and her staff were able to offer me an important and very valuable awareness of the world of arts and antiques and where endangered species items may fit within it. Since fraud and counterfeiting are not at all unknown in the realm of antique buying and selling, and is something that firms such as Sotheby's work very hard to eliminate, I believe we were able to share expertise, gain an understanding of each other's problems and establish good relations.

Seizure data shows us that Thailand is now, as I write this in 2013, apparently second to China as a destination for smuggled ivory. Thailand has not been undergoing anything like the same economic boom as China. True, it has a history of ivory carving and legal domestic markets but they bear little comparison to those of China or Japan. So, is Thailand truly an illicit ivory destination or is it, more significantly, a transit country and organized crime base? From being the major destination for many years, Japan hardly features at all these days in seizure data. Is this another indication that what may seem to be the final demand and consumption location may not necessarily be determining what is happening and that we have yet to understand completely the nature of the demand?

Even where in-plain-sight demand exists, sale of ivory remains a fairly specialized marketplace. Bangkok, Beijing, Guangzhou, Hong Kong, Kyoto, Shanghai and Tokyo are not full of men sidling up to you in dark alleys going, 'Hey, mister, wanna buy a cheap chop?'

And even if they were, how many buyers would they attract? We would all probably like to pay fifty per cent less for our mobile phone than the cheapest deal in the mall but how many of us would actually buy one if we suspected it was stolen? Several surveys in China have shown that, when questioned by researchers in the street or by phone, its citizens are apparently interested in purchasing ivory and would want to pay as little as possible. Similar surveys regularly show a continuing interest in acquiring other unlawful animal products, such as tiger bone wine. But, again, how many would really be willing to cross the line between a lawful and a black market purchase? The market for wildlife is not like that of drugs; there simply is not the same number of potential customers.

It is not at all difficult, however, to find illegal-origin ivory in Asia or Africa. You can find it in Europe and North America, too. A lot of it seems to be small carvings, pieces of jewellery, bracelets and charms, what might best be described as trinkets. And I have yet to see queues of people at any of these outlets. It is certainly possible to find illicit high-quality carvings or whole tusks of raw, unworked elephant ivory. Indeed, I am sure many people will have seen television documentaries illustrating this very effectively, using hidden camera footage. The film makers captured those scenes with hidden cameras and, posing as buyers with big budgets, by deliberately seeking out black market operators. I have done the very same myself in relation to a range of wildlife products. Such footage illustrates the often highly clandestine nature of the trade and reinforces the existence of a limited consumer base for the truly undercover product. It further demonstrates that, unlike the drug dealer, the unscrupulous ivory trader must sometimes wait for a significant length of time before attracting or identifying a buyer.

Although, as far as I am aware, China has yet to uncover significant criminality amongst its licensed manufacturers and retailers, experience in Japan indicates that some of these people will succumb to temptation. There, a few major figures in Japan's ivory industry have in the past been caught purchasing raw ivory, which they presumably intended to launder through their lawful manufacturing and retailing. It has been suggested to me that they were motivated by frustration at the decreasing stocks of raw ivory held by companies and their belief that access to fresh, legal stocks was unlikely, especially given the never-ending debates within CITES. This has certainly been a constant concern raised by representatives of the ivory industry on the many occasions when I have visited their facilities. But circumventing internal ivory trade controls is, or definitely ought to be, high risk. Many of the trading companies, in both China and Japan, have been in existence for decades. In China, many were, and to a degree still are, state-owned ventures. They employ highly-skilled craftsmen and women who only build up their talents and abilities over years of practice under the direction of master craftsmen, several of whom one finds working well into old age. If you are a craftsman or the head of an ivory business, finding alternative employment will not be at all easy if your trading licence is revoked. They conduct their business openly and ought to know very well that, any day of the week, an enforcement officer can stroll in the door and inspect their premises. They operate in modern societies, policed by professional agencies which, if they are doing their duty, should be capable of enforcing internal trade controls.

Historically, many traders from China and Japan travelled to Africa and to countries in Asia with elephant populations and were used to dealing direct with ivory dealers there, particularly in those African nations with their own ivory carving and trading industries. Some of those nations, such as the Sudan, had elephant populations within their territory whilst others, such as Egypt and some Gulf States, did not. Those two countries were major locations for ivory trading, partly historically but primarily because of their geographical locations and their ports, long important as exit points from the African continent. I am referring here to the days pre-CITES and up to the late 1980s. These traders knew each other well and some of their fathers and grandfathers had traded together. The relationship between the traders on these two continents altered dramatically, however, after CITES imposed a trade ban in 1989. When the experimental and one-off sales subsequently took place, the Chinese and Japanese were not dealing with their old counterparts any more but, instead, travelling to auctions organized by governments and at which they had to deal with national parks officials. The dynamics of the ivory trade had altered completely.

Between 1989 and 1999, did the long-established ivory traders organize the poaching of elephants? Were they organizing it between 1999 and 2008, when the flow of legal ivory was haphazard and unreliable? Have they been organizing it since the last sales in 2008? The motivation to do so must certainly have been there; without fresh raw ivory they would be out of business. On the other hand, some of them had very considerable stocks within their premises in cities such as Guangzhou and Kyoto. I know because I have inspected them. We do know that members of a Taiwanese family were operating in Douala in Cameroon during the 2000s and were organizing the smuggling of very large quantities of ivory from West and Central Africa. There is a suggestion that the family may have been involved in ivory trade for a long time but I am not aware of specific links between them and the legitimate traders of China and Japan.

Those time-served Chinese and Japanese traders undoubtedly knew their stuff and could, for instance, immediately tell the quality of an individual tusk and quickly determine how best it might be used, be it for intricate carving or for chops and hankos. But did they know the difference between an AK-47 and M-16 assault rifle or how to recruit those who did and who were willing to use them to kill elephants? I doubt it. It is human nature to welcome a bargain and I am sure those in the ivory industry are no different from anyone else in that sense. But buying something behind closed doors, and moving into the organization of large-scale poaching and the subsequent sophisticated smuggling of the proceeds across many international borders, are two very different things. Additionally, we are considering a time period during which almost all ivory trading and processing was, in China, the business of state-owned companies. What was the likelihood of their managers moving, in a self-initiated manner, into criminal enterprise? Fairly remote, I would suggest, unless we think that there was some Communist government plot behind what began to take place, and I am not a great believer in elaborate conspiracy theories.

I personally think that this period, especially from the early- to mid-2000s, was when organized crime moved into this arena and that its presence and impact could be seen more and more as time passed. The figures seem to back this up. To quote from a CITES press release of March 2013:

> At sites monitored through the Monitoring Illegal Killing of Elephants (MIKE) programme alone, which hold approximately 40 per cent of the total elephant population in Africa, an estimated 17,000 elephants were illegally killed in 2011.

Initial data from 2012 shows that the situation did not improve. However, overall figures may be much higher.

Large-scale seizures of ivory (consignments of over 800 kg) destined for Asia have more than doubled since 2009 and reached an all-time high in 2011.

Globally, illegal ivory trade activity has more than doubled since 2007, and is now over three times larger than it was in 1998.

The sheer scale of the poaching and smuggling is mind-boggling. And the quantities of ivory being shipped from Africa to Asia are astonishing. In 2011 alone, 17 separate large-scale interceptions resulted in the seizure of more than 26 tonnes. The UN Office on Drugs and Crime calculates that the interception rate of smuggled goods may be anywhere between 17 and 40 per cent. Even if we were to accept 40 per cent as the wildlife law enforcement community's success level, it still means that a horrifying amount of contraband is getting past the various risk assessment, targeting and profiling methods that are being deployed.

The organized and sophisticated nature of what is occurring surely cannot be being directed by those who manufacture and retail the final product but, rather, more likely demonstrates the involvement of similarly organized and sophisticated crime groups and networks. After all, organized crime groups working in, for instance, narcotics trafficking, have again and again shown themselves able to co-ordinate and manage every link along the chain, from the harvest of opium in a far corner of the world to its initial processing, its concealed shipment over many international borders and finally its conversion into street-level drugs and their delivery to consumers. They also clearly have the funds to pay off law enforcement officials, politicians and the judiciary, wherever and whenever they need to, and have their own enforcers to maintain discipline and ensure productivity, payments and silence within those links. Everyone seems to agree on this. That said, I do not imagine, should all the links one day be uncovered, that we will find some Corleone-like family firm behind it all. I do not believe that we have yet unearthed the explanation for what prompted, and presumably continues to prompt, organized crime to take over what was previously a steady trickle of poached ivory to a probably limited number of illicit dealers, most of them based in the southeast and far east of Asia, and turn it into what threatens to become a torrent, one that may carry elephants over the cliff and down into extinction.

So what is motivating those behind the illegal trade? Why are they apparently willing to engage in criminality, the dynamics of which differ so markedly from other forms of trafficking? The quick return does not seem to exist. I have asked myself these questions for nearly a decade and a half. I have also put them to the media and to the CITES and law enforcement communities but, so far, no one seems inclined to seek out answers. Regrettably, my previous workload did not allow me to uncover an explanation for myself and it remains a mystery. But we certainly need to know who it is and why there are doing it.

Media reports in 2012 recorded hundreds of elephants killed in just a few weeks in Cameroon. Within a week of the CITES meeting in March 2013, 89 elephants were apparently killed in just one overnight poaching operation in Chad. Many other countries are reporting increased rates of poaching. I talk elsewhere of the suggested involvement of heavily-armed and terrorist-like militias. There are several examples, in South and Central

America, for instance, of organized crime networks establishing and exploiting links with rebel and guerrilla groups. It is speculation on my part but what is to prevent the very same thing happening in Africa? The routings and concealment methods for smuggled ivory grow increasingly sophisticated and, in themselves, require a not insignificant expenditure on the part of those managing shipments. And it is important not to overlook the very significant losses being suffered by organized crime during some of those contraband movements. We are not speaking of the odd kilo or two here and there, but of more than 26 tonnes intercepted in just one year. Regardless of how many clandestine transport arrangements are successful, 26 tonnes is a massive loss to record on any balance sheet. The smuggling and the poaching goes on, though, so presumably the profits to be made are massive too, to the extent that crime groups are prepared to write off regular seizure shortfalls.

Whilst the extinction of elephants throughout continental Africa remains extremely unlikely, several geographical populations have vanished and it seems highly likely that others will follow. The future for forest elephants, in particular, seems bleak. I have seen researchers speculate that some criminal groups, engaged in the poaching of and illegal trade in tigers, look forward to the total extinction of these big cats, which would push prices through the roof and allow them really to reap the rewards of their criminality. I find it hard to believe that such an investment plan is behind what is happening currently with elephants but the harsh reality is that we simply do not know.

In the meantime it is simply not enough to call for a ban on trade in ivory. Many conservationists hark back to the 1989 cessation of ivory trade adopted by CITES and claim that it saved elephants. They will tell you that recent experimental and one-off sales, authorized by the Convention, have prompted the resurgence in poaching and smuggling. I am far from convinced, primarily because that is too simplistic an approach. While the 1989 ban did seem to reduce criminality, it certainly did not wipe it out, as a steady trickle flowed on. What's more, analyses conducted using MIKE and ETIS data have yet to show any specific or demonstrable link between decisions made by the CITES community and the major upsurge of poaching and smuggling in the past few years.

Until we truly understand why organized crime has been attracted to the ivory trade - and it cannot now be disputed that it has - we will not be able to make any dispassionate assessment of what should be done, not only in relation to whether to authorize trade or not, but to determine effective enforcement responses. And the latter will be needed, perhaps desperately, whether legal trade occurs or not; history has shown us that only too well.

Much more needs to be done to eradicate the open display of and trade in ivory in parts of Africa. To see shops and stalls full of glistening ivory products, as I have done in cities such as Conakry and Kinshasa, is to see not only a glaring example of inadequate law enforcement but also a message to every person who walks past: it is OK to harvest elephants and that they remain in good numbers. Surely they must be doing well, if ivory is so widely available? What else can we expect passers-by to think? Perhaps, though, we need to educate, or re-educate, law enforcement officials too.

I recall a senior West African customs officer telling me, in 2011, that his staff simply did not consider the sight of animal or plant products as a matter of concern to them. 'Remember, Mr Sellar,' he said, 'Many of these men and women have grown up in small towns and villages where they walked through forest areas every day on their way to school. They have heard birds singing and primates calling. They've spotted elephants, cat species, antelopes or snakes from time to time all their lives. They don't think of these as being endangered.'

I had a similar experience in Indonesia in the late 2000s. While orang-utans were listed in the most highly-protected category of the country's wildlife legislation, they did not appear to be prized as such by the ordinary person. Even officials whose job it was to protect these animals, and bring to justice anyone who sought to kill or capture them, did not strike me as truly appreciative of just how endangered they were as a species. Time after time, I heard stories of forest officials or police officers who were apparently satisfied with confiscating orang-utans which were being kept as pets, but who seemed to have little inclination to instigate prosecutions. At the time of my visit, some 1,000 orang-utans were being kept in rescue or rehabilitation centres in the country. The majority of them will never be suitable for release into the wild, which is probably just as well, since appropriate release areas are diminishing constantly. Talking to someone who has been particularly successful in great ape rehabilitation, I expressed my bemusement over this disparity between the species' legal status and what one saw on the ground. 'It's simple, John,' he said. 'You look at an orang-utan and you see an endangered species. Someone who lives in rural Indonesia looks at an orang-utan and thinks it's just another fucking monkey.'

That may be a dreadfully unfair and brutal assessment of some Indonesians' awareness of conservation concerns but I believe that there is enough truth in it to make us stop and think. We need to think about where we should carry out most public education or awareness-raising work, and how we may need to structure capacity building in some enforcement agencies. And, as I always thought, what works in relation to one animal or plant is likely to have beneficial implications for all fauna and flora.

We know that not all the illegal ivory leaving Africa is being intercepted. So where is the rest going, the shipments that sneak under customs' radar, with its 17-40 per cent efficiency, and reach Asia? I have already questioned whether there is a sufficiently large consumer base to justify the smuggling and there seems little evidence of huge quantities flooding black markets. So what is happening to it? It's yet another mystery.

Personally, I could not care less whether ivory trade is authorized or not. But it frustrates the hell out of me that we continue to drift along without tackling the underlying problems in a meaningful way and without understanding what is driving the never-ending and seemingly ever-increasing killing of elephants and trade in their tusks.

Either someone, somewhere must be making very significant profits, in a manner which defies most other forms of trafficking, or there are organized crime groups out there with so much cash that they believe laundering it through trade in ivory will, in the long term, more than compensate for the lack of the usual immediate quick buck. Another explanation may be that organized crime is stockpiling raw ivory as an investment, which could account for the fact that those undetected smuggled shipments have not yet appeared in the markets.

IMPROVING OUR RESPONSE

The one thing that the law enforcement community absolutely must do - I see it as the number one priority - is to stop wasting the opportunities with which it is presented. Time after time I sat in my office in Switzerland and read reports of contraband cargo shipments being intercepted at air- or sea ports or couriers being detained. And time after time I saw no rapid exchange of information, either back down the chain along which the ivory had moved or forward to its destination, which would have enabled speedy follow-up investigations to identify those responsible or bring them to justice.

Doubly frustrating was the fact that I regularly read of these incidents not in emails coming to my in-box or in faxes arriving in Geneva, but in media reports. So too did my counterparts in Interpol and the World Customs Organization. As a result, we did not have access to detailed information relating to the circumstances of incidents, which we could have distributed via our communication channels. We would each offer our assistance, often accepted, but we often learned of the incident hours, sometimes days, after it had happened. By then, the media had splashed the news around the world. Worse still, it was not uncommon for some agencies to allow reporters and TV channels to film the ivory, the containers and the concealment methods. I have sat and looked at online images of crates on which the details of the consignee and consigner could be read without difficulty. Details of shipping agents and airlines would be released during some of these press conferences. I recall one seizure where, two days later, journalists reported on information they had obtained after interviewing cargo managers at a major Middle East airline hub through which the ivory had transited. Had any law enforcement officer spoken to the cargo managers? No, or at least they had not until I requested they be interviewed. No such request was made by the authorities in the country where the seizure had been made.

Releasing information to the media before contacting agencies that could have a role to play is like playing hide and seek. To criminals up and down the chain, it's a way of saying: 'We're going to count to one hundred and then we'll come looking for you.'

It should be stressed that some agencies handled seizures carefully and professionally but that was not - and as far as I can see is still not - happening each and every time. Until it does, we are letting chances slip through our fingers, chances that may not necessarily end up with people in handcuffs but which at least ought to help fill in the blanks in our current understanding of these crimes, what is driving them and who is in the driving seat.

In December 2011, the then recently-formed International Consortium on Combating Wildlife Crime organized a large training event in the Shanghai Customs College. Some 50 enforcement agents and prosecutors from 18 countries in Africa and Asia attended. The purpose was to highlight to the participants the important role that Controlled Deliveries might have in combating wildlife crime. This is a technique designed to allow contraband, detected during the shipping phase, to continue its journey but under close surveillance and management by law enforcement officials. It has been used very effectively against, for example, drug trafficking and helps identify who is behind the various links in the smuggling chain. The countries invited to nominate attendees had been carefully selected, as they were those who were regularly affected by illicit trade in wildlife, especially ivory, rhino horn and timber. The event was sponsored by the World Bank, a partner in the Consortium. A year later, it appeared that none of those countries, apart from South Africa, had made use of the technique, although some major interceptions of wildlife had taken place in some of those countries in the meantime. And, in the South Africa case, it was an in-country controlled delivery, so may not really count. I hope I am wrong about this, and that regular covert delivery operations have been managed that have not come to my notice, but if I were the World Bank, I think I would be wondering if my money had been well spent.

There are other elements related to law enforcement that did not seem to be followed up, at least not in my day. While some interceptions of ivory contraband resulted from excellent targeting work by customs, several significant shipments were uncovered as a result of tip-offs, either direct to customs agencies or through their confidential hotlines. On a number of occasions, I wondered what was prompting these and, although I occasionally posed the question to some customs officers, no explanation was ever forthcoming. I suspect that some of these warnings came from rival organized crime groups, seeking to disrupt the activities of their competition. I saw this happen several times with those behind the illegal trade in caviar. Indeed, one individual who posed as a *bona fide* dealer regularly called me with information about other companies. I used to welcome his tips and would pass them on to relevant national agencies. They resulted in a number of seizures and prosecutions. What the individual did not know, however, was that I was receiving information about him too and was feeding that on in a similar manner. I wonder if the realization finally hit him when he was sentenced to jail by a court in New York.

Informants, and the information they supply, is a very sensitive subject among customs and police officers. There is an understandable reluctance to share information between agencies and an even greater resistance to sharing information about the informants themselves. However, this secrecy brings its own problems. It can, for example, result in the same informant being paid by both customs and police, the two agencies being unaware that the informant is providing them both with identical intelligence. This is why many countries have created national intelligence databases that, while protecting the identity of informants, do allow a degree of cross-referencing. Such systems are not in place, to the best of my knowledge, in those countries most seriously affected by wildlife crime. I also believe that, in combating wildlife crime, we have yet to use the most contemporary approaches to informants. All too often, when I asked national agencies about their intelligence-gathering, I would be told that they were unable to engage in any because they had no budget for such activities. There is a widespread misconception in parts of the law enforcement community that information has to be paid for and that informants have to be bought. That need not be the case. I never paid a single penny to some of the most effective informants I used over almost four decades of enforcement and investigation.

When I was a young detective, informants were seen as an important source of intelligence, but I do not think we directed informants in quite the way that the police do today. The prevailing approach to the acquisition of intelligence and the use of informants owes much to the tactics used by security services and counter-terrorism units, which are best not described in detail here. But these must be brought to bear against wildlife criminals too, together with the controlled delivery, surveillance, communication interception and anti-money-laundering and asset recovery enforcement practices that are regularly used to bring drug smugglers and dealers to book. And such methods will be at their most effective if they are used in a multi-agency approach, which also involves cross-border liaison and collaboration.

Even if the agency which is controlling a particular informant cannot or will not share everything that he or she provides to them, perhaps they can at least disseminate information which can help fill in the gaps in the overall understanding of the illicit trade, be it in ivory, tiger or rhino. For the moment, though, it seems the silence will continue. I remember being introduced to the officer-in-charge of a customs post in East Asia that had made a very significant ivory seizure. Having congratulated him and his staff, I asked how they had managed to uncover the shipment. He said it had resulted from risk-assessment and profiling. Much of our conversation, however, was taken up with him insisting that either the CITES Secretariat or the country of origin should pay a reward to his staff. I explained that we had no budget to do so and that, even if DNA profiling were able to pinpoint the geographic source of the tusks, it was likely to be a nation that was considerably poorer than his own. He was not pleased and said that, in that case, his agency should be allowed to sell the ivory. I explained that this, too, was not allowed. His response was that, aside from a financial reward for his officers, he needed money to reimburse his own budget as he had had to pay an informant who told them about the shipment's impending arrival. Puzzled, I reminded him that he had told me the interception came about through risk-assessment work. Our meeting broke up at that point; he said he had another engagement to attend.

Another possible source of support which the wildlife law enforcement community has yet to exploit fully is the DNA profiling mentioned above. For many years it was thought impossible to extract DNA from ivory but technological advances now allow us to do so and, by comparing the profile against samples obtained from the countries in Africa where elephants are still present in the wild, determine the geographical origin. This has enabled a picture to be developed, aside from and in addition to in-country elephant population surveys and routine patrol work, of where poaching is taking place. However - and very importantly - what DNA profiling does not tell us is when that poaching happened. For that, we have to turn to another forensic science technique.

Scientists have noted that the atom bomb tests which were conducted towards the end of World War Two, and for some time thereafter, produced levels of radiation that spread across the globe. Unless you were in close proximity to the test sites, the levels were not especially dangerous to life, whether animal or human. They were, however, absorbed into all human, animal and plant life. The radiation continues to exist and continues to be absorbed. Its presence and its strength allow scientists to determine the age of anything, including an elephant tusk or a piece of ivory, although it is degrading, so levels are reducing over time. And there are limits to what can be ascertained. If the piece of ivory came from an elephant that lived prior to World War Two, for example, then the radiation level will be zero. Forensic scientists have also told me that this test will soon be of no use because of the way in which levels are constantly falling. A time will be reached, and it may not be that far off, when they will again reach zero and the chance to carry out ageing tests will have gone. That may be a simplified description of the process, but if there is a time limit on it, one can only hope that forensic scientists will come up with an alternative.

This makes it all the more important that we exploit such techniques now, and to their fullest. If we can calculate both the geographical origin and age of the ivory that is being seized then we can begin to fill in considerable holes in our current knowledge. The results, though, can throw up even more mysteries. I recall one seizure, for instance, that occurred in the late 2000s in which some of the tusks appeared to date from the early 2000s. That, of course, raised all sorts of questions, chief among them where the tusks had been in the meantime.

It is well recognized in anti-poaching work that tusks taken from illegally-killed elephants are sometimes buried by poachers before they make good their escape from a park or reserve, planning to collect them later. It is one reason why agencies such as the Kenya Wildlife Service have sniffer dogs trained to detect ivory underground. This surely will not account, however, for tusks seized in 2008 or 2009 having been harvested more than half a decade previously. It is, though, further evidence that stockpiling is taking place, and in Africa as well as Asia, and it also underlines my central question: why are some criminals apparently willing to forgo the quick buck that is normally an important feature of crime?

Before leaving the subject of forensic science, I wish to express a further concern. Although there are a very small number of wildlife crime-related laboratories around the world whose focus is truly forensic, their work wholly devoted to science associated with the law, many of the other facilities engaged in wildlife-related research are more academic in nature. This does not make their studies and results any less important, significant or potentially valuable, but it does leave them open to challenge in courts of law, particularly in criminal courts. The whole realm of forensic science has, in recent years, come under very considerable scrutiny by criminal courts and courts of appeal. As a consequence, laboratories engaging in examinations resulting in evidence that may be presented in court are increasingly having to adopt time-consuming and expensive norms and practices which place burdens upon them that few pure research institutes could cope with, or would wish to. I recall participating in a meeting convened by the Food and Agriculture Organization of the United Nations at its headquarters in Rome, intended to consider a greater use of forensic science in combating illegal, unreported and unregulated fishing and attended by several of the leading fishery researchers and scientists in the world. Many of them were regularly using DNA techniques in their work. However, when specifically asked about their personal willingness, or that of their institute, to engage in criminal work, few responded positively. Most remarked on the costs associated with bringing their facilities up to the standards expected of forensic laboratories but several also spoke of their personal reluctance to subject themselves to the pressures of giving evidence in court.

I am also conscious that several of the research facilities which are currently producing highly interesting results receive items for examination in a fashion that would not comply with the chain of custody requirements which must be satisfied before evidence is presented to a criminal court. The manner in which their sample and specimen libraries and profile compilations, against which examined items are compared, have been collected and obtained might also fail to stand up to judicial scrutiny. I am not for a moment suggesting that scientists have engaged in anything improper, but am simply alluding to the scrutiny to which any evidence is subjected under most criminal trial procedures. Indeed, it will inevitably be attacked by defence lawyers, given the devastating influence that forensic examination conclusions, particularly those resulting from DNA profiling, can have upon the determination of guilt or innocence. One only has to look at major cases such as OJ

Simpson or, more recently, the South African Olympic sportsman charged with murdering his girlfriend, to see how the collection of evidence is challenged. Lastly, I worry that there may be individuals involved in this field whose passion for the topic may lay them open to having their objectiveness questioned by trial attorneys.

I have always been an active proponent of a greater use of forensic science in combating wildlife crime but, while urging this, have tried constantly to emphasize an appreciation of the judicial obligations that must be borne in mind. Having undergone training as a scenes of crime officer, it was a message that was drummed into me as a young detective and which I have never forgotten. I think, too, that the wildlife law enforcement community sometimes gets distracted by the most modern scientific methods of crime detection, such as DNA, but overlooks the basic tools that often bring ordinary criminals to justice. While I sometimes saw elephant tusks dusted for human fingerprints, for example, I struggle to recall cases in which documents, permits, waybills or packaging were similarly examined. Once again, opportunities went unexploited. Thinking back to my days as a detective, I solved several cheque fraud cases by treating those documents with a chemical that produced beautifully clear finger impressions, which subsequently matched those in our criminal record files and databases.

I must temper any apparent criticism, however, by acknowledging that this is an area where much more could, and should, be done in relation to training and awareness raising. While some commendable capacity building has been done, and is ongoing, in forensic science and scenes of crime work, there remains scope for a lot more. I think we need to cast our training net more widely. It would be surprising to find a police officer who did not know the importance of calling a scene of crime officer to the scene of a burglary; that would have been part of his basic training course. By way of comparison, I am not sure that summoning a scene of crime officer to a major contraband interception at a sea or airport would feature in the guidance issued to customs officers.

Regrettably, when examining the poaching and illegal trade of elephants and other species, we must also consider the question of corruption. As we've seen, law enforcement personnel and others are open to corruption or may deliberately choose to move to the dark side. I think, understandably, focus is placed upon those people operating at the beginning of the chain - anti-poaching staff, customs, police, CITES permit issuers, cargo managers, airline check-in staff and the like – and there is also a focus on the opposite end, where people may be paid off to facilitate illicit trade or clear contraband cargo for import. We must not lose sight of what may be happening in the middle. On at least two occasions I was contacted by someone who had become aware of significant interceptions of ivory as it was being smuggled from Africa to Asia. In these cases, customs, at two different ports in southeast Asia, had detected the smuggling and had detained the shipments. I use the word 'detained' because they had allegedly yet to seize the contraband. Word of each incident came to me in its immediate aftermath. In the first, I was told that a local politician was bringing pressure to bear for the shipment to be allowed to proceed. It was said that he was acting on behalf of the individual, elsewhere in Asia, whom I describe in another part of this book as apparently untouchable. In the other incident, it was said that the customs officers were seeking someone to whom they could sell the ivory.

I do not know whether these allegations were accurate. What I do know is that when, through one of our partner agencies, I asked that the interception be confirmed, it appeared that the relevant national customs headquarters knew nothing of the actions, despite them involving very considerable quantities of ivory. I do know, however, that both shipments were subsequently seized.

As well as ensuring that people do their duty, we also need to monitor closely what happens to seized contraband. There seem to be constant rumours of ivory, in particular, 'leaking' or disappearing from customs or other agency stores. There are two well-known cases in the Philippines where large quantities of seized ivory were stolen or vanished from what should have been secure storage. Did people in the agencies responsible for seizing the ivory criminally seek out a buyer or did the organized criminal group behind the shipment approach them and purchase release of the goods? I suspect we will never know. I understand that some customs officers were charged in at least one of these cases but I have never heard whether or not they were successfully prosecuted and, if they were, what sentence they received.

To trade or not to trade?

If nothing else, I trust that these reflections on almost a decade and a half of trying to monitor both the legal and illegal trade in ivory will demonstrate that the work is far from straightforward and that many questions need to be answered if we are to move forward effectively. Do I regret the part I played in the processes that led to China and Japan being designated as trading partners and importing raw ivory from southern Africa? No, I do not. I still believe the internal trade controls adopted by those two countries were adequate and complied with what the CITES community said had to be in place. But if a chain is only as strong as its weakest link, then the robustness of a control system relies upon it being implemented adequately. It is the work of the chef that makes a meal delicious, just as much as, if not more than, the ingredients used. Am I satisfied that each country has adequately and rigidly implemented their system? No, I am not. I am sure people who attended CITES meetings will recall that I often spoke about the tendency of countries and agencies to take their eye off the ball. Should I have predicted that any, or all, of the countries might not implement their control systems adequately? I do not believe that it was my position to do that. I spent almost four decades of my working life guided by the principle that all are equal before the law and that everyone is innocent until proven guilty. I had to swallow hard at times to abide by that principle. Some people, even those who know me very well, may not appreciate just how firmly and utterly committed I am to the rule of law. In my opinion, it is vital that those who make our laws and those who enforce them must, absolutely must, be wholly independent of each other. This approach may not always produce the results that we would all like but to do otherwise produces hellish ones.

As I near the end of examining the subject of elephants and ivory, I might as well throw in my penny's worth on one of the core questions, even though it is bound to bring the critics down on me again.

Should the trade in ivory, both at national and international levels, be banned? I honestly do not know. Much as I would like, especially in retirement, to be able to claim the 64,000 dollar prize, I would not presume to have the answer that has eluded most of the international community for nearly as long as CITES has been in existence. All I can do is provide an enforcement perspective. I believe, and I think many in policing circles would agree with me, that one of the worst pieces of legislation ever enacted was the Volstead Act. Adopted by US legislators in 1919, this introduced prohibition, the banning of the manufacture and sale of alcoholic beverages. Many people in the fields of law enforcement and criminology think that it was prohibition which did much to establish organized crime groups in a manner that remains with us today.

Prohibition, regardless of what is prohibited, together with the enforcement effort required to implement it, does not enjoy a terribly good track record. That is part of the reason why the debate over decriminalizing drug use rumbles on, with fairly convincing arguments on each side. There are, of course, certain forms of behaviour that almost all humanity believes must be proscribed without exception: murder, rape and drunk driving are just three obvious examples. Where I am less inclined towards prohibitions is when it is used to try to address issues that would perhaps be better tackled through other means. As I said before, I do not see the demand for ivory disappearing any time soon and, for at least the foreseeable future in parts of Africa, sources of legal-origin ivory will exist. I do not believe that we have done enough to find ways of connecting the legitimate demand and the lawful supply. This will probably have to involve adopting trade regimes which will differ from the CITES practices of old.

Several years ago, I had a casual conversation with the then CITES Secretary-General in which I postulated whether there might be potential to consider adapting the approach taken in regulating trade in diamonds. I wondered if, for instance, individual countries should not trade directly with importing countries but that all ivory should instead pass through some form of central exchange, with strict regulation of the amount of ivory entering markets and of the companies and traders licensed to process and sell it. This would, of course, require personnel to staff such a central exchange but imposing a levy on trade could presumably fund what would be needed. The Secretary-General thought there was value in looking into this further but felt that it was not the right time for the Secretariat to come forward with such an idea. I agreed and neither of us took it any further.

However, I still think such mechanisms are worth exploring and that we need to get away from the current 'ban or no ban' approach. We would need to work with both the exporting and importing countries. If the governments of consumer nations are convinced that there is a legitimate demand, and they wish to see it supplied legitimately, then perhaps the time has come for ivory truly to be given the value it may deserve. One could restrict raw ivory's delivery into the hands of the craftsmen and women who have the skills to convert it into meaningful, desirable and significant *objets d'art*. These would be sold for prices which reflect the craftsmanship that went into creating them and bring proper financial returns for the exporting countries, helping to fund their conservation programmes and including levies and taxes to finance adequate and rigidly enforced internal trade control systems in the importing countries. Techniques such as DNA profiling and up-to-date marking methods would need to be incorporated into the control systems more than they have been to date. It may be time to get rid of the cheap and shoddy bangles, pendants and other tourist tat that are found in so many stalls and inferior retail outlets in Africa and Asia. No one expects to find a real diamond amongst the inexpensive dross cluttering so many souvenir shops and other outlets where poorly worked, cut price ivory items are currently on sale. In future, they should not expect to find genuine ivory in such places either. And we will have to find ways to bring some benefit to the elephant range states that are currently excluded from trade. Elephant populations in Appendix I of the Convention do not die any less frequently than those in Appendix II. If ivory is of legal origin, let it be traded. I know that cannot happen under current provisions, but so what? Amend the provisions. Do we want to safeguard these species or not? There seem to be precious few existing incentives, and even fewer financial resources, to motivate those states currently omitted to protect the ever-decreasing numbers of elephants in their countries. It will take better brains than mine to design adequate systems but it strikes me that we have to start thinking outside the box.

The average price paid by traders from China and Japan who purchased raw ivory in the CITES-approved and supervised sales in 2008, was 156 dollars per kilo. If it is really correct that a kilo of raw ivory could fetch up to 8,000 dollars on the black market in 2013, then something, somewhere is badly wrong. What seems irrefutable is that the current approach is not working, at least not for many elephant populations. I sometimes thought that the never-ending debates in CITES, and not just on elephants, were like Nero fiddling while Rome burned. If the international community is truly committed to saving endangered species, then the various factions must pull themselves out of their trenches, cross no-man's-land and, like the soldiers of World War One at Christmas, come together to play the game.

TIGER TRAFFICKERS

While the principle motivation during my period with CITES remained what it had been while I was with the police - to bring criminals to justice - there were times when I saw only too clearly what was prompting others to devote years of effort to saving endangered species. The most striking of these took place in the summer of 1999.

I had been appointed to lead teams examining the poaching of, and illegal trade in, tigers. This called for visits to what are termed in CITES as range and consumer states. A range state is where a species can be found in the wild, whilst a consumer state is where that species (or products made from it) is used. Consequently, for tigers, the teams travelled to several countries in Asia but also to countries in Europe and North America where tiger bone products where being used, primarily by Asian ethnic communities, as part of traditional medicine. In three phases, between January and June, I made my way to Cambodia, Canada, China, India, Indonesia, Japan, Malaysia, Myanmar, Nepal, the Netherlands, the Russian Federation, the United Kingdom, the United States and Viet Nam. Six other individuals, with law enforcement or conservation backgrounds, joined at different stages but I was privileged to be the sole team member to call on all 14 nations. I was subsequently able to visit every tiger range state in the course of my CITES work, with one exception, which I will describe later.

It was in early June 1999 that I found myself sitting beside the manager of the Sariska Tiger Reserve as he drove an open-topped jeep along one of the many dusty tracks of this jewel among India's national parks. In the seats behind me were the director of Project Tiger, a man who had spent his entire working life with the Indian Forest Service and who was highly respected, nationally and internationally, for his efforts to conserve both his country's forests and wildlife, and one of the park guards. While we discussed the difficulties of patrolling 800 sq. km and the crime issues he and his staff faced, the manager was doing his best to provide me with views of some of the parks' inhabitants. The Project Tiger director's keen eyesight had spotted a leopard making its way up a rocky hillside, despite the gloom created by the trees, and I was grateful that his years of experience gave me a sighting that I would certainly have otherwise missed. The sure-footedness of these graceful large cats is a wonder to behold and the manner in which they are able to move fluidly and steadily across uneven ground is incredible. I could have watched this beast for hours but the manager was determined that we should see a tiger and he drove on.

We had spent several hours traversing the park without success when the manager decided to put his local knowledge and experience to the test. He announced that, before giving up for the day, he would try one last area, which he thought a young male tiger was in the process of making his own territory. He had only seen the animal there on two occasions before but was relatively sure that it was determined to brand that part of the park its exclusive fiefdom. We headed in that direction but saw nothing to begin with on the twisting and turning tracks. The manager told us to hold on as he intended to go off-road, towards a spot where he had seen the tiger previously. He believed the young male might still be nervous of approaching the reserve trails and that we would need to search him out in the more thickly-wooded habitat. He turned sharply and we began to thrust our way through fairly dense thickets, which reached up to the height of the jeep doors and windshield. However, we had only gone about twenty metres from the track when the guard in the back seat suddenly reached forward, grabbed the manager's shoulder, and hissed something which I could not catch. Since the guard was talking in Hindi, and also in what seemed to be a stage whisper, I did not understand what was said but it prompted the manager to bring the jeep to a sudden halt.

I looked over my shoulder and saw the guard's attention was fixed on a point just off to the right front corner of the vehicle. Then I noted that the manager, too, was staring in the same direction. I could not see what was fascinating them both. Leaning forward, I looked past the body of the manager and straight into the eyes of a tiger. It was so close to the jeep that if the reserve boss had leaned over the driver's door and stretched out his arm, he could almost have touched its nose. The striped king of the jungle was standing between two thorn bushes and had been almost invisible as we had approached. The guard's raised position in the rear of the jeep had enabled him, however, to just catch sight of it from above. Exhilarated as I was by this encounter, the feeling of stress emanating from the three other occupants was palpable and I realized that we had probably stopped where we shouldn't have. The tiger was not happy and I could sense that my companions were not either. I am ashamed to say that the thought passed through my mind that the tiger was surely bound to go for the manager first and that that might give me some opportunity for escape. And 'bound' was the operative word, as it would have taken only the slightest leap for the animal to become the fifth occupant of what I was very conscious was a vehicle without a roof or side windows. We all, including the tiger, sat or stood motionless. A long time seemed to pass, although it was probably only 20 seconds, before the tiger made its displeasure obvious by opening its mouth, displaying its teeth in all their marvellous but lethal glory, and hissing violently. I imagine most people have seen how nasty a domestic cat can appear when it hisses. Believe me, it is nothing, absolutely nothing whatsoever, compared with the impression made by a full-grown male Bengal tiger.

Anxious as I was to get out of the situation, I understood that none of us wished to do anything to prompt an attack. And so we remained silent and utterly still. Then I noticed that the bushes between which the tiger was positioned were apart around its body and rear quarters but had grown together somewhat in front of it. To reach us, it would have to press forward through a few tangled and thorn-strewn branches. The same thought appeared to have struck the magnificent creature too as, with a final dismissive but aggressive tooth display and hiss, it backed out of position, turned and strode slowly off. It showed not the slightest alarm and its retreat was roundly dignified as if to show us that it had decided to change direction but that the choice had nothing at all to do with us.

Nervous smiles and quiet laughter broke out within the jeep and we began to congratulate each other, not just on the most amazing sighting, but also on avoiding what could so easily have become a very nasty incident. It was agreed that a stiff drink would be appropriate and we decided to head back to our base. The manager turned the jeep and we swept back to the track in a semi-circular manoeuvre. However, as we swung up and onto the trail again, the manager once more brought the 4x4 to a sudden stop. There, standing about 15 metres away in a small group of trees just off to one side of the track, stood a large sambar deer stag. This is a large species of deer and, when fully grown, individuals are similar in size to the red deer found in Scotland's mountain and forest areas. The voice of the Project Tiger director came from the rear. 'Why isn't it moving off?' I, too, was puzzled by the deer's total lack of reaction to our sudden appearance. Instead of looking at us, the deer had its head turned almost completely around, seemingly staring back over its left shoulder. We all followed its gaze. 'My God,' whispered the reserve manager. 'Can you see it?'

There, on the opposite side of the track, was the tiger from which we had just had the fortunate escape. Its eyes were firmly fixed on the deer. It was crouched down in a semi-stalking and semi-attack posture, with its ears pressed down and back in what I understand is a clear sign that it is about to spring. The four humans and two animals were mesmerized by each other. I think one of us in the jeep probably said something too loudly because the sambar's head swung round in our direction, as if finally becoming aware of our presence. And in that split second the tiger reacted. Aware of the deer's distraction, the tiger covered the ground between them in just a few bounds. Its speed was breathtaking and the deer never had a chance. Its head did begin to swing round again but too late, far too late. Just before the gap finally closed, the tiger leapt up and its claws closed around the lower neck and shoulder area of the deer. Its teeth, which had, less than two minutes before, been bared in warning at us, closed around the back of the sambar's neck. We were so close that we could hear the crunch as the tiger's jaws bit down onto its prey, followed quickly by an almost gunshot-style crack as the deer's spine was broken. The deer collapsed and, motionless apart from some twitching of its limbs, appeared to have been killed instantly. The tiger lay down alongside the felled prey and kept its jaws firmly in place. As it did so, its eyes swivelled towards us and low growls emerged from its throat, as if to caution us to mind our own business and not interfere. It need not have worried; there was no way I was getting out of that jeep until it was parked beside human habitation.

A full minute seemed to pass before the tiger appeared satisfied that dinner was ready and that the deer was dead beyond doubt. Rising up, it moved its feet so that it was astride the deer and, keeping its teeth clamped where they had been from the moment of interception, it began to move forward dragging the carcass beneath it. I wondered whether there was to be no end to these astounding sights; it was amazing that a tiger could haul an animal larger than itself in what was, while not effortless, nonetheless an impressive display of strength. The tiger and its prize slowly disappeared from view into the vegetation of the forest. The human observers remained silent. I think each of us was wondering whether what we had witnessed had really happened right in front of our eyes. Finally, the Project Tiger director broke the silence and told me, as if I needed telling, that I had just viewed the most remarkable spectacle. He went on to say that, in forty years of service in the forests of India, he had never been so close to a tiger kill.

When we returned to the hotel where I was staying on the edge of the reserve, itself very impressive as it had previously been a maharajah's palace, and my team mates told me that they had not seen a single tiger all day, I provoked considerable envy when I recounted what we had witnessed. However, we were able to take them early next morning to the kill site and found the tiger nearby, sated after what appeared to have been an all-night meal judging by the greatly-reduced deer remains and the tiger's swollen belly. What none of us knew then was that, within a few years, poachers would kill all of the tigers in the Sariska Reserve.

In the course of my travels I have been charged by a rhino in Nepal and an elephant in Tanzania. On both occasions, these were the bluff attacks which these animals sometimes make to warn off intruders to their territories and in which they turn away at the last minute. These two species are impressive by virtue of their very size and one is left in no doubt as to their power and the destructive effect they could have on human skin and bone. But the big cats of the world seem to have an extra something and a lot of it has to do with their vocal abilities. I recall being on the edge of the headquarters compound of Namibia's Etosha National Park late one night when a lion roared nearby. The sound literally vibrated through my body and the sense of force and strength was nearly overpowering. I was similarly struck one day when I was shown to a wooden crate at the back of the main offices in Chitwan National Park in Nepal. As I drew near, the most incredible noise emerged from within and the box began to shake violently. Keeping my distance, I was finally able to see that it contained a leopard. The snarls and growls made it plain that I might be very badly mauled if the cat managed to get out. This particular leopard had attacked livestock owned by villagers living on the edge of the park and had been captured by rangers. It was the third occasion on which they had had to do so. Each time, they had transported the animal many miles away and released it back into the forest. However, it appeared to have developed a taste for beef and would always make its way to some population site and begin to savage and eat cattle. The park authorities intended to make one more effort at relocation but acknowledged that this would be the last attempt. If the leopard had to be captured once again, they would employ euthanasia.

It is the tiger, however, which seems especially to deserve the regard and respect given to it by both man and the animal kingdom. I once approached an enclosure within a rescue centre in Thailand where a male tiger was being kept. With the war in Iraq being fought at the time, staff at the centre had named the bad-tempered tiger Saddam. Although the enclosure was concrete, with sturdy metal bars across its front, I involuntarily stepped back when Saddam sprang at the railings and gave out a deafening and spine-chilling roar that seemed to shake the earth around me. They truly are the most amazing of species and I find it almost incomprehensible that we have allowed tigers to come so very, very close to extinction. Indeed, the current status of the tiger offers many lessons to be learned by the law enforcement and conservation communities.

In the early 1900s, tigers ranged across much of Asia and are thought to have totalled at least 100,000. By 2013, numbers of tigers in the wild were estimated to have fallen to somewhere between 3,200 and 3,500. Tigers now occupy only 7 per cent of their historic range. This startling decline resulted from a number of impacts (in no order of priority): reduction in, and fragmentation of, suitable habitat; falling numbers of prey species;

encroachment by humans into tiger landscapes; legal hunting (during part of this period); deliberate eradication through government policies in some areas (for part of this period); conflict between tigers and humans and livestock; poaching and illegal trade.

Apart from one sub-species, the species *Panthera tigris* has been listed in Appendix I of CITES since the treaty entered into force on 1 July 1975. The remaining sub-species (the Amur or Siberian tiger) was listed in Appendix I on 22 October 1987. Consequently, international commercial trade in tigers is prohibited. Since the late 1990s, domestic trade in specimens of tiger has been banned in each country that historically engaged in such trade. There were, originally, nine sub-species of tigers but three of those are now extinct. There was a time when tigers could be seen in areas immediately to the west of the Caspian Sea and their habitat stretched eastwards across the whole of Asia but those days are long gone. DNA profiling, as I understand it, suggests that several of the existing and extinct sub-species may, genetically, be almost indistinguishable but morphologically, i.e. in appearance, they look very different. The Amur tiger, for instance, is the biggest of all the world's cats and its thick coat, which protects it within the harsh climates of the far east of Russia, makes it look all the larger. Just over a week after my encounter with a Bengal tiger in India, I saw two Amur tigers in a rehabilitation centre a few hours' drive from Vladivostok and they were truly impressive.

The tiger has an incredible status in mythology and history and is perhaps, among all fauna, the species that features most prominently in religion, art, literature and legend. It is often the very symbol of power. Yet, despite its sometimes deserved reputation as a man-eater, it is not necessarily viewed as malevolent. The Hindu goddess Durga is often depicted riding a tiger to reflect her unlimited power but she is also regarded as using it to protect virtue and destroy evil. In January 2011, I was fortunate enough to climb up to the Taktsang Buddhist Monastery at over 3,000 m in the Paro valley of Bhutan. Also known as the Tiger's Nest or Tiger's Lair, legend has it that this is where a Buddhist guru landed, having flown on a tiger's back from nearby Tibet. Many people believe that the monastery and its location deserve to be on a list of the wonders of the world. The eminence of tigers in India is reflected in the way that the species there is called the Royal Bengal tiger. The tiger is one of the symbols in the Chinese zodiac and is one of the years in the Chinese calendar. Historically, it was one of the most important ingredients in Chinese medicine.

However, despite all this, the tiger has suffered terrible persecution, even in countries where it has been most highly prized for centuries. Whilst the British Raj in India witnessed hundreds of tigers hunted down as trophies by military and civil service officers, for example, the killing continued in 'sporting' shoots conducted by maharajahs and other wealthy Indians after the country gained its independence. In China, Chairman Mao Tse-tung appeared to have mixed views on tigers. On the one hand, they feature in some of his well-known quotes, such as 'In waking a tiger, use a long stick' or when referring to the Soviet Union as a 'paper tiger'. On the other hand, Mao is said to have been behind a policy to eradicate as many tigers as possible in China, in order to free up land for cultivation and agriculture.

It was in the early 1970s that the conservation community began to appreciate the rapid loss of these animals and wake up to the fact that the tiger was on a path to extinction. In 1973, Indira Gandhi, then Prime Minister of India, established Project Tiger and this seemed to halt for a period, or even reverse, the drop in numbers, at least in that country. However, despite efforts by India, other tiger range states and the international community, the continuing decline of the tiger has seemed almost unstoppable. Although relevant countries established protected areas and tiger reserves, numbers continued to fall regardless of setting aside tracts of land where the animals ought to have been safe. Indeed, between the early 1970s and the early 2000s, hundreds of thousands of dollars must have been spent in the name of tiger conservation, yet if tiger numbers were to be used as a gauge of success, then one could reach hardly any other conclusion but that it had all been an abject failure, aside from allowing a few dwindling populations to maintain a tenuous grip in pockets where total extinction was avoided. Pondering why such reserves were apparently not safeguarding the species, alongside other research, gradually made clear that the most significant and devastating threat to the survival of tigers was poaching and the subsequent illegal trade of tiger skins and other body parts.

Almost every part of a tiger has a value in the black markets of illegal trade in wildlife. Its skin is prized for decorative purposes or may be incorporated into the traditional clothing of some ethnic minorities. Its bones have historically been used as ingredients in a wide range of traditional medicine, particularly in responding to rheumatism and arthritis. Its whiskers have been used to treat toothache. The animal's brain was believed to cure laziness, while the eyeballs were employed in dealing with epilepsy and malaria. Its nose could treat convulsions in children and its fat could heal haemorrhoids or scalp conditions. Its collar bones are regarded as good luck charms by gamblers. Its feet, mounted on the outside of a house, are believed to ward off evil spirits. Its claws and teeth are regarded as talismans. Its penis, dissolved in alcohol, is claimed to be an effective aphrodisiac. Its tail can be processed to create a treatment for skin cancer. Illegal trade in tiger meat for human consumption appears to have increased in recent years. There is almost no end to the variety of ways in which those who trade in this animal can profit. Trade in live tigers, although limited, also occasionally occurs, primarily for private collections of exotic species or as a status symbol, sometimes by senior figures in organized crime groups.

In 1999, when I led the teams engaged in what were termed the CITES Tiger Technical Missions, the distinction between range and consumer states seemed very clear. Range states were where tiger poaching occurred and consumer states were where the illicit trade took place. While we noted that there was evidence of overlap between the two, i.e. trade was also happening in countries where tigers were being poached, it seemed restricted in nature. Just over a decade later, a very different picture could be seen. The nature of the trade was also to alter over time. In the late 1990s, tigers appeared, in the main, to be poached for their bones and other body parts but not particularly for their skins. The seizures of tiger specimens that were taking place in Europe and North America were almost invariably of traditional medicine products. Those products were primarily plasters, adhesive poultice-like treatments for joint pain, or sometimes tonics used as general health-promoting liquid drinks. Some of the seizures that were taking place involved many hundreds of plasters. The prices charged for these items prompted the technical mission teams to question whether they could truly contain actual tiger ingredients; the costs did not seem to reflect what one would expect of a black market product. Additionally, the sheer scale of the apparent illicit traditional medicine trade made us wonder how it could possibly be that tigers had not already been wiped off the face of the earth, such was the apparent demand for their body parts. We were not the only people considering that question.

DNA profiling techniques for wildlife were still not widespread in 1999 and certainly not for tigers. Even as they were developed in coming years it was noted that, to be reliable, the product being tested would require a tiger ingredient to be present in quantities that traditional practitioners had never used. The US Fish and Wildlife Service's forensic scientists shared our doubts as to the authenticity of the tiger bone products on sale and being seized around the world. Unable to distinguish tiger from other species ingredients, they determined instead to seek out evidence of bone. Calcium being a significant constituent of bone, they set about testing for its presence. In test after test, products turned out to be calcium-free. This appeared to substantiate that what was actually taking place was fraud on a massive scale. This also seemed to confirm the teams' suspicion that the real trade in tiger bones was taking place very clandestinely and involved specialist medicinal practitioners supplying consumers who demanded, and were willing to pay for, the real thing.

I was able to corroborate this in subsequent investigations and missions. I spoke with a traditional medicine shopkeeper in Bangkok in 2002, for example, who admitted that he travelled, once a year, to the Myanmar border where he would purchase tiger bones from illicit dealers in small towns adjoining Thailand. He was not particularly reluctant to discuss this with me and I wondered why not. I then discovered that, whilst trading in tigers or tiger parts was against Thailand's wildlife legislation, its Food and Drug Administration had yet to outlaw tiger parts as an ingredient in medicinal products. Fortunately, this legal loophole was closed soon after.

Apart from that oversight, domestic trade in tigers and their products had been banned across the world by the late 1990s. The only exception was Japan and the technical missions' team found that, while its use in some traditional medicines was continuing but declining, the main source of interest on the part of consumers appeared to be in its use as an aphrodisiac. I will never forget, as a result, visiting stores on streets that ran parallel to the main thoroughfare of Ginza. Ginza in Tokyo is Japan's answer to London's Oxford Street or New York's Fifth Avenue. However, just a short distance away were sex shops stocked with some of the most bizarre items that I had ever seen. Alongside other virility aids, shops offered seal and tiger penises for sale alongside Chinese hard liquor. Customers could purchase these items, together with large bottles, and were instructed to place the seal or tiger penis in the bottle, add the liquor, leave this for about two months until the body part had dissolved, then drink and expect a really good time for all. Alternatively, ready-made seal or tiger penis wine could be purchased by the bottle or by the glass. One shopkeeper offered to pour me a complimentary glass of tiger penis wine but I declined, especially as no information seemed to be available as to just how quickly its effects might be felt. The attention that the mission team's work brought to this commerce led, soon after, to a change in Japan's laws and tiger trade ceased there too. Japan was not, though, the only country where the tiger mission technical teams had bizarre encounters.

During a visit to Vladivostok which the tiger team made in June 1999, I found that the hotel which had been arranged for us offered an extra service that did not appear in the directory of facilities. My companions consisted of a US-born woman, a French-Canadian man and a Chinese male colleague from Geneva. Every night, at a quarter to midnight, the telephones would ring in each of our rooms. The Canadian would be asked, in French, whether he wished for 'female company'. The same offer was made, in Mandarin, to my Chinese colleague. And I got an identical proposition, but in English. Our US female team member was never awakened by a late-night call. I did not feel it my place to raise the matter of this blatant discrimination with hotel reception staff.

We were told that Vladivostok in those days was regularly suffering from outright wars between the various mafia groups that were battling for control of the city. The sound of semi-automatic and automatic gunfire could apparently be heard on many nights, as scores were settled or fresh outbreaks of violence took place. We were told by local wildlife law enforcement officials that such fights were never broken up by the Militia. Instead, the Militia waited for the shots to cease and would then move in to pick up the pieces (or corpses).

We were also told that it was easy to spot mafia members, as they all tended to travel around in brand-new Toyota Land Cruisers with blackened side and rear windows. Driving in Vladivostok being somewhat chaotic, not helped by high levels of drunken driving, accidents were fairly commonplace. We were warned, should we ever be involved in a collision with one of the dark-windowed Toyotas, to get out and run away as quickly as we could, in case the Land Cruiser's occupants feared that we were actually a rival group intent upon battle. Thankfully, we never had to put this advice into practice.

The same wildlife officials took us one day to a city bar and restaurant that was the haunt of local professional hunters. There is a major commercial sport hunting tradition in the provinces around Vladivostok, with many men making their living either from killing animals for their meat or skins or by acting as guides for sportsmen from other parts of the country and abroad.

It was such professional hunters that had a major detrimental impact upon tiger populations in the far east of Russia long before trade in tiger skins and body parts became profitable. Any hunter coming across a tiger would be almost bound to shoot it dead. In times gone by, the carcass might simply have been left to rot. Tigers were targeted in this way because they have a fondness, in that part of the world, for eating dogs. Since most hunters used dogs as part of their activities, for tracking game or recovering downed geese and other bird species, they were prized companions. Leopards, including the increasingly rare Amur leopard, risked suffering the same fate.

But tigers were not the only thing that tended to be shot on sight. The hunters' bar, its walls decorated with the heads of deer, bear and other trophy animals, its shelves filled with mounted specimens of birds and small mammals, was the watering hole where the professionals would gather. There they would meet up with their counterparts after trips into the nearby taiga forests. Some trips might be for only a morning or afternoon, whilst others – especially if they involved guiding wealthy clients into the remote neighbouring Kamchatka region in search of bear and other large mammals – might be of several weeks' duration.

I was told that these hunters would often put the same question to each other as they raised their first glass of vodka or beer: 'How many Chinese did you kill this trip?'

Allegedly, although it would be difficult to verify this, professional hunters had the same approach to Chinese poachers as they did to tigers. Poachers who crossed the border into

Russia from their homes in provinces such as Heilongjiang, in the northeast, were fired upon just as promptly as big cats. It seemed that life, human or animal, was cheap in those parts, an area I have heard described as Russia's answer to America's Wild West. Did this really happen? Who knows? Whatever the truth, I certainly found Vladivostok to be something of a frontier town.

However, it seemed that hunters were not only at risk from each other. Officers of Inspection Tiger, the specialized anti-poaching and environmental crime unit which had its headquarters in Vladivostok, described to me how they were once contacted by the wife of a local poacher after he had failed to return from a hunting trip. She knew that he had set off to try and get a tiger and knew roughly where he had planned to go. However, 48 hours after what was meant to be an evening's hunt, he still was not home. Inspection Tiger staff, several of whom had themselves been professional hunters, headed towards the area in question. After a lengthy search, they came upon the poacher's body. His rifle lay by his side. It had been fired but seemingly not quickly or accurately enough. He had been badly mauled, and partly eaten, by a tiger. The photographs of the scene were by no means the worst I had viewed in my police career but they were certainly not pretty.

Interestingly, the poacher's head and face were not especially disfigured. This brought to mind conversations I'd had, just a few weeks before, with tiger anti-poaching officers in Indonesia. Whilst not exactly common, attacks by tigers upon villagers in rural Sumatra were certainly not unheard of. Forestry officials had noted a recurring feature: that someone killed by a tiger had had their face 'ripped off'. Although that phrase was used repeatedly, it did not reflect the facts. What would actually happen, apparently, is that the tiger, using its claws, would tear into the back of its victim's scalp. This led to the scalp being pulled forward, exposing the skull, and squashing and compressing the face downwards into the neck area. It would create the impression that the face itself, although still attached, had been removed. This was perhaps also linked with the fact that tigers commonly grasp their prey by the neck during the initial stages of an attack, as I had seen for myself in Sariska Tiger Reserve. As it happens, pathologists employ a similar technique when conducting human autopsies. They use a scalpel to cut through the skin at the back of the skull and 'fold' the face forward to reveal the top of the skull, which is then removed with a saw, allowing the brain to be taken out for closer examination.

Some villagers in Sumatra believe that the tiger removes the face of its victim so that it cannot be watched as it devours the torso. This belief seems to mirror, in some respects, one which existed centuries ago where some murderers gouged out or damaged their victim's eyes, thinking that, at the moment of death, the iris somehow captured the image of the attacker. The poacher located by Inspection Tiger had not been disfigured in such a manner but since attacks upon humans in the USSR and modern-day Russia happen very rarely, it would seem impossible to determine tiger man-eater behaviour.

On the other hand, the human face in itself is possibly enough to ward off attacks by tigers. In the Sundarbans areas of Bangladesh and India, villagers working in the mangroves and forests sometimes wear masks with human faces painted on them. They wear them, however, on the back of their heads, convinced that a tiger will think it is being observed when approaching them from behind. Given that the Sundarbans suffers some of the worst attacks on humans by tigers, I suppose anything is worth trying. Personally, I do not think I would volunteer for any experiments to test its efficacy. I was told by some locals in the area that tigers acquire a taste for human flesh by feeding upon the body parts that float downriver following cremations that take place upstream, often hundreds of miles away. I suspect this may be more folklore than fact.

It was during a visit to the Sundarbans that, with hindsight, I should possibly have worn a face mask. Local forest guards offered to show me recent tiger pug marks that they had observed the day before. Given that they indicated that the tiger might still be in the area, and that a sighting could be possible, I readily agreed to accompany them. A few of us set off walking towards the forest, in single file, with one forest guard in front and another bringing up the rear. We began to skirt the forest itself and passed along a narrow trail that ran through an area of elephant grass. This vegetation is well-named as it is almost as tall as the average man and very thick. The guard in front called out that there was not far to go before we would arrive at the paw mark site. I was happy to hear this as I was starting to become rather anxious about the terrain through which we were walking. It had occurred to me that any tiger which might be present would be completely concealed in the long grass and, having seen the effects of a tiger attack, I was somewhat nervous about becoming a meal. We passed safely through the area, however, and arrived at a clearing where, in a muddy patch of ground, the distinctive impressions of a large cat were shown to us. Our curiosity satisfied, and there being no sign of the animal that had left them, we made our way back to the patrol base.

That night, I was chatting with the District Forest Officer and told him of my nervousness. I said how reassuring it had been to have the armed guards at the front and rear of our little expedition. 'Actually, Mr Sellar,' he commented, 'Most of my staff couldn't hit a barn door with their rifles.' He then went on to relate a story that had occurred the previous year when a documentary camera crew had spent time in his area trying to film tigers in the wild. The crew and the film producer had been adamant that any footage was to be of free-ranging tigers and they wished to avoid any subterfuge in gaining good pictures. However, they had spent almost three weeks without seeing a single flash of orange or black stripes. At last, utterly dejected and exasperated, it was agreed that something would have to be done if they were not to leave without a single frame of tiger footage. It was decided to try and lure a tiger into a clearing where it might be captured on video. The producer negotiated with local villagers and persuaded them to sell the crew a cow, which could be used to attract a tiger. The villagers agreed to do so but insisted that the beast not be used as live bait. The animal would have to be killed and its carcass laid out as bait. The residents refused to kill the cow themselves, however, and indicated that the film crew would have to arrange its death. Not having any expertise in the slaughtering of cattle, the producer sought the assistance of the forest guards.

This, however, led to another problem. It was agreed that one of the patrol staff would shoot the cow and he stepped forward with his rifle. I should explain that the weapons issued to these anti-poaching officers were Lee Enfield .303 rifles, the very same model carried by British soldiers in World War One. The guard aimed and pulled the trigger. Nothing happened. The bullet in the chamber had failed to discharge. Another was loaded and he took aim once more, with the very same result. The rifle was reloaded 14 times before a bullet fired and the cow dropped down dead. Although the story was related with a smile, I could see that the District Officer had told it very deliberately to illustrate how poorly-equipped he and his men were. But at least this patrol actually had rifles; I was to visit one reserve in India where the scenario was even more ludicrous. There, I asked the park manager whether his patrols had access to weapons and was assured that they did. I inquired whether I could see one, to determine the type in use. 'Ah, that might be difficult,' said the manager. I asked why. 'Well, the department's rules are that our weapons have to be stored in the local police armoury.' I asked whether the patrol staff went to the police office each day to withdraw the weapons. 'No, we are not allowed to patrol with guns as a matter of routine,' came the reply. 'If there is a specific need for weapons, we request that the police issue them.' What form might such a 'need' take? I wondered. 'Oh, if the staff were fired upon by poachers, we could ask the police to deliver our rifles.' How long might that take, I asked. 'During the day? Maybe half an hour. But, at night, probably a lot longer.' What was perhaps most troubling of all about the conversation was that the reserve manager appeared to regard the arrangement as perfectly acceptable.

This was referred to some days later when I took part in a press conference with my boss in the nation's capital. Unfortunately, one report lost something in translation and a newspaper item subsequently appeared with the comment: 'Secretary General witnessed patrol staff walking around without arms.'

Although the technical mission teams were able to identify a number of suggestions and recommendations on how tiger poaching and illegal trade might be combated, and eventually prepared a report that ran to over 100 pages, the main concern that I had, having visited all 14 different countries, was whether (especially in the range states) there was sufficient political will to save the tiger. It was a concern that I would feel many times in the years to come and not just in relation to tigers. Russia was perhaps the country in which the team felt most confident. Its then recent establishment of Tiger Brigades, dedicated to combating poaching and trade in tigers, had impressed us all. Anti-poaching work, previously conducted by forest department staff, was transferred to the Brigades and they proved to be a force to be reckoned with. Composed of professional hunters, ex-military and some ex-Militia officers, they benefitted from funding donated by several international NGOs. They appeared to fear no one and, on several occasions, arrested government officials, including one Militia commander who was engaged in selling tiger and leopard skins. Unfortunately, as time passed, considerable jealousy and envy emerged, especially between people who had previously managed wildlife law enforcement, and Brigade activities and government funding were allegedly restricted in the late 2000s. I encountered Brigade officials on several occasions in the years after our initial meeting in 1999. They were, inevitably, individuals with considerable personal presence and not the kind, as the saying goes, that you would want to meet in a dark alley at night. The technical mission team believed that the Brigade approach was something that was well worth copying by other tiger range states.

These units were subsequently re-named Inspection Tiger and their remit was expanded to cover illegal logging and other forms of environmental crime. Three of their number attended a training course that I coordinated in India in 2002 and, on their arrival, I noted that one of them was sporting a massive black eye, which he was attempting to conceal behind a pair of sunglasses. I commented on this to the senior member of the trio and remarked that I was surprised that anyone had managed to bruise the eye of an individual who would not have looked out of place in the front row of the Scottish rugby squad. His boss grinned quietly and said to me, 'If you think he looks bad, you should see the man responsible.' Later in the training course, I was to have my own physical encounter with the Inspection Tiger man-mountain.

I had noted, in most of the countries I visited, that whilst wildlife law enforcement officials might have access to weapons, very few agencies equipped their staff with the standard equipment that would be carried by police patrol staff in Europe or North America. I never saw any official with a telescopic or side-handled baton, for example, and neither did I observe anyone with the modern rigid handcuffs carried by each and every Scottish police officer. These have been specifically designed not only to tether a prisoner's wrists together but, very usefully, to allow a pressure to be brought to bear that ensures compliance with instructions and renders one's captive less likely to resist arrest. This can be achieved even with just one cuff around only one wrist. To demonstrate the rigid handcuffs' capabilities, I called the Inspection Tiger officer to the front of the class one day and asked him to grasp my jacket lapel in one of his fists. My jacket was grabbed by his right hand, a hand the size of a spade with fingers like sausages. Meantime, I held the rigid handcuffs at waist level in my right hand. 'OK,' I told him, 'When I say 'Go', I want you to try and drag me across the room.'

I am not particularly tall and I am not well-built. This bear of a Russian towered above me. He grinned and many giggles broke amongst his classmates. He began to bring pressure to bear when I called 'Go' but it took me only a second to flick one cuff onto his wrist, apply pressure and bring him, helpless, to his knees. If the class was stunned, it was nothing to the look of amazement on his face. But this rather silly demonstration had a definite purpose. I went on to explain to the students that, while many NGOs or government donor agencies refuse to pay for firearms and ammunition, they might very well be willing to purchase less lethal restraint and self-protection equipment. I encouraged them to ask their agencies to seek funding to acquire such devices. I do not know whether any subsequently did.

Whilst writing this book I revisited the team's 1999 report and was troubled by how prophetic some of the comments have proved to be.

> Intelligence quoted to the team appeared to more than justify suspicions that organized criminal gangs, including the Russian mafia and Chinese triads, may well be involved in wildlife crime. Although several enforcement agencies told the team of their concern over the existence of such organized trade and routes, little appears to have been done to research or infiltrate illicit criminal activity at that level. The team acknowledges that the lack of specialist wildlife crime units in Asia severely restricts the ability to tackle this aspect of trade but is strongly of the opinion that such research and infiltration is necessary if any significant progress is to be made.

Another matter that concerned the team was whether, with all the attention that was being given to tigers, other species might be suffering unnoticed. The situation for one animal was particularly worrying:

> The team firmly believes that poaching of and illicit trade in leopard should be of great concern for the Convention. It repeatedly hears of conflict between leopards, humans and livestock that results in attempts to poison or otherwise kill such animals. The species appears to be increasingly popular for traditional medicine and seems to be regarded in some areas as a valuable alternative or replacement for tiger. Leopards also seem to be popular in the illicit skin and exotic pet trade. Team members heard of leopard poachers on the Russian Federation/Chinese border who killed a Russian Federation border guard who had tried to intercept them.
>
> The team gained the impression that comparatively little work is being done in relation to leopard population surveys, particularly when compared to what is being carried out for tigers. Yet comments from workers in the field and NGO staff indicate that leopard populations may be experiencing rapid reductions through the very same factors that impact upon the number of tigers.

I do not want to enter the realm of 'we told you so' but I do wish more attention had been paid to our concerns, especially as, within a few years, seizures would start to be made of horrendous numbers of leopard skins being smuggled into China. However, I do believe it deserves to be said that the wider conservation community at that time paid relatively scant regard to what was being reported by the CITES Secretariat or those who, like the technical teams, were operating on its behalf. A few non-governmental organizations, particularly those which had a focus on illegal trade issues, welcomed the teams' report and made regular reference to it in years to come. Unfortunately, I think there was an institutional arrogance among a number of the major conservation bodies that led them to believe they knew best and that they could not learn from others. In my opinion, the same arrogance remains in some quarters today. This resulted partly, I believe, from the fact that those organizations had staff which had spent years, and in some cases lifetimes, studying species in the wild and who, albeit understandably, thought they knew just about everything there was to know. This situation was probably also aggravated by the situation existing at that time where the greatest threats to endangered species were thought to be habitat-related and that was very much the primary focus of those engaged in conservation. The impact of wildlife crime was yet to be fully understood or appreciated, to a large degree because few, if any, in the conservation world had a relevant perspective to bring to bear. In recent years, the situation has changed and focussing on wildlife crime has almost become flavour of the month. It is hard not to look back and realize how much time we lost and how the headstart of organized crime grew and grew in the interim.

This disjuncture between the CITES Secretariat and conservationists was also very apparent in what came after the technical missions. It was decided that supplementary missions should be conducted to certain countries visited by the technical team, countries which might benefit from encouragement at a diplomatic level. Consequently, high level political missions were performed by a three-person team consisting of the CITES Secretary-General, the Chairman of the CITES Standing Committee and myself. The missions took place in early 2000 and the team's report had to be finalized very shortly before the eleventh meeting of the Conference of the Parties to CITES, which was held in April of that year. One of the countries visited by the team was India. The technical team had expressed concerns about the situation of tigers there and the high level team fully endorsed these. However, what the high level team saw and experienced indicated that things were even worse in some places than had initially been thought. Among other issues, it was noted that anti-poaching staff in the reserves visited by the team were grossly under-equipped and that funds allocated to tiger conservation by the central government seemed to be stuck in state and provincial bureaucracies and were not reaching the field level. The team was also told of cases where 4x4 vehicles, donated by international conservation groups and charities for patrol purposes, had been diverted by field managers to their own personal use. Everywhere it went, the team heard of corruption at all levels.

It fell to me to draft the team's report and I had great difficulty in finding ways to describe diplomatically how bad some of the experiences had been. I had also been asked to prepare recommendations and suggestions. Worried that I had gone too far, I passed the draft to my colleagues, only to be told that it was not strong enough. I redrafted the document and it was published for the conference. None of the team was particularly surprised when the manure hit the air conditioning unit. India, understandably and expectedly, went on the defensive. However, what disappointed us was that the conservation organizations and tiger experts, or most of them, sprang to India's aid. The recommendations were roundly rejected and the document had to be reworked again before the conference formally accepted it. It was a perfect example of politics coming into play. However, some of the politics were bizarre and puzzling. I was particularly baffled by one country, a strong supporter of both tiger conservation and the CITES Secretariat, which chose on this occasion to object to the report. A member of its delegation quietly and informally explained everything to me. The report remarked upon the situation in one of India's states where the team had learned of a plan to reintroduce the Asiatic lion. This species of lion, once fairly widespread in India, had been reduced to a small population confined to just one state in the whole country. It was apparently intended to try and expand the lion's habitat by relocating a breeding stock into one of the states visited by the team. The team had remarked upon this, commenting that it seemed risky to introduce another big cat species when existing tiger protection efforts appeared seriously inadequate. The delegate advised me that his country's foreign aid programme had donated large sums to the lion reintroduction project. Politics and diplomacy apparently dictated that, rather than acknowledging that their aid was perhaps poorly directed, they should join in shooting the messengers.

While I do not regret what I drafted in terms of the team's opinion of the situation existing then in India, I do somewhat regret India had to be singled out in that manner. The scenario there was probably not much worse than in many other range states. Indeed, it was better than several. On the other hand, India was home to the world's largest populations of tigers and was, in many ways, perhaps the most advanced nation in terms of its economy and infrastructure. However, it was with no pleasure whatsoever that I subsequently learned that the team's concerns had been more than justified.

FROM BAD TO WORSE FOR TIGERS

In 2005, word began to spread of another 'tiger crisis' in India, one which was rumoured to be as bad, if not worse, than what had led to the creation of Project Tiger in 1973. So serious did the situation seem to be that India's Prime Minister ordered the Central Investigation Bureau, the nation's FBI, to examine what was happening. In March of that year it reported that not a single tiger had been seen in Sariska Reserve since July 2004. This national park, which was capable of sustaining up to 20 tigers, had been wiped clean by poachers. And it was just one of the country's reserves that suffered similar fates. It seemed that India, or at least some of its reserve managers and staff, had taken their eye off the ball. What depressed and frustrated me most about the whole affair was that during the technical and political missions, and in the time thereafter, I had met so many dedicated and committed individuals who seemed determined to safeguard this magnificent species and respond against those who wished to criminally exploit it. I was at a loss to understand why their efforts apparently continued to go unsupported or be rendered ineffective by poor management and strangling bureaucracies.

My thoughts went back to a training event I had co-ordinated in 2002 at the National Police Academy of India in Hyderabad. Over the course of two weeks, we brought together 28 enforcement officials from tiger range states across Asia and provided them with training in policing skills. The event made use of academy instructors but we also flew in enforcement and prosecution experts from Canada, the Netherlands and the United States. I wondered if we had wasted time, money and effort and whether the students, who had participated so enthusiastically, were also struggling back in their home territories with the same hurdles seemingly faced by enforcement officials in India. Thinking of the time I had spent at the academy brought to mind three other distinctive experiences which occurred during that fortnight. The first was the heat of Hyderabad. During several days in the middle of the course, the outside temperature reached 52 degrees C. Many people died throughout the State of Andhra Pradesh in that period. The temperatures were hardly conducive to anti-poaching patrol work.

The second related to the conduct of the training and an evaluation form that we asked all the students to complete at its conclusion. One of the questions posed was, 'What did you like most about the course?' As I scanned through the completed questionnaires, I came across a startling response. Although the forms were to be completed anonymously, the answers given by this particular student led me to believe I knew who had filled in the form. He was a man in his late twenties from southeast Asia. Most of the answers I had read to that point referred to the practical exercises or highlighted a particular subject or lecturer. What this person had liked most about the course was having his own room; each student had occupied a single bed-sitting room in the academy's accommodation blocks. It brought home to me, very starkly, what a different life is led by people in developing countries; that a government official, well into adulthood and presumably receiving a reasonable salary, had for the first time in his life been able to go to bed at night and sleep in privacy without sharing the space with other people.

The final incident also demonstrated to me how different lives and careers were for a senior police officer from Scotland and one in India. My main focal point in the National Police Academy, both whilst arranging the training course and during its delivery, had been one of its Assistant Directors. To show my appreciation, I asked him to book dinner for the two of us in Hyderabad's finest restaurant one evening in the final week. We enjoyed a very pleasant time together and our conversation ranged over a variety of subjects. As the night drew to a close I asked him why he had decided to join the Indian Police Service (IPS). 'Oh, I never wanted to be a policeman, John,' he replied. Surprised by this response, I pointed out that he had managed, for someone who apparently did not want such a career, to have reached senior rank and a very responsible position in his nation's force. 'Very few IPS recruits ever wanted to be in the police, John.' I was, by then, utterly bewildered and asked him to explain. His answer was remarkable.

He described how, in India, when men and women graduated from university and wished to work in a government post, they were obliged to sit a standard civil service entry examination. The results each entrant gained determined their career path. Those who achieved the highest marks were destined for a life as a diplomat. The choices diminished in line with poorer marks. Consequently, although policing was seen as a good job, it was somewhat down the marking ladder and the majority of entrants would have hoped for a higher score. The Assistant Director, for example, was not at all reluctant to admit that he was very disappointed when he was told this his marks entitled him, at best, to a career in either the customs or police service. He went on to say that relatively few of his classmates, when he had first entered the Academy as a brand-new recruit, had ever wanted to put on a law enforcement uniform. He also admitted that this recruitment practice was reflected in the poor motivation and poor policing that could sometimes be seen in parts of India. I do not know whether the same approach is taken in today's India but I found it astounding that such a responsible public duty could be allocated in that way. My dinner companion told me that he understood this had originally been instigated by the British colonial power and presumed I had passed through similar processes. I rushed to assure him that Scotland recruited volunteers and volunteers alone and that, aside from the civil service itself, such standard exams were not used in Britain. I cannot think why, during the days of the Raj, such a system would have been introduced. I sincerely hope the British did not use it in other countries, since it leaves behind a dreadful legacy.

Prior to the depressing news of 2005, we had already started to appreciate that the illegal trade affecting tigers was going through dynamic changes. Whereas the demand had previously seemed to be driven by the need for tiger body parts to be used in clandestine traditional medicine practices, it gradually emerged that the tiger's skin appeared to be the primary part of the animal now being traded. It was also noted that leopard and otter skins were being smuggled alongside those of tigers and seizures taking place, especially in Nepal and China, demonstrated this on several occasions. There were also very significant and very substantial seizures of big cat skins in towns in India where the tanning and treatment of animal skins, including of livestock, were traditional industries. With hindsight, the number of skins being intercepted ought to have rung alarm bells that poaching must also have increased markedly. However, no bad news was emanating from the reserves. To this day,

I do not think any meaningful explanation has emerged as to what was taking place in, for example, India's national parks and why the disappearance of tigers was not noticed sooner. It is difficult, though, to avoid suspecting that the sheer scale of poaching could only have taken place had some degree of corruption and collusion been present.

Intelligence emerging from some of the seizures often indicated the involvement of Tibetans in the skin trade. The names of people from Tibet were discovered in hotel registration paperwork in the towns in India where skins were being tanned. Some of the skins seized by the authorities were seen to bear what appeared to be signatures in Tibetan script. Skin tanners and dealers, when questioned, disclosed that traders were arriving, via Nepal, from Tibet. These individuals would inspect the skins in stock, select what they wanted, negotiate a price and, before leaving, mark the relevant skins to ensure they received in due course, once they had been smuggled out of India, what they had ordered during these purchasing visits. More pieces of the jigsaw were falling into place but the whole picture could not yet be seen. One of the significant gaps was the answer to the question, 'Why Tibet?' Although its geographical position along the smuggling chain linking India to China made its involvement perfectly logical and feasible, and there was evidence (although mainly anecdotal) that some bartering had historically taken place in which tiger bones might be exchanged for the wool of Tibetan antelope, significant commerce within Tibet itself was not really known of. The intelligence emerging from India and Nepal, though, indicated that some Tibetans appeared to be controlling the trade in a manner not encountered previously. In August 2003, I found myself staring at one of the missing jigsaw pieces but, infuriatingly, I did not appreciate its full significance.

I was in Lhasa, the capital city of the Tibet Autonomous Region in western China. I was about to complete one of the most memorable missions of my period with CITES, which had taken me from luxury hotels in Bangkok to Thimpu, capital of Bhutan, and onwards to Beijing. The primary focus of this trip had been to examine illegal trade in the wool of Tibetan antelope. From Beijing, I flew to Xining, the capital of Qinghai Province. Once there, a Chinese government colleague with whom I had spent many days during numerous visits to his nation joined me in climbing into a 4x4 vehicle alongside local wildlife law enforcement officials. We then set off to traverse the Tibetan Plateau, diverting en route to visit bases of the Forest Security Bureau whose staff were tasked with conducting anti-poaching work to safeguard the antelope. The fact that Kekexili National Park, located on the plateau, is larger than Switzerland gives some impression of the scale of the problem faced by patrol staff. The Naqu district of Tibet contains a national nature reserve which is larger than Bulgaria, Cambodia or Malawi. The reserve had 32 law enforcement officers and they had 16 vehicles. However, in August 2003, only three of those vehicles were serviceable. It took us four days to travel from Xining to Lhasa and we covered over 2,000 km. Most of the route was at altitudes between 4,000 and 5,000 metres and we spent one entire day at over 5,000 metres. Another day, due to a lack of accommodation on the chosen route, we spent over 20 hours driving before we reached a town where we could grab some sleep before moving on again. There were places where we saw Tibetan antelopes, a very rare sight for foreigners, and also construction underway to build the railway line that would eventually cross the plateau. Speeding across that terrain in a pressurized train carriage seemed very attractive, given the bone-shaking sections we crawled across in a Land Cruiser, but that mode of travel would not be available until 2006. I was just pleased to avoid the worst of the effects of high altitude, especially as there was no turning back once we were committed to the trip. There is no air ambulance evacuation from the Tibetan Plateau.

How fortunate I had been was brought home to me when we arrived in Lhasa, a mere 3,400 m above sea level, and discovered that it was not unknown for some visitors to the city to have to fly back out immediately as pulmonary oedema started to affect them. In Lhasa, I assisted at a training course that was conducted for customs, police and forest bureau officers from around Tibet. However, I also had time to visit the Barkhor area of the city. Barkhor Square has been the scene of many of the self-immolations carried out in recent years by those seeking independence for Tibet. This part of Lhasa, aside from the famous Potala Palace, is the most popular section with tourists. A one-kilometre walk encircles the Jokhang Temple, a site of pilgrimage for Tibetan Buddhists, and shops and stalls are situated all around. It was in several of these shops, which were primarily doing business with local people, that I encountered the jigsaw piece.

The traditional clothing of Tibetans, especially men, is called the chuba, a long sheepskin jacket, designed to protect its wearer against the harsh Tibetan climate. Some chubas will be decorated with colourful panels of woven silk or dyed wool, sewn most commonly onto the front. Such additions are particularly popular with female wearers. As I wandered along Barkhor, my attention was drawn to shops selling these jackets and what really caught my eye was that some of these coats seemed to have animal skin panels in them. Entering one shop, I was astounded to see a rail of jackets openly on display and that each garment had large panels of what was clearly leopard skin. The jackets also had fur trim around the collar and lapels. Bringing my poor species identification skills to bear, I struggled to think what type of fur this could be but then realized that I was looking at otter pelts. I called my colleague from Beijing across and pointed out what I had stumbled over. He seemed as shocked as I was at the blatant exhibition of endangered species. He, in turn, summoned local officials to view this spectacle. They, however, did not seem to appreciate the criminal significance of what we were looking at.

In later discussions with local officials, I learned that it was something of a tradition in times past in parts of Tibet for a brave warrior to be presented with a piece of animal skin to attach to his chuba, just as a European solider might be awarded a medal. I was told that different levels of courage might be recognized by the presentation of tiger, snow leopard or leopard skin. I gathered, however, that this had historically involved a small portion of animal skin and I asked the official to explain why the chubas I had seen had large panels of leopard skin. He was not sure but said that he expected this reflected the increasing affluence of some Tibetans and the way in which this sometimes led them to spend significant sums on items reflecting their history and culture. This theory certainly seemed to reflect what we were seeing elsewhere in China with regard to increased interest in elephant ivory and rhino horn. Before I left Lhasa, I stressed to local officials how important it was to crack down on and eliminate this trade immediately. They appeared to understand and I left with the impression that action would be taken. In the official mission report that was subsequently sent to the Government of China, I also highlighted this issue and emphasized the urgency for action, both through enforcement and public awareness campaigns. I failed to appreciate, however, just how extensive this form of trade had become and how, once again, politics would come into play.

Before 2003 was out I would learn how seriously this form of trade had escalated. In October, a customs Anti-Smuggling Bureau unit in Sangsang, Tibet, checked a truck carrying what appeared to be a load of wool. Concealed beneath, however, were 31 tiger, 581 leopard, 778 otter and 2 lynx skins. I saw a picture of the skins, which had been laid out in the large car park at the rear of the customs building. The entire area was covered. The scale of the killing, smuggling and dealing was astonishing. There was no way that species such as tigers and leopards could sustain this level of harvesting. Worse was to come. In the next few years, surveys by NGOs, especially the Wildlife Protection Society of India and the Environmental Investigation Agency, would disclose widespread sales of skins across Tibet and neighbouring provinces. The open display and wearing of chubas incorporating big cat skins were also encountered at large festival events where Tibetans gathered together to engage in cultural occasions, often involving horse racing and other displays of equine skill.

Where politics came into play was the sensitive concern on the part of some in central government that a number of those wearing such garments might be doing so in order, directly and deliberately, to flaunt Tibetan traditions in the face of what some local citizens regarded as Chinese oppression. Instead of cracking down on trade, information I received indicated that enforcement officials in Lhasa seemed to be doing little to reduce sales of animal skin garments and that these were continuing to be conducted openly. The CITES Secretariat again urged the Chinese authorities to act. I learned through informal channels, however, that government officials in Beijing, especially in the Public Security Bureau (police) and internal security agencies, were reluctant to bring strong enforcement responses to bear in case they would be interpreted, both by Tibetans and external observers, as some form of ethnic discrimination or repression. While I sympathized with their quandary, I could not help also thinking of the tigers and leopards, especially in India, which were being pushed all the closer to extinction. Eventually, the government of China settled on trying to take enforcement action against those engaged in the trade itself while introducing a scheme requiring anyone possessing skins for personal use to register that ownership. Personally, I do not believe these approaches worked very effectively and, if nothing else, left confusion among potential consumers and loopholes that could be exploited by unscrupulous traders.

What was most effective, but which really threw a political cat among the pigeons, was when NGOs brought what was happening to the attention of the Dalai Lama, in exile in nearby India. He immediately issued statements reminding his followers, and all Buddhists, that it was against the teachings of the Buddha and his disciples that animals should be exploited in this way. The response, especially in parts of Tibet, was dramatic. Large crowds of people came together and lit bonfires upon which animal-skin chubas were thrown. At some of these gatherings hundreds of robes were destroyed. Unfortunately, the nature of one or two of these assemblies appeared to be misunderstood by nervous Public Security Bureau and military officials and rumours spread that excessive force was being used to break up crowds. There were also rumours that independence activists might have hijacked some of the rallies. There can be no doubt, however, that the Dalai Lama achieved very significant reductions in the trade. A few Chinese officials have also told me informally, and they could not possibly say so publicly, that they were grateful for his intervention. I would have loved to have had the opportunity to thank him personally. As it happens, I almost bumped into him, quite literally, as he left and I entered the elevator of a hotel in New Delhi, but his protection officers hustled him away before I could speak. It was an ironic encounter, given that I was in the process of conducting a meeting there of the CITES Tiger Enforcement Task Force.

TIGERS: TO TRADE OR NOT TO TRADE?

Whilst the reduction in the sale and wearing of tiger and other big cat skins in Tibet was welcome, the crisis in India and other range states indicated that any significant recovery in tiger numbers seemed highly unlikely. As we entered the second half of the 2000s, another issue began to cause anxiety and considerable debate. The government of China let it be known that it was reviewing its complete ban on all domestic trade in tigers. In 1993, responding to pressure from the CITES community, China had outlawed the use of tiger and rhinoceros ingredients in all traditional medicine. Given the centuries-long use of such medicinal constituents, this had been a major step. Although the medicine industry acknowledged that alternatives were available, there were many practitioners and consumers who believed that both tiger bone and rhino horn were potentially life-saving components of treatments and there was considerable pressure from some quarters for trade to be resumed.

I recalled being asked to speak at an event in Beijing in 1999, organized by the Worldwide Fund for Nature (WWF), which brought together conservationists and traditional medicine practitioners. During a coffee break shortly after my presentation I was approached by a very senior figure from the association representing China's traditional medicine. He told me, in essence, that he could not understand what all the fuss was about and asked why we should be concerned about tigers in the wild. 'After all, Mr Sellar,' he said, 'we have farms where tigers breed very readily. Why do we also need tigers in the wild?' I found it difficult to answer. I think one either is happy with animals being behind bars, or in other forms of captivity, or one believes they should be allowed to run free and enjoy a natural existence. Conservationists will also tell you that the presence, or absence, of what are sometimes referred to as mega-fauna species such as tigers, is one of the best indicators of whether areas of biodiversity are healthy or not. But the conversation I had that day was a good illustration of the way in which some cultures and races have very differing views on wildlife. I saw another demonstration of this not long afterwards in Hong Kong. I had been inspecting shops selling wildlife products and was making my way back to my hotel. I passed through an area where a street market was thronged with shoppers. Most of the stallholders were selling foodstuffs. I had paused to look at a stall selling mainly fish, when I noticed that off to one side there was a large glass-sided water tank in which turtles were swimming around. As I stood there, a woman who looked like your average housewife conducting her household shopping appeared and spoke to the stallholder. She pointed to a particular turtle in the tank and he reached in and brought it out. Placing it upside down on a wooden board atop his counter, he grasped a meat cleaver and began to hack the animal out of its shell. Once clear of its carapace, he dropped the still-alive 'meat' into a plastic bag, and handed it over to the lady, who paid him. I was appalled by what, to my mind, was outright cruelty but neither the shopkeeper nor his customer batted an eyelid.

The Chinese government was not suggesting at all, in the late 2000s, that wild tigers would, or should, be harvested for commercial use. Instead, it was believed that the existing captive breeding centres would be able to supply the demand. Additionally, one proposal was that the use of tiger products would be restricted solely to traditional medicine hospitals. During the tiger technical missions in 1999 I had visited a tiger farm in Harbin in northeast China, not far from the Russian border. At that time, when the government policy remained firmly anti-trade, the facility, one of the country's largest, had become something of a public attraction and it was not being operated with any view to commercial animal production. In 2007, it was arranged that I should visit the other major captive breeding location.

This was the Guilin Xiongsen Tigers and Bears Mountain Village in Guangxi Zhuang autonomous region. It was a massive complex which presented a public image of being partly a place of entertainment and partly a form of zoo. However, behind the scenes it was very much a commercial operation in abeyance and it was also a place which was the focus of allegations by several NGOs, but also of a media investigation, that it was engaging in illegal trade involving its inhabitants. A television reporter was claiming to have witnessed tiger meat being supplied to customers in the Village's restaurant. There were many animals there. At the time of my visit, the Village contained 1,306 tigers and 210 lions. I met with the owner and spent quite some time in conversation with him as he led me around the premises. He said that the facility had been established in 1986 with the aim of breeding tigers for commercial purposes, primarily by supplying the bones of dead animals for traditional medicine. By 1993, the facility had bred 400 tigers and was regularly supplying ingredients to the medicine industry. However, in that same year the government introduced its ban on the use of tiger parts and derivatives and the company had no outlet for its products. Instead, it became a place of public interest and entertainment and apparently relied solely upon the income from visitors.

The owner explained that 117 tigers had died on the premises between 1993 and 2003 and that their carcasses had been stored in a deep freeze. However, they had all been destroyed in 2003 following a period of financial difficulties which resulted in the freezer being switched off. The destruction had apparently been overseen by government officials. Although I could understand why defrosted skins and meat might have rotted and needed to be destroyed, I did wonder why it had apparently not been possible to retain the skeletal remains. However, my task was not to look into what had occurred in times past, even if it seemed suspicious that potentially valuable items had been deliberately wasted. Since 2003, 43 tiger carcasses had mounted up and I inspected the freezer in which they were stored. What immediately struck me was that the majority of them seemed to be either cubs or juvenile tigers. I asked what had caused the tigers' deaths and was shown the facility's records. To my surprise, not being acquainted with what is involved in keeping large cats in captivity, I discovered that 75-80 per cent of deaths were recorded as being as a result of fighting between tigers. It struck me that if the aim of the facility was commercial breeding, it was not doing a very good job either in keeping offspring alive or of keeping them alive long enough to grow into adulthood, when their bones and skins might attract an appropriate financial return. It was also hard to believe, if this was a good example of Chinese tiger farms, how the current animal husbandry practices could possibly supply demand in the way that some people were arguing would be possible.

The owner told me that he had very substantial bank loans and was facing bankruptcy. He insisted that he ought to be compensated for having to close the commercial arm of his business in 1993 and had calculated that an appropriate sum would be the equivalent of 150 million US dollars. He said that he had been demanding compensation from the government for years but had received no response. I found the figure quoted incredible and pointed out that, in my limited experience of civil law litigation, I believed he did not have much of a case. He grew quite angry and asked me to justify the comment. Before doing so, I asked him to explain why, following a ban on commercial trade in tigers in 1993, he had continued, in the face of such a prohibition, to maintain his captive breeding operations. He replied that he hoped, and continued to hope, that the ban would be lifted. I observed that, in my opinion, had he sought compensation in 1993, he might have had a strong case to argue. However, putting it bluntly, I went on to say that he had essentially engaged since then in a financial gamble and, not to put too fine a point on it, he had lost the bet. He was not pleased.

The visit to the Village posed almost as many questions as it answered. I had hoped to visit an ancillary operation of the company, the production of bone-strengthening wine. I was particularly keen to see how this was conducted, as it was alleged that this product, which was sold in tiger-shaped bottles, contained dissolved tiger bones. However, when I expressed a desire to do so, I was told that this took place in an off-site location many hours distant and that it would not be possible. The owner assured me that the wine was produced using the skeletons of lions that had been bred in the Village. When I queried why, in that case, the wine was not supplied in lion-shaped bottles, he answered that the tiger shape was adopted for marketing purposes. It had been my experience that any captive breeding operation, unless very strictly monitored and regulated by the authorities, is open to unscrupulous exploitation, either by its operators or by organized crime. In the formal report that I subsequently prepared, I recommended that supervision by local enforcement officials be tightened. While not implying that I was not told the whole truth, I could not help but find aspects of the Village somewhat suspicious.

One matter that I did not raise in my report, for diplomatic reasons, was a thought that occurred to me regarding the ownership of the premises and its operations. While it seemed perfectly acceptable for such a substantial company to be in private ownership in 2007, I wondered whether that would, or could, have been the case when it was established in 1986. It seemed more likely that it would have been a state-owned enterprise at that time. Over the years, I have heard it suggested that certain government officials have a personal financial interest in tiger farms but I was never provided with any evidence of this.

The actions of certain individuals during my stay in Guilin did little to dampen my suspicions that all was not in order in relation to bone-strengthening wine. Whilst waiting for the several local and central government officials who were accompanying me everywhere, I was wandering around the foyer of my hotel first thing one morning and strolled into what I took to be some form of souvenir shop. I was fascinated to discover, though, that it was actually selling medicinal products, and had many tiger-shaped wine bottles on display.

Unfortunately, the shop assistant spoke no English and my Mandarin was not sufficient for a meaningful conversation. Looking back into the lobby area, I saw the colleague who had travelled across Tibet with me and I called him over. I asked him to ask the assistant where the bottles were produced, what was in them and what they cost. Having worked with this official over many years, I knew I could rely upon him to provide an accurate and honest interpretation. However, as the girl replied to his questions I could make out the Mandarin word for tiger and my interest rose. My colleague informed me that the bottles came from the Village we had visited and that they contained tiger bone wine. I asked him to repeat the question about the ingredient and also to ask her if she was sure that the liquor was made with genuine tiger bones. During the exchange that followed, I once again heard the Mandarin word for tiger used several times. The shop assistant was adamant that the wine in the bottles had been made using genuine tiger bones. I noticed that another government official watched and listened from the shop doorway as this conversation took place.

It was intriguing, upon returning to the hotel that night, to find that the shelves of the lobby shop, which that morning had displayed numerous tiger-shaped bottles, were now empty. A different assistant was on duty and my Chinese colleague and I spoke with her. She informed us that 'senior hotel management' had instructed that the bottles be removed. It was incidents like that, together with what I had seen in the Village, which inevitably made me wonder whether illicit trade was occurring and, further, whether it might be being condoned or ignored. The period, lasting several years, during which China's government reflected on its tiger trade ban caused a lot of consternation in the conservation community and did the country's image abroad no good whatsoever. Several conversations I had with officials indicated that they were conscious of the opposition but I formed the impression that many thought it came solely from within non-governmental organizations. I think some of them were taken aback when they subsequently discovered just how strongly some national governments around the world were opposed to any resumption of the tiger trade.

The CITES Secretariat recognized, however, that internal trade was wholly a question for China and we took no public stance in relation to whether it should occur or not. We did, however, observe that reopening trade would be such a significant U-turn in policy, especially after the years of effort which the Chinese government had put into public awareness campaigns promoting alternative medicines, that it was bound to cause confusion. Personally I believed, and still do, that any resumption of trade would be inappropriate. This may appear to clash with my views in relation to trade in ivory and I must admit that I base my opinions, to a degree, on my gut instincts. My primary concern related to the risks involved of laundering through purportedly *bona fide* captive breeding. Unlike elephant populations, the numbers of tigers in the wild are so low that it may not take much to push them over the tipping point and into extinction. From what I had personally observed, I also questioned the effectiveness of captive breeding. Like my colleagues, I was also very concerned that a change in policy could send out negative and confusing messages after a period, dating back to 1993 in China, during which the communication to the public had emphasized how terribly endangered the species was. Lastly, I had in mind that indications that it was acceptable to trade in tigers might have knock-on implications for other big cats such as leopards, and I was only too conscious of how they were already suffering. Intelligence to which I had access was indicating that lions in Africa were perhaps being poached so that their bones could be smuggled to Asia for medicinal purposes and I viewed legal bone trade as a Pandora's box.

Concerns related to the captive breeding of tigers seemed to be more and more justified in the late 2000s as seizures occurred in countries such as Thailand and Viet Nam, where either live animals or large pieces of carcass, some frozen, were discovered being smuggled across borders. It also became more common for tiger meat to be found in some specialized restaurants in the southeast and far east of Asia. Word reached me of increasing numbers of privately-owned facilities where exotic species, especially big cats, were being bred in captivity, with no apparent conservation purpose and in premises that were neither zoos nor public entertainment venues. It appeared that the motivation was commercial profit, although no legal outlet existed for such farming. It was particularly troubling when at least one of these breeding operations was linked to an individual already suspected of connections with the illegal trade in ivory and rhino horn. Although tiger poaching was still taking place, some of the seizure locations suggested that it was unlikely that the animals involved were wild tigers. The increasing use of DNA profiling by some enforcement agencies corroborated this. For example, one seizure of several tiger carcasses took place in Thailand, near its border with Malaysia. Although Malaysia remained a range state, its tigers were very seldom seen, were difficult to track down and were also very limited in number. It seemed improbable that these specimens could have come from the wilds of Malaysia. DNA profiling confirmed this when one of the carcasses was shown to be that of an Amur tiger. Whilst the tigers of the far east of Russia have the largest territories of any of the sub-species, I had yet to hear of them wandering southwest into the Malaysian Peninsula. It was yet one more piece of evidence demonstrating that captive-bred tigers were being used for illicit trade.

When the CITES parties met together for their regular conference in June 2007, the conservation of tigers received considerable attention. Indeed, I saw that non-governmental organizations seemed to band together around the tiger in a way I had not seen previously in relation to a single species. Many NGOs, but also country delegations, made plain their opposition to any reopening of domestic trade in tiger products and I doubt if China looks back on that meeting in The Hague with much fondness. (China was subsequently to announce, before the end of the decade, its decision, 'for the present', as they put it, not to reopen trade.) Despite the high profile that tigers had achieved within CITES, I remained unconvinced that sufficient political will existed in all range states to safeguard the future of the species. This was reflected in the very poor reporting rates demonstrated by some of these countries. Each had been asked to update the CITES Standing Committee on tiger conservation progress but the reports of several range states failed to materialise at meeting after meeting. To be honest, I was never wholly convinced that this reporting operation was productive and I do not think some of the reports received were particularly enlightening or helpful in identifying ways in which more progress could be made. I struggled to find constructive comments to incorporate into the Secretariat's documents for these meetings, too.

I was also running out of ideas as to how the Secretariat might do more to promote tiger conservation and, in particular, combat crimes affecting the species. What I found especially frustrating was that, unlike what often happened with trade in other wildlife, such as caviar and ivory, I received very little specific information with regard to illicit trade in tigers and I had been unable to acquire the type of informant that had proved so useful in other CITES crime types. I was left feeling that I was not contributing as usefully as I might have been and seemed stuck on the sidelines, simply offering encouragement or technical advice. Some of my colleagues in Geneva were also beginning to think that, as with sturgeon, we were perhaps engaged in a losing battle and that unless greater buy-in could be achieved from the countries where increasingly fewer tigers were roaming, it may have been to move on to other things. More than one colleague told me I was wasting my time. I was not, however, ready to give up and there was one area in which I believed that there was scope to provide constructive assistance.

One exasperating aspect of the under-reporting by range states was that it meant we had no effective overview of crime affecting tigers and other Asian big cats. We knew where some of the poaching was occurring, where some contraband was being intercepted and where some of the sales were taking place but the picture was not complete. As with other species, there also did not seem to be effective follow-up or exchange of information between agencies and countries. This could be particularly irritating when one took account of the fact that, unlike ivory, which was being smuggled intercontinentally, most illicit trade in tigers involved neighbouring countries or certainly countries within the same geographical and political region. Indeed, from the somewhat limited overlap between range and consumer states in the late 1990s, the situation in the late 2000s was that the range states had moved to become the primary consumer states as well. This seemed to reflect the socio-economic changes being experienced and enjoyed by most of Asia. It was somewhat ironic that the media and financiers sometimes referred to countries in the region as 'tiger economies'. Along with counterparts in Interpol and the WCO, I was constantly harping on about intelligence and the need for its collation, analysis, exchange and dissemination. It then occurred to me that, if operational staff needed advice on the questioning of smugglers, perhaps they also need capacity building in the field of intelligence. I set about raising funds and tried to identify an organization in the region that might undertake training for us.

Eventually, it seemed best if CITES and Interpol did this work and I organized a week-long course in Jakarta to which we invited all tiger range states. As with other specialized training I had arranged in the past, I asked countries to nominate students but stressed that the instruction would be intense and that only suitable people, in terms of their ability to receive training and later to apply the skills they learned, should be identified. Eleven of the 13 range states participated, although unfortunately representatives from the twelfth and thirteenth nations did not show up. One, although nominated by his police force, failed to get travel approval from his government while the other was unable to obtain a visa in time. The participants were generally well motivated but some struggled to cope with what was clearly a completely new and quite complex subject for them. I was also concerned whether some of them occupied positions in their home nations in which the newly-acquired skills would truly be put to good use. What really troubled me, however, were comments one student made to me as people filed out of the classroom at the completion of the course. This man, a police officer in a large city near a major border in one of Asia's largest countries, approached me and asked for advice. He explained that he and his colleagues had details of a number of people, foreign nationals, who they knew were visiting their country on a regular basis. They were convinced that illegal trade in wildlife was the purpose of these visits and desperately wanted to communicate with the police agencies in relevant countries to provide this intelligence and to ask for information about these people in return. I explained that Interpol communication channels were probably the best way to achieve this. The officer said that he already knew this but clarified that his problem was that his line manager would not allow it. He went on to say that his agency's policy, dictated by central government, was that only certain ranks were authorized to communicate abroad and only in relation to very specific crime types. Wildlife was not one of those types. The official refused my offer to address this with his government. He did, however, show interest when I explained how I could act as a confidential channel on his behalf but, unfortunately, I never heard from him again.

At the completion of the course, we encouraged the students, as something of a practical exercise, to return home and gather information relating to tiger crimes that had occurred in their nations over the course of recent years. Interpol's Crime Analysis Section offered to receive the data and bring their expertise to bear. No such analysis was possible as so little data was submitted. I was determined, though, not to be put off and the fifteenth CITES conference adopted a formal decision calling on range states to participate in another such exercise and to submit relevant information. Just over half the range states responded. It was not enough. Interpol did its best but the resulting analysis was not especially enlightening. I subsequently reported to the Standing Committee in the following terms:

> … this exercise, intended to provide an international overview of poaching of and
> illegal trade in tigers, cannot be regarded as having been particularly successful.

Looking back, I think this was probably yet another nail of frustration hammered into the career coffin of John M. Sellar.

POLITICAL WILL AT LAST?

Around late summer of 2008, I began to hear more and more about something called the Global Tiger Initiative (GTI). From what I could gather, it appeared to be a partnership between a number of conservation bodies and tiger research experts, aimed at making something of an almost last gasp push to engender commitment to saving the species. What appeared bizarre, however, was that the World Bank seemed to be closely connected to the initiative. I, like several others who had knowledge of this field, wondered what on earth tigers could have to do with the World Bank. I subsequently learned that it was the then President of the Bank who had a personal interest in tiger conservation and who apparently had scope within his mandate to bring the organization's resources, human and financial (the latter in only a limited way) to bear on worthy causes. The president intended to use his own considerable influence to generate greater public awareness of the plight of the tiger and also to reach out to senior government figures and attract political attention to the subject. He had created a small team from within his staff who might be the right people to help push the project forward. The people selected were to show themselves, over the course of the coming years, to be indefatigable in their determination to make the initiative succeed. In some respects, these people with next-to-no previous experience of species conservation achieved more than major conservation bodies had achieved over decades. I believe it was also very helpful to introduce a completely fresh perspective as conservation efforts were reviewed. However, as I had seen before in relation to other species, it appeared, despite the recognition that it was poaching and illegal trade which were driving tigers towards extinction, that the Initiative had yet to reach out to the enforcement community. Neither had any significant contact been made with the CITES Secretariat, the International Union for Nature Conservation (IUCN) or the Global Tiger Forum. The latter was an intergovernmental organization that had been established among tiger range states but which, frankly, seemed somewhat marooned at that time, affected like CITES by poor political will on the part of some range states and yet to attract all range states into its membership.

In September that year, I met with World Bank officials in Washington DC. We were joined by the Secretary General of the Global Tiger Forum and a senior IUCN representative. While I think the latter individuals, whom I had known for many years, were pleased, as I was, with the enthusiasm displayed by the Bank, they also shared my concerns that its officials may not have realized the scale of the task that lay ahead of them. For my part, I made no secret of the many frustrations and difficulties that I and CITES had encountered over many years of attempting to move tiger conservation forward and, in particular, to respond to crime directed towards the species. The Bank officials told us of the outreach in which they were engaging at senior levels of tiger range states' governments and that this seemed to be producing encouraging enthusiastic responses. Although I did not voice it at the time, I could not help wondering cynically whether this was because those governments thought that the Bank would be bringing its cheque book to subsequent meetings. One thing that did impress me was that the Bank's core team included one of the world's leading experts on tiger conservation and research. While I could not claim to know this individual well, he had always struck me as a no-nonsense person and I thought his presence demonstrated a belief that something meaningful could be achieved. I reported back positively to Geneva, albeit with some reservations.

In due course, the CITES Secretary-General met with the World Bank President and I was asked to prepare a confidential tiger enforcement briefing for Bank officials. As a result, the CITES Secretariat was invited to be the principle adviser to the Initiative on enforcement matters and it was agreed that we would also help co-ordinate assistance from Interpol, the UN Office on Drugs and Crime and the World Customs Organization. Since reference to the CITES Secretariat meant reference to me, I was to spend a considerable number of days devoted to tiger issues and trying to co-ordinate input from my enforcement counterparts in other regional and international bodies. However, I also found myself entering a phase in my career where, more than in any other, I moved from being an enforcement officer into becoming dangerously like a diplomat.

Enforcement remained my primary focus, however, and I often found myself almost the only person at meetings or conferences with any experience or detailed knowledge of this field. I recall, for instance, one of the early GTI events, hosted in Kathmandu in 2009 by the Prime Minister of Nepal, where the only enforcement community representatives in the room were me and the head of India's Wildlife Crime Control Bureau. (Despite it being recommended by a review body back in the early 1970s, it was only in 2007 that India's government finally established a multi-agency body to respond to wildlife crime.) The Kathmandu meeting followed a conference in Pattaya, Thailand, in April the same year, which its government's Minister of Environment had called to discuss wildlife crime in Asia and which brought together law enforcement officials from throughout the Association of Southeast Asian Nations. Expecting just to provide advice from the sidelines, I ended up instead being asked to take the lead in preparing a formal declaration, adopted by delegates, in which the nations committed to doing more to combat such crimes.

From an early stage, World Bank officials and the GTI partners had ambitions of convening a summit at which high-level government representatives would come together to agree upon actions to save the world's tigers. As time passed, ambitions grew and the event seemed to take on greater and greater significance. Before too long, Bank officials began to speak of this becoming a Heads of State meeting. I have to be honest and admit that I thought this was most unlikely ever to happen. I was to be proved wrong. In January 2010, the pace seemed to quicken when a ministerial meeting took place in Hua Hin, Thailand, where a UN Office on Drugs and Crime (UNODC) colleague and I helped co-ordinate enforcement-related discussions.

I was, by then, working more and more closely with UNODC. It had long been my intention to establish working relations between our two offices but, aside from occasional contact, I had never found the time to interact meaningfully and closely with my counterparts in their headquarters in Vienna. Links were overdue, however, as UNODC, especially in some of its regional and country offices, was doing excellent work in raising the profile of environmental crime, especially wildlife crime, and many of its officials were keen to do more and work collaboratively with CITES. Our combined efforts for the GTI were also pushing us together and I finally decided to take a step that I should have taken many years before.

In late 2009, UNODC agreed to host a meeting in Vienna at which I was invited to chair a coming-together of CITES, Interpol, UNODC, the World Bank and the World Customs Organization. While these agencies had all, in one way or another, had some interactions over the years, they had never sat down together and discussed joint strategies. We all agreed that each organization had an interest in wildlife crime, several of us had very clear mandates from our member countries to operate in this field and we each had specific expertise to offer to countries to assist them in combating criminal exploitation of their natural resources. It made perfect sense that we ought to combine our efforts and find ways to work more collaboratively. While the World Bank was present because of its involvement in the GTI, my purpose in inviting its participation was partly because of its interest in helping to reduce illegal logging but primarily because of its specialized knowledge in the fields of combating money laundering and in recovering stolen assets. Everyone in the room that day acknowledged that there was huge potential if we could combine forces. I was asked to continue to act as chairman and guide the agencies into what would finally emerge as the International Consortium on Combating Wildlife Crime (ICCWC, pronounced 'eye-quick'). However, the agreement reached in Vienna had yet to be endorsed by the heads of the partner agencies and a lot of work lay ahead of me before that was achieved.

In the meantime, work relating to the GTI seemed to take more and more of my time, although it also had to be fitted into the already busy schedule of my ordinary CITES duties. I was also spending considerable time with the new CITES Secretary-General, who had come on board in May 2010. Like his predecessor, he recognized the importance of combating wildlife crime and was determined to do all he could to raise its profile. He was very enthusiastic about GTI and shared my enthusiasm over the potential of ICCWC. In July 2010, tiger range states met in Bali to discuss arrangements for the summit. Although little was being said in public, World Bank officials had high hopes that this would indeed by a heads of state event and that it would be hosted by Vladimir Putin, who was then Prime Minister of the Russian Federation. It was thought that it would take place in St. Petersburg. A central theme of the Bali meeting was the preparation of a formal declaration which it was intended that leaders of tiger range states would adopt in Russia.

A draft declaration had been prepared but delegates in Bali were uneasy about the wording and some tense discussions ensued. It looked as if agreement on wording for a declaration might be problematic and concerns began to be voiced that this would not be achieved before the meeting ended. I was completely taken aback when a Russian diplomat approached me and asked that I take over the negotiations. He explained that I was well known personally to most of the participants, both because of the lead I had taken with regard to enforcement issues but also because of the years I had spent visiting tiger countries. He went on to say that I was recognized for my blunt, no-nonsense approach but that this was tempered and complimented by my being from an international treaty secretariat. The final card in his hand was that, as a senior United Nations official, I would be seen as being wholly independent. He had apparently discussed this with other governments and they also wanted me to take on the job. It seemed I had no option. Aided by one of the Bank's consultants, who also happened to be the partner of the bank's tiger expert for whom I had such respect, I set up a small working group of delegates to go over the draft declaration. However, despite working for the whole of one afternoon, it became clear that agreement would never be reached based on the existing wording. I could also sense that the group members were losing patience and wanted, too, to finish for the day and head off to a grand function planned for that evening. Calling a halt, I told everyone to go and enjoy themselves and that I would have a new draft for them to look at the following morning. The Bank's consultant and I then sat late into the night preparing what was to become the St. Petersburg Declaration on Tiger Conservation. It was a very considerable relief to us both when working group members liked what they saw the next morning. With some amendments by the group, and some final adjustments from the whole conference, the draft was agreed upon and people left Bali looking forward to the event to come.

Back in Geneva, I continued work on ICCWC, which involved more drafting, this time of a Letter of Understanding that would formally establish the Consortium. The Secretary-General and I hoped that this might be signed in St. Petersburg to coincide with the heads of state conference, which had by then been called the International Tiger Forum. It was with disappointment that we learned that the Secretaries General of Interpol and the World Customs Organization had pre-existing commitments which prevented them from joining us in Russia. Consequently, my boss and I travelled to Lyon, where we got the Interpol chief's signature on the Letter, and I carried it alone to Brussels, where the head of the WCO added his.

The International Tiger Forum took place in November and it was a bitterly cold St. Petersburg that greeted hundreds of participants. The CITES Secretary-General and I knew that the President of the World Bank would definitely be in town but we could not be so sure about the presence of the Executive Director of UNODC. A new person had very recently been appointed to that position, coincidentally a Russian. He had been the Russian Federation's ambassador to the United Kingdom and his selection to head the Office on Drugs and Crime had surprised many people. A career diplomat and civil servant, he had limited experience of law enforcement or crime issues. Colleagues in Vienna were not at all confident that he would be interested either in going back to Russia so soon and, more importantly, attending a tiger conservation event and becoming associated with wildlife crime matters. I understood that some of his advisers were perhaps recommending that their new Executive Director should not involve himself with what was still regarded as a low-priority crime type, compared with the high-profile drug, firearms and human trafficking on which UNODC usually focused. We need not have worried, as he showed considerable interest in both tigers and wildlife crime and spoke very effectively during the Forum. Furthermore, he has gone on since to regularly speak out about the seriousness of wildlife crime and how more needs to be done to tackle it. He has also become a stalwart supporter of ICCWC.

It was with considerable personal pleasure and satisfaction that I stood in a building within the grounds of the Konstantin Palace on the outskirts of St. Petersburg, a short time before Prime Minister Putin announced the adoption of the Declaration on Tiger Conservation, and watched as the signatures of the heads of CITES, UNODC and the World Bank were placed on the Letter of Understanding and ICCWC came formally into being. It was, however, the first day of the forum that, in many respects, was to be a personal highlight for me. The conference took place in the opulent surroundings of the Marinsky Palace, adjoining the grand St. Isaac's Square in central St. Petersburg. The event had been formally opened and proceedings had started when a senior official of the Russian Environment Ministry came up to my seat, situated in the middle rows between government delegations and non-governmental organizations and observers. 'The Russian government intended to surprise you, Mr Sellar, but we have just realized we need to give you some warning.' I asked what he meant. 'We are about to propose you as Chairman of the Drafting Committee of the Forum. We were not going to tell you in advance but we remembered that you will have to give an acceptance speech.' I enquired when this would happen. 'Oh, there's lots of time. It won't happen for another five or ten minutes.' Very flattered, but equally very flustered, I just had time to stumble a few words of thanks as he turned and walked away. True to his word, less than ten minutes later a spokesman strode to the podium and announced that the Russian Government wished to propose John Sellar of the CITES Secretariat to be elected as Chairman of the Forum's Drafting Committee. I was still desperately thinking about what I would say by way of acceptance and only half-heard what was being said to justify my selection, but I was deeply honoured when the speaker announced that he was confident I would be accepted by acclamation, as I was 'recognized by the international community as a man of great integrity.' A round of applause indicated that I was elected unopposed.

I cannot recall now what I said in my acceptance speech, other than expressing how honoured and privileged I felt and that I would do my utmost to be worthy of the trust governments were placing in me. As it happens, thankfully, I had no further drafting to undertake and, other than chairing a few discussion sessions, the conference passed uneventfully for me.

It was remarkable and unprecedented to be able to convene such an international gathering with a focus on a single endangered species. It undoubtedly demonstrated that political will had been garnered for the iconic tiger. The forum took place in the Chinese Year of the Tiger. The next Year of the Tiger occurs in 2022. One of the goals to which range states committed themselves was to double the number of tigers in the wild by that year. Given the breeding capacity of tigers, that could certainly be reproductively possible. Will it happen? Frankly, I would not wish to bet on it. However, the Global Tiger Initiative produced levels of enthusiasm and expressions of commitment from governments that I had certainly not witnessed during my previous decade's work on the tiger. One has to hope that the momentum which GTI generated will be maintained.

My major disappointment during the many GTI meetings which I attended was that the positive reports delivered by range states were seldom challenged. I was, at times, reminded of the Caspian Sea countries where an atmosphere of 'we won't contest your statistics if you don't contest ours' seemed to prevail. I also heard no open reference to rumours that some range states, such as Cambodia and Viet Nam, may no longer warrant that description, as it is thought that tigers may have become extinct in those nations. It was interesting to see a delegation from the People's Democratic Republic of Korea present in St. Petersburg. Historically, this country, better known as North Korea, was home to tigers. The tiger conservation community, however, seemed to decide that they became extinct there many years ago and one never sees North Korea listed as a tiger range state. In the late 2000s, I wrote to its government and asked whether it believed that it should be regarded as one. I received a reply indicating that, whilst there had not been any sightings of tigers for many years, a survey two years previously had noted tiger pug marks in a rural area. Unfortunately, it appears that North Korea's leaders have priorities other than wildlife conservation. It is not a party to CITES and I am not aware of any encouragement for international conservation bodies or individuals to conduct research there. It seems unlikely that opportunities to seek out tigers in that territory will develop in the foreseeable future. If North Korea does indeed deserve still to be classed as a tiger range state, then it will, annoyingly for me personally, be the only one that I have not had the chance to visit. Another interesting development at the forum was the involvement of countries such as Kazakhstan, which would historically have been range states and which were considering the reintroduction of tigers. As more and more suitable habitat is enclosed and encroached upon by human development, one may well have to look to countries that still have areas of wilderness, such as Kazakhstan, if a future for the species is to be secured.

I have yet to be convinced, despite the success of GTI, that the international community appreciates just how close to extinction tigers have come. It is hard to be optimistic. The war against crimes targeting tigers, as with the war against drugs, is likely to be a lengthy one, with major and minor battles along the way. But tigers cannot afford for it to be too long. If we were to win the war but lose tigers along the way, it would not be much of a victory. It would surely be a terrible indictment of the human race if our children's only chance to see a tiger was in a zoo behind bars. As I once wrote in a speech for the CITES Secretary-General, it is the poachers, smugglers and traders who should be behind bars, not the magnificent tiger.

Regrettably, one must also acknowledge that there are constant shifts in the attention of politicians and the conservation and enforcement communities. The welcome focus that benefited tigers in the late 2000s was soon to shift to other species, particularly rhinoceroses, and it is to that animal that I now turn my attention.

RHINO RACKETEERING

Although illicit trade involving caviar had certainly involved corruption, and anti-poaching staff on the Tibetan Plateau had been obliged to face violence and what is probably the world's harshest and most challenging workplace, these were perhaps nothing compared to the levels of organization and sophistication which emerged as rhinos, in the latter days of my CITES career, came into criminal focus, often through the sights of a rifle.

What rhinoceroses do have in common with caviar is that, like sturgeon, they have been around since pre-history. I was surprised to learn recently that woolly rhinos used to inhabit parts of what is now Scotland in around 25,000 B.C. It was, however, the Ice Age and not organized crime that brought about their demise. There are currently five species of rhinoceros existing in the wild. The black and white rhinoceros are both found in sub-Saharan Africa, although now mainly in eastern and southern Africa. Both species have two horns. The great Indian rhino, which has only one horn, can be found in Bhutan, India, Myanmar and Nepal. The Javan rhino, also with only one horn, is restricted solely to Indonesia and Malaysia. The Sumatran rhino, despite its name, is found not only in Indonesia, but also in Malaysia, Myanmar, Thailand and, possibly, Viet Nam. It is thought, however, that the last remaining representative of this species in Viet Nam was killed by poachers in a national park in early 2011. Unlike other Asian species, the Sumatran rhino has two horns.

All rhinos are listed in the first appendix of CITES, which means that their commercial trade is prohibited. However, the geographical populations of white rhinos in South Africa and Swaziland are listed in Appendix II. This has significant implications, to which I will turn later.

WHY RHINO HORN?

The horn of a rhinoceros, unlike the horns of many other animals, does not contain any bone. It is primarily keratin, a fibrous structure that is also the main constituent in human hair and nails. Indeed, if one burns a piece of rhino horn, it gives off an odour very similar to the smell of burning human hair. This can sometimes be a simple, but helpful, field test to distinguish real rhino horn from fake items. However, unlike hair or nails, what protrudes from the head of a rhino is so dense and compacted in nature that it is not surprising that it might be thought of and described as 'horn'.

Historically, there have been three distinct reasons why people have wanted body parts of the rhinoceros, and an additional, but less important, fourth reason. Most rhinoceros horn was probably absorbed by traditional medicine, especially Asian medicine. It has long been regarded as an important ingredient in treatments for fevers, to the point where many practitioners regarded it as potentially life-saving. I have heard of experiments where crushed rhino horn allegedly did reduce the temperature of patients who ingested it. I have also been told, however, that something like aspirin was much more effective and that the experiments referred to were inadequately or unscientifically conducted. Perhaps less well known is the belief that rhino horn can act as a highly-effective response in cases of cerebrovascular disease. It is said that, administered soon after the onset of what we would more commonly speak of as a stroke, it can reduce both the spread and degree of paralysis. Like tiger bone, rhino horn is now banned in all countries where its use was previously common. China, which had formerly been the most significant country of consumption, outlawed usage in 1993.

As recently as early 2011, however, I spoke with a representative of China's traditional medicine community who told me that she believed the prohibition had been a retrograde step and that she, and many of her colleagues, would immediately return to using tiger bone and rhino horn if the ban were to be lifted. I was often intrigued by the stark differences in the messages I received when speaking to spokespeople for traditional medicine based in Asia, when compared with what would be said by their counterparts in Europe or North America. The latter appeared to have set aside any reliance on animal ingredients such as tiger or rhino, preferring instead to use alternative plant components, whilst the former clung vehemently to the importance of historical constituents.

The second most important use of rhino horn, at least in more modern memory, was around the Red Sea and Gulf of Aden. This was focussed in Yemen, and to a lesser extent in some parts of neighbouring Oman and Saudi Arabia. On reaching adulthood, men in Yemen have traditionally been presented with a dagger called a jambiya. The dagger will be worn every day in a sheath on a belt around their waist, and forms part of Yemeni traditional dress. One quickly notices, on arrival in Yemen, that at least half the male population wears traditional dress and is consequently armed with such a dagger. The dagger is not worn, however, if western-style clothing has been adopted. A top-quality jambiya has a hilt or handle of intricate construction, with the finest known as saifani handles, traditionally made from rhinoceros horn. Historically, only the most wealthy citizens or people of social or political importance, such as judges, would have worn a jambiya with saifani handles. However, during the 1970s and 1980s, the discovery of oil deposits in Yemen led to significant socio-economic changes, especially for young people, and the demand for rhino-horn daggers increased sharply.

I visited Sana'a, the capital of Yemen, in November 2008, to try to assess any continuing use of rhino horn. The nation was at that time experiencing significant civil unrest in parts of its territory, although the emergence of what would become known as 'al-Qaeda in the Arabian Peninsula' was yet to be appreciated. It was, though, regarded as something of a high-risk destination and this required, in accordance with normal practice in such situations, that I be briefed by the United Nations Security Section upon arrival. These in-person briefings, designed to alert UN staff to potential problems and provide relevant guidance, were meant to be attended before one did anything in the relevant country. Having arrived in the middle of the night, I set my alarm so that I could phone the security office first thing, hoping to make an appointment as soon as possible and move on with the real task in hand. I found myself talking to the head of the section, who was intrigued by the purpose of my visit. I do not think UN security officials often encountered staff members combating wildlife crime. 'What sort of background do you have to get appointed to that type of work?' he asked. I gave a brief summary of my previous police career. 'For goodness sake,' he responded, 'you should be briefing me.' I was told that a face-to-face appointment would not be needed and was given some general advice, with a special warning not to travel alone in the city centre at night. 'You shouldn't encounter any problems,' the security chief told me. 'Things are pretty quiet at the moment.'

As I replaced the receiver on the bedside telephone, I heard the sound of gunfire from at least three automatic weapons in a nearby street. Thankfully, I heard and saw nothing else of concern over the course of the next few days.

Although the wearing of jambiyas remained widespread in Sana'a, I could find next to no sign of rhino-horn handled daggers. Especially during the 1990s, considerable international attention had fallen on Yemen and its citizens' use of rhinoceros horn. Public awareness campaigns, national legislation and enforcement all began to have an effect and trade reduced. The generally poorer state of the country's economy had also played a part. One significant factor had also been the issuing in 1992, by the Grand Mufti of Yemen, of a fatwa calling for a halt to poaching and illegal trade in rhinoceros horn. Since rhinos are not to be found in Yemen, the intention of the fatwa, in relation to poaching, was presumably to discourage any citizens that might have been engaged in organizing or participating in it elsewhere in the world.

I was able, twice, to tour the souk in the old centre of the capital city, where many jambiya traders were located. While there were many retail outlets, there were also several large shops where dagger manufacturing took place. Most jambiyas appeared to be bought off-the-shelf but they could also be made to order, especially with regard to the design, construction and the handle's materials. The jambiya handle, sheath and belt each make a clear statement about the owner, readily distinguishing his social standing. Traders told me that the most commonplace substance used for carving dagger handles had become buffalo horn, much of it imported from Asia. A customs official subsequently corroborated such imports. The average price for a dagger, sheath and belt seemed to be equivalent to 20-30 US dollars. Not, perhaps, a lot but still a not-insignificant sum in the Yemen of 2008.

I heard, though, that antique jambiyas, especially those with a rhino horn handle, were highly prized and might sell for tens of thousands of dollars. Trade in antique rhino-horn handled jambiyas remained permitted. Apparently, a dagger previously owned by someone important or famous might attract a huge sum. I was told, by several people, of one jambiya for which the buyer had paid a million dollars. What I did come across, repeatedly, was fraud. Many of the traders that I called upon offered to sell me a rhino-horn handled dagger and would thrust a jambiya towards me. I would be assured that the asking price, usually anywhere between 1,500-2,000 dollars, was a bargain. Not a single one of these daggers had, in my opinion, a genuine rhino horn grip. I did, however, see one handle that I would have been confident was from a rhinoceros; it had the translucence which is so striking in the authentic article. It was not for sale. A carver was altering its design, the new owner having inherited it.

The authorities were, at that time, promoting the construction of dagger handles using agates mined in Yemen, especially for high-quality jambiyas, and I saw some very impressive examples. Here too, though, the economic downturn was inhibiting this initiative.

Before leaving Yemen, I participated in a workshop convened for enforcement personnel, and traders were invited to one of its sessions. An NGO representative who was assisting, and who kindly acted as my interpreter, made some statement regarding allegations of continued use of rhino horn. In contrast to the quiet and dignified manner that I was used to seeing from Chinese and Japanese ivory traders, the jambiya industry representatives responded with utter outrage and the most incredible shouting match developed, with them demanding that evidence of their violation of the law be presented. The workshop ground to a halt and considerable efforts had to be made to stop them storming out. The sheikh in overall charge of the souk was particularly vocal, ranting at length at my colleague. As soon as he quietened, the most senior jambiya trader took over and lambasted the poor man too. Even though I could not understand what was being said for most of the time, the performances were impressive and convincing. It all seemed spontaneous and it struck me that these men were taking quite some chance, should it subsequently be shown that they were protesting falsely.

An aspect of Yemen that did worry me was its geographical location and the importance of its seaports. It struck me as, potentially, a significant smuggling transit country. Given the focus of its law enforcement authorities on civil unrest, terrorism and the piracy being conducted by Somalia-based criminals off the country's shores, I imagined that all these factors could be exploited by criminals.

Before turning to the third, and distinctive, use of rhinoceros horn, I will briefly mention the fourth, minor practices which, although of interest, do not seem to be driving poaching or illegal trade. In parts of Asia, there appears to be some demand for rhinoceros skin, although what use it is put to is unclear. In Nepal, there have been some seizures of skin when horn-smuggling cases were intercepted. In the late 1990s, whilst visiting Kathmandu in relation to tiger matters, I was told that the carcass of a rhinoceros used to feature in the coronation ceremony of the nation's kings, but the days of a monarchy in Nepal are behind us. I have heard it said that, in the Philippines, some people believe rhino horn to be an effective treatment for cases of snake or dog bite, as it draws out the venom in the former and counteracts disease in saliva, such as rabies, in the latter. As with the use of tiger bone, I remain deeply puzzled over what, seemingly centuries ago, prompted someone inflicted with a disease or other troubling physical condition to think, 'I know, what I need is a good dose of crushed rhino horn.' While necessity may be the mother of invention, surely a giant leap of faith or imagination is required before one would reach for a tiger bone or a rhinoceros horn.

The final distinct historical use of rhino horn, which I found increasingly worrying and to which I thought too little attention might be being given, related to *objets d'art*, particularly the carving of rhino horn. It seems that, as long ago as the eighth century in Japan, rhinoceros horn was being carved into a variety of objects, including ritual implements, plectra for musical instruments, knives and bowls. This would seem to fit well alongside the traditional Japanese carving of ivory. Despite what is at first sight a rough and ugly appearance and texture, rhinoceros horn, when polished and smoothed, takes on a translucent façade and lustre that matches that of ivory, jade or lacquer. It also benefits from a strength of composition that lends itself to incredibly intricate carving. It was to be in China, however, that the carving of rhino horn would reach its zenith and where it would remain popular for several centuries. It may well be that the extinction of the species in China, together with its long use in medicine, added to its interest and attraction.

As I understand it, ownership of the finest rhino horn carvings, from the earliest practice of this art form, was rigidly restricted to emperors or their closest and most senior courtiers. Rhinoceros horn bowls were particularly highly prized. This resulted from a belief that poisoned liquid coming into contact with a rhino horn bowl would effervesce and alert the drinker to the danger. From simple items, desired for their life-saving potential, such bowls evolved into magnificent works of art, with sides or bases carved into delicate patterns, incorporating detailed historical and legendary figures or tiny flowers, petals, animals or dragons. A difficulty for the antique world, and its salerooms and auction houses, was that, unlike many other items, these bowls, often referred to as Chinese libation cups, seldom bore any makers' marks and establishing their provenance and age can be problematic. A colleague in South Africa first alerted me to an auction of cups which took place in Hong Kong several years ago. The more I researched this field, the more troubled I became about the opportunities for fraud and counterfeiting. It was this which led me, as described elsewhere, to seek a meeting with Sotheby's legal staff in New York in 2011. It also took me into 1 Police Plaza, the headquarters of the New York Police Department. I had discovered that any antique fraud incidents would land on the desks of the NYPD's Major Case Squad detectives. I would not have been surprised had those officers shown me the door and told me not to waste their time. As it happened, they could not have been more welcoming, co-operative and interested, as I outlined my fears about the potential for fraud in rhino horn antiques. Indeed, they were keen to get in their car immediately and set about inspecting possible outlets with me. For the moment, though, I was content simply to brief them on the possibility of such crimes occurring. I will return later to this nagging concern, which would not leave me, but there was plenty elsewhere that warranted my attention.

It was in England in the late 2000s that a marked interest and increase in the sales of rhino horn products had already been noted among auction houses. This seemed to apply to any rhinoceros horn item. Although Chinese libation cups featured, walking sticks with carved handles and other objects all began to fetch high prices. In each case, Asian customers were observed or Asian countries were noted to be the intended destination for the items purchased. I heard of several auctions where Asian buyers bid by telephone. But it was antique whole rhino horns that were really selling furiously, again destined for Asia. Most of these had originally been acquired as hunting trophies, often by big game hunters of old. Their shipment to foreign parts could comply with UK laws, European Union regulations and with CITES. However, suspicions grew that these items were destined for the clandestine markets of Asia and the UK government began to impose tight restrictions on their re-export. Other EU member states followed Britain's example.

RHINOS IN PERIL

Feeding the demand for horn, to supply medicinal markets and for dagger handles, had led to significant levels of poaching throughout the 1980s and early 1990s. It was also a period in which civil unrest, battles for independence and military units sweeping back and forth across parts of Africa, especially eastern and southern Africa, led to the slaughter of hundreds and hundreds of rhinos, and other species like elephants, for their body parts. The military of South Africa, in particular, or what might be described as rogue groups and criminally-motivated personnel within it, was accused of substantial involvement. However, as political upheaval eased off and Asian and Yemeni markets were cracked down upon, with consumers being encouraged towards alternatives, the future for the rhino looked much brighter. Indeed, rhinoceros numbers began to creep up encouragingly. Poaching did not go away, of course, as it never does completely. Some consumers in Asia continued to insist on being treated with rhino horn ingredients, just as some customers continued to want tiger bone products. But the demand was at nothing like previous levels and the organized nature of it, especially, reduced markedly. The late 1990s and early 2000s passed with a degree of calm which enabled some populations of the animals to increase significantly. From being viewed as a base of poachers, or their controllers, and an exit point from Africa for contraband elephant ivory and rhinoceros horn, South Africa changed into a shining example of conservation. Elephant and rhino numbers there grew and grew, with places like Kruger National Park thought of as world-leading examples, visited by thousands upon thousands of local and foreign tourists. It was all too easy to think that everything in the garden was rosy. Unfortunately, the calm came before one of Africa's, and the world's, worst illegal killing and harvesting storms.

In the second half of the 2000s, rumours began to emerge of a new form of demand. It appeared, unusually, to be centred in Viet Nam. It was unusual because, while Viet Nam certainly had, like neighbouring China, a centuries-long tradition of traditional medicine use, it was perhaps not seen as quite so deep-seated there. Although, for instance, illegal bear farms seemed to operate in parts of the country, the international law enforcement community did not regard major urban locations, like Ha Noi or Ho Chi Minh City, as significant destinations for medicine-driven illicit trade. We were wrong. Looking back, as many enforcers and researchers have, it now appears impossible to pin down who or what prompted the emerging interest in rhinoceros horn. The most common story told to me related to a very senior person in Viet Nam's government who, it was said, claimed to have been cured of terminal cancer by dosing himself with crushed rhinoceros horn. It probably does not matter what started it: what mattered was that the belief appeared to spread unbelievably fast.

In November 2008, increasingly alarmed by the growing levels of poaching and illegal trade, we convened a CITES Rhinoceros Enforcement Task Force. It met in Nairobi and brought together officials from mainland China, Hong Kong SAR, Kenya, India, Mozambique, Nepal, South Africa, Thailand, Viet Nam, Yemen and Zimbabwe. Interpol and UNODC joined us, as did the Lusaka Agreement Task Force, a multi-nation wildlife crime response unit based in Kenya. Everyone agreed that crime affecting the species appeared to be escalating in an almost unprecedented fashion but that its seriousness did not appear to be sufficiently widely appreciated. It was decided that the CITES Secretariat should take the lead in spreading word of what was happening and, particularly, to stress the organized and sophisticated nature of these crimes. Although I was used to preparing CITES Alerts, distributed to enforcement agencies worldwide and intended to help them target wildlife criminals, these were usually documents of three pages at most. That approach would obviously be inadequate.

Instead, I prepared a restricted-circulation briefing document, incorporating the intelligence available to us at that time and providing a comprehensive overview of what appeared to be driving the poaching, smuggling and illicit trading. It also contained suggestions as to how these crimes might be tackled. It eventually ran to 13 pages. We distributed it to our normal CITES and enforcement focal points but also decided to send it out through diplomatic channels. We specifically asked that it be disseminated to financial and serious organized crime units, as the Task Force had acknowledged that wildlife law enforcement agencies would not have the resources or expertise to respond effectively. This clearly warranted a multi-agency and multi-national response.

In August 2009, I visited Viet Nam and met with representatives of customs, police and wildlife law enforcement agencies. Everywhere I went I took with me, and distributed, copies of training materials and the intelligence briefing, which I had specifically arranged to have translated into Vietnamese. Whilst I was generally satisfied with the various encounters I had, and the expressions of willingness to co-operate, I headed back to Geneva with the impression that the seriousness of what we faced had yet to hit home in Viet Nam. In December 2010, I was to pay another visit there, along with ICCWC partners, to assist at a multi-agency seminar where enforcement officials discussed how they could better co-ordinate their response to wildlife crimes. Colleagues from the ASEAN Wildlife Enforcement Network were also present. Illegal trade in rhino horn, not surprisingly, was emphasized. At one point, at the end of one of my presentations, I held up copies of the documents I had had translated into Vietnamese and which I had distributed the previous year. I asked for a show of hands from those who had read any of the documents. There must have been almost fifty people in the room. Two hands were raised.

In 2010, I also learned that, in certain sections of Vietnamese society, almost everyone seemed to know someone, or had heard of someone, who was using rhino horn. Although no longer regarded as necessarily a cure for cancer, more and more stories were circulating of people claiming they had entered a period of remission after ingesting horn, or that a cancerous tumour had shrunk as a result of this treatment. I was told of cancer sufferers who were travelling abroad for treatment, for instance to oncology clinics in Singapore or Thailand, where, alongside chemo- and radio-therapy, their relatives would smuggle them daily doses of rhino horn. It was no surprise, of course, that the price of horn was also jumping up apace. The amount of fake horn on offer was increasing too, along with specially-constructed dishes upon which horn would be ground down before being mixed with liquid and swallowed. These were openly on sale in towns and cities across Viet Nam. I spoke with a relative of a cancer victim who told me that he and his relatives would consider doing anything, and paying anything, to be free of the diagnosed death sentence. Organized crime was preying upon people when they were at their weakest, both physically and mentally, in the most cruel and exploitative manner.

However, any frustration I might have felt over what was happening in Asia was nothing compared to what was being experienced by those tasked with protecting rhinos. Animals in Kenya, Mozambique, South Africa and Zimbabwe were being hunted down regularly and stripped of their horns. In the Democratic Republic of Congo, rhinos appeared to have been driven to extinction. Rhino poaching was noted to be increasing in parts of India, too. But in South Africa, the numbers killed were staggering. In 2007, 13 rhinos were poached. By the close of 2008, the year's total had leapt to 83. 2009 saw 122 killed, while 330 died in 2010. Numbers increased in 2011 to 448 and 2012 ended with 668 rhinos dead. Even though the authorities were responding effectively, with 267 people arrested in 2012, the slaughter went on and on.

At one of the final CITES meetings I attended, in 2011, despite such significant numbers being affected, a conservationist described the poaching levels as 'sustainable'. This was because South Africa had the largest number of rhinos in the world and they were, for the moment, breeding sufficiently regularly and successfully to replace the numbers poached. And yet, from the law enforcement perspective, what an incredible term to use. The world's population of *homo sapiens* recently passed the figure of seven billion. Is there a 'sustainable' number in relation to murders of men and women? For what other form of crime do we think in terms of sustainability? I wondered whether there was perhaps some clue in that word as to how some people view the seriousness of wildlife crime.

South Africa was battling other forms of rhinoceros crime too, however. I mentioned earlier that white rhino populations in the country were listed in Appendix II of CITES. Because the nation's numbers of that species remained biologically healthy, at over 18,000 in total, South Africa was entitled to engage in semi-commercial trade in white rhinos. This was, however, strictly restricted to two forms of trade. Firstly, rhinos could be taken during legitimate sport hunting, in which their horns and other body parts could be retained as trophies of the hunt and subsequently exported. Secondly, live rhinos could be exported to 'appropriate and acceptable destinations'. This was intended to enable the movement of animals abroad for reintroduction or zoological purposes. In due course, rumours would emerge that some live rhinos, shipped to allegedly zoological premises in China, were having their horns shaved or trimmed and that the pieces were entering illegal trade.

It was on hunting, however, that concern started to focus. The number of foreigners arriving to hunt rhinos, and seek the horns to take home as trophies, began to rise. Since hunting licences and export permits were issued at the provincial level in South Africa, it would be some time before the central CITES authorities in Pretoria noticed that anything was amiss. In the meantime, more and more hunters arrived and the prices charged by professional hunters and sport hunting companies rose too. Although they came from a country with next to no history or tradition of big game hunting, the majority of hunters were Vietnamese. Professional hunters noted that most clients had no experience of hunting or tracking. Many had clearly never picked up a rifle in their lives. Some in South Africa's sport hunting community expressed their concerns to the authorities and related their observations. Others kept quiet and just pocketed the ever-increasing fees. There were, however, others still who recognized the huge profits to be made, turned their back on the conservation principles of their profession and actively engaged in poaching. Since they had the marksmanship skills, the ideal weaponry, tracking ability and - a massive advantage - knowledge of where to find rhinos, their impact was considerable. These gamekeepers-turned-poachers were also joined, on occasions, by the owners of some reserves and game ranches, on which rhinos were legally kept, who supplied horns to illicit traders. It was rumoured that some of these people even colluded with poachers or staged faked poaching incidents. There were also rich pickings to be made by anyone who happened to own a rhino horn and wanted to dispose of it, no questions asked. Since South Africa had always had large numbers of rhinos, and sport hunting had always been a popular national pastime, many legitimately-held horns in private ownership found their way into the hands of smugglers.

Finally awake to the substantial pseudo-hunting that was taking place, the South African authorities moved to tighten controls. In particular, they reached out to their CITES counterparts in Viet Nam and sought their co-operation and collaboration. The number of Vietnamese hunters began to drop off as movements of horn between South Africa and Viet Nam came under increasing scrutiny. Now also awake to the substantial imports of horns, accompanied by CITES documents obtained through fraudulent applications, the authorities in Viet Nam struggled to catch up. However, as so often in the past in relation to other wildlife crime and other countries, Vietnamese enforcers blamed lack of progress on legislative difficulties. They explained that their CITES-implementing law did not allow them to regulate wildlife items that had been cleared for entry into the country. Although they did visit the homes of alleged hunters, and found rhino horn trophies no longer there, they claimed to be powerless to act. Personally, I found this infuriating. To my mind, any number of criminal or customs law provisions could have been employed, from tax avoidance to import misdeclarations, from money laundering to conspiracy. It was yet another example of people with backgrounds primarily in conservation trying to co-ordinate law enforcement and combat sophisticated crime. Viet Nam and South Africa went so far as to spend months and months drafting, and agreeing upon a memorandum of understanding intended to aid collaboration and co-operation between the two nations. Since each country was already a member of both Interpol and the WCO, I could not understand why existing communication channels and means of co-ordination were not employed. I could also see that field level investigators and anti-poaching personnel shared my frustration. Several hundred horns must have left South Africa in the course of just a few years, under the guise of being hunting trophies.

While this stumbling and fumbling was going on, organized crime - not to be deterred, and certainly not willing to give up the substantial monetary returns - simply recruited different stooge hunters. Czech citizens started to apply for hunting licences, as did people from Thailand. In one fraudulent hunt, subsequently well publicised by the media, Thai lap-dancing girls from a club in South Africa were pictured, rifle in hand, standing over the carcass of a rhino which had actually been shot by their guide, wholly contrary to hunting regulations.

One aspect of the fraudulent hunting that intrigued me was the very significant cost involved, a tab which was presumably being picked up by organized crime. Individuals purporting to be *bona fide* hunters were being flown from Asia to Africa, in itself a not insignificant expense. There would be accommodation and living expenses to pay, and the fees associated with hiring guides, organizing hunts and the acquisition of licences and permits were constantly rising. It appeared not unreasonable to estimate the costs associated with some hunting trips as being equivalent to 100,000 US dollars. Some of the people posing as hunters were arriving in South Africa ready to make payments in cash, avoiding national currency controls, providing yet another possible ground for investigation in South Africa and in the country from which the traveller had come. The total sums paid seemed higher than the potential return, if and when horns could be brought back to, for example, Viet Nam and entered into illicit trade. Financially, none of it seemed to make sense. I wondered why the networks did not simply focus on poaching. It then struck me that what I was looking at was money laundering, and on a massive scale.

One of the major hurdles facing organized crime is how to spend the illicit profits gained. Sometimes these proceeds are beyond imagination. Particularly in the field of narco-trafficking, stories abound of police raids on rooms which are, quite literally, stacked from floor to ceiling with cash. Disposing of this cash, at least in a manner that does not attract the attention of the authorities, has always been a problem for criminals, which is why they engage in money laundering. Ill-gotten gains are washed through a variety of processes, often involving bank accounts in different countries. At each stage of the wash, a percentage of the money will be lost, but it is always getting cleaner and cleaner. Because organized crime groups will sometimes have so much money that they almost do not know what to do with it, even a small amount of clean money emerging from the laundry, compared with what first went in, will suffice. I believe that this was what happened in some of the pseudo-hunting. Since it was possible to obtain a clean rhino horn, i.e. one accompanied by a genuine CITES document and so one which the authorities in Viet Nam had no reason to question or legal authority to seize, it was worth investing considerable sums of dirty money to acquire it. Thinking back, it had many similarities with what the Russian mafia had done in relation to illegal trade in caviar. I discussed my views with a colleague, someone who was perhaps the world's leading expert in this field and who was, at that time, employed by the World Bank. He agreed with my assessment.

As the flow of falsely-declared rhino horn trophies slowed, the pace of poaching quickened. Regrettably, the profits to be made became as attractive to some government officials as they had been to professional hunters. Police, military and anti-poaching personnel all began to feature in the arrest statistics. So, too, did criminals who had previously specialized in cash-in-transit robberies and vehicle hijackings. The violence associated with poaching and patrolling increased. In the first quarter of 2011, 14 poachers were shot dead by law enforcement officers and many others were wounded. In what had been called the rhino wars of the 1980s and early 1990s, it was said that some countries adopted a shoot-to-kill policy for anti-poaching patrols. Politicians, park managers and enforcement agency chiefs deny that similar strategies exist today. They insist that strict rules of engagement are in place and that they expect them to be complied with. Field staff that I have spoken to confirm this. But they also admit that, in the moonlit encounters in the backwoods of a park or reserve, there exists an unspoken game plan of 'shoot first'. Each of them has seen too many colleagues seriously wounded or killed for any other response to be appropriate. As someone who, in a previous life, patrolled dark streets and entered buildings in search of sometimes violent criminals, I have some concept, albeit remote, of what these people face when they set out on their tours of duty. It is unbelievably hazardous and remarkably commendable. I know very well what it is like when the radio bursts into life and you are directed to respond. Whether the uniform worn is police black or park camouflage, those who don it undertake to react, whatever the nature of the call. Those who have not put on such a uniform can never know what it feels like. That some people put it on daily in defence of our natural resources is something for which we need to be truly thankful.

AN APPARENTLY UNCEASING DEMAND

As if pseudo-hunting and poaching were not enough of a problem, what was taking place far from the parks of Africa or Asia demonstrated that the demand for rhino horn appeared insatiable. It seemed, for every finger pushed into the leaking dyke of rhino horn supply, another breach would occur elsewhere. As countries tightened up controls and rejected applications for permission to move antique horn trophies obtained at auction houses and hunting fairs, organized crime groups spread their tentacles further. Taxidermists' premises were broken into and horns stolen. A store housing elephant tusks and rhino horns in a national park in South Africa was robbed at gunpoint. Auction houses and antique dealers' properties were broken into. Museums were burgled; in one incident, security staff had tear gas sprayed at them. In Europe alone, 82 horns were stolen during 2011, together with other rhino carvings, including Chinese libation cups. A stuffed rhinoceros on display in a natural history museum had its horns cut off. During 2012, many museums in Europe began to replace with replicas any horns on display, either on taxidermy specimens or mounted separately. Police issued warnings to zoos to guard live rhinos.

Intelligence indicated that people of Asian origin were touring Europe, Canada and the United States, seeking out possible sources of old or new rhinoceros horns. Examples of fraudulent and forged CITES documents were uncovered. Members of Irish organized crime groups appeared to latch on to the potential for profit and several horns were intercepted by customs as they were smuggled into Eire. Smugglers were intercepted in various parts of Asia as they returned from picking up horns in other parts of the world. Several of these couriers were transporting up to eight horns at a time. China, Thailand and Viet Nam began to make more interceptions at their borders. Some of these detections indicated that China was re-emerging as a consumer destination. It became increasingly common to see rhino horns concealed within contraband shipments of elephant ivory.

Innovative and imaginative use of DNA profiling spread, to help link seized horns with poaching incidents and to help uncover false claims of legal origin.

A number of prosecutions, particularly in South Africa, resulted in penalties that ought - one would have hoped - to have acted as a deterrent. One Thai national, accused of organizing pseudo-hunting and illegal trade in horns, was sentenced to 40 years' imprisonment. Gaol terms of between eight and twelve years were handed down on a number of poachers. Assets of a value equivalent to over 6 million dollars were confiscated from three people within an organized crime syndicate. However, the rhino racketeering was relentless. What did not help was when members the judiciary seemingly failed to appreciate the serious criminality involved. In March 2013, two brothers were fined 500 euros for trying to smuggle eight rhino horns into Ireland, even though the value of the contraband was estimated at half a million euros.

What struck me as bizarre throughout all this was that, if rhino horn truly was an effective response to cancer, why were major pharmaceutical companies not rushing to bring out products with such ingredients, or synthesizing alternatives? It seemed that my incredulity was not shared by sufferers, however. In April 2011, whilst attending a workshop in China relating to snake trade, I encountered a representative of the traditional medicine trade and discussed rhinoceros horn with her. She confirmed that there was no history of it having been used as a treatment for cancer. In that case, I suggested, would her association be willing to help the CITES Secretariat in promoting the fact that it was not effective as a cure? She declined, saying that any such statement would be inappropriate, since the association had never conducted research into its efficacy for cancer and that it might actually prove to be effective. During our conversation, she, like others before her, told me of how effective she believed it to be for stroke victims and bemoaned its prohibition. This exchange came to mind, a few months later, when a delegate to a CITES Standing Committee meeting proposed conducting research which, he hoped, would demonstrate that ingesting rhino horn, in response to disease or other medical conditions, is as useful as chewing one's own nails, given that the same constituent is in each. I questioned whether such a finding would actually have any useful influence on consumers. Belief in traditional medicine is so ingrained in some parts of the world that it is almost religious in nature. To my mind, telling a traditional medicine practitioner or consumer that there is no scientific evidence to justify their belief that rhino horn is valuable in responding to cerebrovascular disease is like telling an evangelist that there is no scientific evidence to demonstrate the existence of God.

Focussing on prevention rather than cure, the managers of some parks and reserves in Africa have instigated de-horning among rhinos in their areas, believing such animals will not be attractive to poachers. Personally, I question the effectiveness of this and I am aware that many others, in both conservation and law enforcement, do too. While the horns of a tranquilized rhino can be relatively easily removed, and this seems to cause no more harm to the animal than we cause to ourselves when we trim our finger- or toenails, some small part of the horn will be left in place. Poachers have been known to kill animals even for what is left behind. Given the current demand, even small quantities of horn are valuable. At night, when most poaching occurs, the hunters may not see that an animal has been de-horned. I have been told that some poachers, on encountering a de-horned rhino, will go ahead and kill it regardless, as it saves them wasting time in future, tracking the same animal to no useful purpose.

One reserve manager claims to have inserted into the horns of his rhinos a toxin that is poisonous to humans but not to rhinos. Large signs around the perimeter of the reserve proclaim that the horns contain poison. I believe this approach to be pointless. As we have seen from repeated examples in the field of narcotics trafficking, organized crime could not care less if adulterated drugs find their way into the marketplace. Many addicts have died through injecting, or otherwise ingesting, toxic substances, believing them to be genuine heroin, for example. I see no reason why the groups and networks that control the illicit trade in rhino horn will care any the more if toxic horn were to reach consumers in Asia. In any case, given the small quantity of horn that constitutes a daily dose, I imagine an individual rhino horn would have to be so laced with poison, to offer deterrence to human consumers, that it would be bound to spread into the animal and affect it negatively.

It was inevitable that someone, at some point, would suggest that the answer to all these problems would be simply to legalize trade in rhinoceros horn. Such proposals began to be voiced in around 2008. Proponents argue that since rhinos can be de-horned, owners should be allowed to do so, and to sell the horn to consumers. It appears that the government of South Africa is considering this approach. One wonders whether there is any link between the major crisis presently facing South Africa and its offer to host the next CITES Conference of the Parties, scheduled for 2016. Several questions have come into my mind when considering the legal trade option:

- Will there be enough horns to meet the current demand, which presumably may continue to increase, especially if prohibitions on consumption were to be lifted?

- Could demand be met if the nature of the demand alters, moving, for example, from crushed horn, which requires small amounts to be taken from a whole horn, to a desire to possess whole horns as status symbols?

- Presumably, if legalized, prices for horn will lower. If so, will the trade be financially viable?

- While South Africa might, in terms of the Convention, argue that it could regulate exports in a sustainable manner, which are to be the importing countries? It takes two to tango and, at present, no country in Asia allows legal domestic trade in rhinoceros horn. Unlike the situation with elephant ivory, there are no assessed, authorized or regulated domestic markets elsewhere in the world to which traders in South Africa could sell trimmed horn. By early 2013, no Asian country and no nation elsewhere in the world had announced its interest in resuming legal trade in rhinoceros horn

- If I were a criminal in Asia, might I not wish to undercut trade from Africa and kill rhinos in my own area instead? Given how close some rhinoceros populations in Asia are to the extinction tipping point, this would require very careful consideration

However, what resonates with me most is that there seems something almost immoral in legalizing this trade. Its purpose, if the efficacy of rhino horn as a medicine is as questionable as it currently appears, would be to sell a non-peer-reviewed treatment to victims of one of the world's most debilitating and fatal diseases, a treatment that would do them no good whatsoever. The fact that rhinoceros horn may, on occasions, have something of a positive, placebo-like impact on a cancer sufferer is surely no justification for making it available to others. I am also troubled by the unspoken undertones in these discussions, involving one part of the world supplying another, which, to my mind, might be seen as straying perilously close to discrimination or, at worst, racism.

IS AN END IN SIGHT?

Regrettably, I see none. Although appreciation of the seriousness, organization and sophistication of crimes affecting rhinoceroses is now much more widespread, rhinos continue to be killed. The numbers poached seem set, as I write this in 2013, to outstrip the totals of previous years. One hopes that the days are long gone when an intercepted smuggler, carrying five rhino horns between Africa and Asia, was allowed to proceed on his way, customs officers having confiscated the contraband. And yet that occurred as recently as 2008. The follow-up to interceptions or the exchange of information between agencies, nationally and internationally, appears at times as dismally inadequate for rhinos as it has sometimes been for elephants, tigers and so many other endangered species.

I remain concerned at the potential for fraud within the antique world. There is clearly a legitimate trade in antique rhino horn products, especially Chinese libation cups. Although some of these products and old trophies, sold through English auction houses, for example, were undoubtedly intended for clandestine purposes, the prices paid for others were far too high for them to be crushed down into powder for medicinal use. This, in itself, is what makes me anxious. As I mentioned before, organized crime has many tentacles and they stretch far and wide. Their aim is to seek out every crevice or corner where another situation can be exploited for profit. Experience has shown us that items carved from fresh elephant ivory have been disguised and passed off as antiques and subsequently sold at high price. Personally, I believe it is only a matter of time before the counterfeiting of antique rhino horn items is uncovered. The very significant increase in both the value of, and interest in, Chinese *objets d'art* offers criminal exploitation opportunities. It was, however, when I learned that a single rhinoceros horn libation cup had sold at auction in the United States in 2010 for over 900,000 dollars that I became utterly convinced: it can only be a matter of time before fraud is detected.

During the period since my retirement from CITES, I have read that crushed rhino horn is now being taken in parts of the southeast and far east of Asia as a treatment for a hangover. Some horns are apparently also being acquired as a status symbol for their owner, just as some buyers seek a tiger skin for display in their homes or offices.

As I prepare to move away from species-specific issues, I am conscious of another concern which has long troubled me. The consumption of wildlife has, over the whole of man's existence, taken a myriad of forms, with many different demands and motivators. Some of these have almost been like fashions, emerging for a period and then drifting away. Who could possibly have predicted that rhino horn would one day be thought of as a cure for cancer? Importantly, who can predict what bizarre or unexpected demand might suddenly appear next?

It is this history of use and abuse which convinces me that we must halt our current species-specific approach. We must stop thinking of wildlife crime but think, instead, simply of crime. If we do not, then we will constantly be running to catch up, as we have done in relation to elephants, rhinos and tigers, whenever some new illicit demand presents itself and begins to drive yet one more species from the conservation-concern category into one of extinction-endangerment.

My very last act as CITES Chief of Enforcement was to finalize an update of the briefing document I had prepared following the first Rhinoceros Enforcement Task Force meeting in 2008. I had convened yet another CITES Enforcement Task Force meeting in May 2011, this time to examine crimes affecting both rhinos and elephants. The same frustrations were voiced that had been expressed almost three years before. We all, once again, recognized that no new wheels needed to be invented. Participants acknowledged that many of the pledges made in 2008 - to increase the exchanges of intelligence and information, to collaborate and co-ordinate better than before - had not been fulfilled. One of the few positives that came from the meeting was that our understanding and overview of some aspects of poaching, smuggling and trading had improved. It was agreed that the 2009 CITES Secretariat briefing document should be updated and re-issued.

As I left my office for the last time, in September 2011, the document had been completed but had yet to be distributed. It had grown from 13 to 19 pages in length. All I could do was hope that it might be more helpful, and more widely read, than the first edition seemed to have been.

WHAT MIGHT WE DO BETTER?

It is all very well for me to carp about what some national law enforcement officers may or may not be doing, but I would certainly not wish to give the impression that there is no scope for improvement in what the international community has done. Indeed, at both the national and international level, I believe we should reflect on existing practices and consider whether new tactics might be more successful. While I am a firm fan of the 'If it ain't broke, don't fix it' approach, it is very rare in life that we cannot learn from what is happening elsewhere.

I think many of the international bodies engaged in conservation or law enforcement assistance have done, and continue to do, excellent work in the field of capacity building and some of the materials developed are of the highest standard. It is increasingly common to see training resources produced, not just in the six official languages of the United Nations, but also in the local languages of those at whom they are directed. Delivery methods are, today, much more regularly inventive and attractive. Interactive, computer-based training is much more commonplace and, thankfully, it is less usual to find students having to listen to a lecturer reading out the text from PowerPoint presentations projected onto a screen. Several agencies offer online courses which can be accessed by enforcement officers many thousands of miles away. Few agencies, though, seem to have developed materials for, or spent time reaching out to, the line managers who determine how the on-duty time of the student is spent. Neither, in my opinion, has sufficient effort gone into convincing the policy makers and priority setters in the law enforcement community of the need for their staff to receive specialized training or, indeed, even of the need for their agency to respond to wildlife crime. I believe that specialized training, certainly in the past, has been delivered inappropriately or has been inadequately targeted.

Although I received instruction in interview techniques at the Scottish Detective Training College, it was a skill I developed watching colleagues questioning suspects and in the hundreds of interviews I subsequently conducted myself. By their very nature, it is next to impossible for international agencies to provide the on-the-job training that actually fosters the skills people need. A few - but to date very few - governments have tried to address this gap by embedding experienced officers in developing country agencies for several months at a time. Exchanges of personnel between countries can also help in this area and there seems scope for these two approaches to be extended and used more often. As a detective involved in general crime investigation, I required an appreciation of the issues connected to money laundering but I did not need intensive training in the subject. Neither does a wildlife law enforcement officer, but he does need the assurance that there will be a response from specialists in this field, in his country's financial crime unit, for example, when he seeks assistance. Both general awareness raising and the specialization of training need to be targeted appropriately. It is reasonable to predict that a customs officer stationed at a major cargo airport will encounter and be asked to regulate legal trade in wildlife, since much of it is transported by air. The same officer is much less likely to encounter trade involving hazardous waste; it will be a colleague stationed at a seaport who will do so, as that moves around the world on container vessels. A blanket approach to training those two officers wastes their time and the time of the delivering agency.

While I found the United Nations and its agencies to be staffed by intelligent, dedicated and impressive individuals, it was noticeable that officials with extensive, practical, hands-on experience were in something of a minority in the offices with which I regularly dealt. Backgrounds in civil service, diplomacy, law, academia and research are much more common and UN recruitment policies and processes favour such applicants. That is all very well, but it does mean gaps in the bridge one hopes may be built with those working on the ground. Graduates in law have much to offer in the field of international relations and the activities of inter-governmental organizations but, if they have never seen the inside of a court of criminal law or come face to face with a criminal, their grasp of enforcement issues is likely to be very limited. And if one doesn't understand the situation on the ground, particularly the problems faced by those attempting to enforce the law, it is next to impossible to design effective responses and identify ways to support the enforcers. After two decades in policing, it might have been tempting for me to think that I had nothing further to learn. I knew nothing, though, of on-the-ground enforcement in, for example, Bangladesh, Bhutan, Botswana or Brazil and so, wherever possible, I spent time with officers on patrol or engaged in operations. To my mind, too many UN officials spent their time in meetings and I encountered several, some of whom had worked for the organization for many years, who seemed to have little interest in visiting the frontline. I perhaps took it too far - by crossing the Tibetan Plateau, for example - but there is simply no other way to appreciate the harshness of that environment for patrol staff unless you set foot in it. My twenty or more years of police experience opened the doors to the offices of customs, police and other enforcement agencies around the world because, regardless of where they worked or what the local dialect was, the people behind those doors and I spoke the same language. United Nations agencies need to recruit more people who 'speak' enforcement.

I believe it is also important that international agencies tailor their support to provide the widest possible benefit. When I made the initial designs for the ICCWC training on the management of controlled deliveries, for example, I tried to stress that these techniques could be used to respond to the smuggling of any manner of contraband, not only of wildlife. If we get things right for protecting tigers, many other species will be safeguarded too. If we can improve the questioning of wildlife smugglers, the interviewing of drug mules ought to be enhanced as well. Training should pass from external instructors and into the curricula of national academies and colleges. The support which is available, and which needs to be brought to bear, has to be 'sold' to law enforcement managers, ideally as part of a package which they will recognize as building the overall capacity of their agencies. For far too long, wildlife crime has been seen as something on the sidelines of general criminality. It must, instead, be treated as being part of mainstream crime. While I understand why some countries have been prompted to introduce special environmental courts, to handle prosecutions brought against offenders and also sometimes to help bring these out of the horrendous backlog of criminals cases in many judicial systems, this approach risks reinforcing the impression that natural resource crimes are somehow different from other crimes. And it is that impression which, to a significant degree, in my view, deters enforcement agency managers and, especially, the managers of specialized organised crime units and units dealing with money laundering, financial crime, technical surveillance and cybercrime from paying attention to them or allocating resources to investigating them.

I have mentioned elsewhere my opinion that we should avoid focussing too much on wildlife crime legislation, both nationally and internationally. I know of no country in the world where such laws provide sufficient powers, penalties or authority to enable investigators, and subsequently prosecutors, to respond adequately to organized natural resource crime. Yet almost every nation on earth has criminal statutes intended to allow enforcement bodies to bring offenders to justice who have engaged in criminal conspiracies, racketeering, smuggling, tax evasion, the corruption of public officials or the laundering of illicit financial gains. The United States Department of Justice, among the world's prosecution authorities, is probably the one that most regularly achieves significant financial penalties and terms of imprisonment when it brings wildlife offenders before its country's federal criminal courts. It places relatively little reliance, however, upon America's Endangered Species legislation, enacted to implement the CITES Convention. Instead, it uses mainstream criminal law statutes and provisions. I have often heard its prosecutors explain that, aside from powers and penalties, this approach also makes it much easier for them when they have to address a judge or a jury. Trying to help a jury understand the complex provisions of international treaty law governing trade in fauna and flora is not easy. On the other hand, no member of a jury has any difficulty in recognizing what is meant by terms such as 'smuggling' or 'conspiracy' and, importantly, they immediately recognize such terms as being associated with serious criminal behaviour.

Unfortunately, the lack of awareness of serious wildlife crime, within some government agencies in particular but also among several inter-governmental bodies, meant, at least until relatively recently, that others were often moved to step in and offer support. In several countries in Africa and Asia, wildlife law enforcement is propped up by NGOs and foreign aid. Historically, next to no wildlife law enforcement would have occurred in some countries had it not been for NGO support and lobbying. The non-governmental organization community, as a whole and also individually, has a vital role to play. Its research, market surveys and in-house expert knowledge of species and trade are strengths upon which government agencies can, and should, draw. I have, however, occasionally watched in horror as media footage pictured NGO personnel participating in law enforcement operations, even physically conducting searches of homes, vehicles and people. There must be a clear distinction between support, the provision of expertise (which may, at times, justify a presence during operations) and actual hands-on enforcement. It is one of the reasons why some of the covert investigations conducted by NGOs occasionally troubled me and I have seen instances in which the evidence uncovered, or the manner in which it was discovered, would be wholly inadmissible in a court of law. What often irritated me most, however, was that NGOs were, not infrequently, doing the work of law enforcement agencies. Indeed, some governments and their enforcement departments appeared almost to abdicate their responsibilities to NGOs in what I regard as a shameful manner. This, too, appeared to reflect the lack of interest in wildlife crime from on high and the manner in which such crimes were seen as separate from general law enforcement duties.

I think there is considerable scope for donor agencies also to reflect upon how they deliver aid in the realm of wildlife law enforcement. In my opinion, too much is channelled through NGOs or directed to be delivered by NGOs. By way of comparison, there are several examples of western governments providing financial aid and human resource assistance, especially in capacity building, to help developing countries to combat trafficking in narcotics. Such support is also provided to help particular nations rebuild policing after major civil unrest or war, usually in the form of instructors, seconded police officers or sometimes retired officers. That the same approach is not taken when attempting to build wildlife law enforcement capacity seems, again in my opinion, to push the issue onto the sidelines and into the lower priority categories. I have, in the past, described the involvement of NGOs as something of a necessary evil. It was a somewhat tongue-in-cheek comment and I do recognize that it was unfair. I enjoyed very close working relations with many NGOs and with many individuals in the NGO community. I have considerable respect for many who have devoted large parts of their working lives, and in some cases their whole lives, to the cause of endangered species, and I include those people who may think of themselves more as conservationists than employees of an NGO. But surely we should all work towards a time when NGOs will not need to support law enforcement so closely, just as we should work towards the time when no species needs to be listed on Appendix I of CITES. I acknowledge, however, that the former goal is perhaps more achievable than the latter.

Since it is probably the only basis from which I am qualified to comment, it is to be expected that my focus throughout this book has been almost exclusively on law enforcement. However, over the years but increasingly recently, I think that we have tended to fall into a trap when considering responses to illegal trade in wildlife: we have focussed too much on enforcement, in the sense of targeting criminality. (For the purposes of this discussion, I set aside prohibition of trade or other forms of bans.) We seldom give enough attention to regulation. I am thinking here mainly of domestic regulation, since cross-border regulation is so difficult, due to the sheer volume of goods and cargo nowadays and the focus on national security and terrorism. It has been shown, time after time, that large amounts of illicit goods which have either been harvested illegally within a country or imported illegally, are openly on view and for sale.

Effective regulation ought to make significant inroads towards eliminating this. I have seldom seen routine and efficient regulatory inspections being conducted at markets, manufacturers, or individual retailers and producers. Where it does occur, it is often conducted by municipal or federal civil servants who have few identification skills and little knowledge of wildlife trade. Effective regulation is also required of the many captive breeding and artificial propagation operations and which may be used to launder illegal-origin specimens. The regulators themselves must also be regulated, of course, since corruption and collusion seem so prevalent in some parts of the world.

Effective trade regulation may also provide us, in appropriate cases, with better opportunities to return specimens to the wild, if they can be intercepted before leaving countries of origin. It should, moreover, bring about increased revenue gathering and encourage and facilitate legal and sustainable trade. Additionally, I hope, it ought to lend itself to poverty alleviation by providing for some of the revenues and profits to pass to those engaged in lawful harvesting. Legal and sustainable trade in wildlife provides a vital source of income to many people in rural communities throughout the world. CITES, I found, is commonly thought of within the law enforcement community as a treaty that prohibits trade in wildlife. It is vital, however, that it is recognized as a convention aimed at controlling trade and ensuring that lawful trade is facilitated and regulated, just as crucially as illicit trade is detected, intercepted and penalized.

If enforcement is often emphasized, the other subject to receive regular attention is demand-reduction. This undoubtedly has a part to play in any response to crime, of whatever nature. Perhaps the finest example of this during my police career was in the realm of drink-driving. As a young constable, I very regularly arrested drivers who had had too much to drink before they climbed into their cars. I recall several occasions when, having pulled over a suspect driver, I would find that they could hardly stand when asked to leave the vehicle; I recall one man who, having opened the driver's door, fell out of the car at my feet. Thankfully, this is much less common today. While drivers who prove to be over the statutory alcohol limit are still intercepted, it is now socially unacceptable to engage in drink-driving in many parts of the world. Although enforcement, including the widespread introduction of roadside breath-test devices, mandatory periods of disqualification and substantial fines, played a part, most people agree that it was public awareness and public education campaigns that really made a difference. I am not persuaded, however, that the same may be achieved so readily in relation to the consumption of wildlife.

The CITES Secretariat, at least during my service, had little public awareness material or other literature explaining the Convention. We struggled to summarize the CITES provisions in simple and easily understood language. Like any law, the Convention has exceptions and exclusions, some of which are generally applicable, while others apply only in certain or specific circumstances. Even fitting the full title of the Convention onto a promotional sticker or poster was problematic. I confidently predict that many people around the world would recognize the initials WWF as relating to the well-known wildlife and conservation charity but few would understand CITES. We found it nearly impossible to encapsulate a simple message without implying that either all wildlife trade was legal or that all wildlife trade was unlawful. I have seen some startlingly impressive campaigns carried out by governments and NGOs, several of which incorporated messages from well-known celebrities and figures from the world of sport. One Thailand-based NGO was particularly skilled in this realm, to the point where it was able to have educational videos shown on the screens above check-in desks at Bangkok International Airport, where they alternated with flight information. But the majority of these campaigns have tended to present a generally anti-trade message.

Of course, it does not always go as planned. Almost two decades ago, a certain country tried to influence its Asian ethnic communities to turn away from traditional medicine, particularly those products with tiger or rhino horn ingredients. The campaign failed because those behind it mistakenly emphasized the use of tiger or rhino body parts as aphrodisiacs, the truth being that, historically, those animal ingredients have primarily been regarded as responses to debilitating medical conditions. The intended target audience was offended by the implications that they and their ancestors consumed such products for sexual purposes and paid the campaign little notice.

My own attempts to enter this realm were not particularly successful either. About halfway through my time in Geneva, I was looking for ways in which we could improve the regulation of legal trade in ivory while dissuading potential customers from purchasing ivory from illicit traders. At that time, the presence of unregulated ivory markets in Africa, even in countries where the sale of elephant ivory was meant to be totally prohibited, was being increasingly recognized as encouraging poaching and smuggling, while the illegal trade of ivory within African elephant range states was, in some instances, more significant than in certain marketplaces in Asia, historically viewed as the root of the problem. One day, I had what I thought was a brilliant flash of inspiration. Recognizing how important the game of soccer is throughout most of Africa, and noting how several of the English Premier League football clubs' stars were of African origin, I wondered whether it might be possible to convince them to participate in some form of public education campaign. Judging by the number of English team football shirts that I saw worn by young and adult men in countries across Africa, it was obvious that these football greats had not been forgotten because they had moved to a different continent. I hoped they might want to help spread the message not to buy illegal-origin ivory. What was particularly appealing about some of these soccer giants was that they came from Francophone nations in West and Central Africa and could send the message in the appropriate language. I telephoned the public relations offices in three of the major English football clubs. When I outlined what I proposed, there was immediate enthusiasm, despite my stressing that I was calling from a UN organization, which meant that we would not be offering payment to the players. Each club representative agreed to speak to the relevant players or their agents and promised to call back. Two of them did. Both apologized that it would not be possible to move forward. Both public relations officer had the same explanation: the player's agent was demanding that a substantial fee be paid. The third club, despite my leaving reminders and attempting to make contact, never called back. I have often wondered whether the agents even troubled to ask the players' opinion on my proposal.

Aside from these negative experiences, I am wary about how much can be achieved in some areas of wildlife crime. I think we must be particularly careful to draft any messages to consumers very carefully. Some of the most eye-catching campaigns I have seen in the past have tended to give the impression that all trade in wildlife is wrong, both morally and legally. Apart from the fact that this over-simplifies the message, I also believe it to be inappropriate. As I explained earlier, I see little reason for an outright and total ban on the sale of ivory. I do acknowledge, though, that there is undoubtedly a place for education campaigns relating to the trade. Where I believe we will face our greatest hurdle is in reaching those people, and there must be many of them, who are currently customers in the highly clandestine markets for wildlife and wildlife products. I have in mind, for instance, the individuals in China who have, since 1993, continued to demand and presumably pay significant sums for the 'real thing' in terms of medicinal products with tiger ingredients. These are people who know very well that they are committing a crime every time they visit their black market traditional medicine practitioner. The two decades' worth of encouragement to use alternatives, alongside the seizures, arrests and prosecutions conducted during the past twenty years, have seemingly done nothing to discourage such consumers. I predict that it will be as difficult to alter their purchasing behaviour as it will be to deter the Vietnamese people suffering from terminal cancer who, along with their relatives, are currently willing, money for the dealer in hand, to clutch at the slightest straw in search of a cure or remission.

Considerable focus in the design of awareness campaigns is often placed upon educating children. I accept there is great value and potential in forming views and attitudes in young people, which one hopes will remain with them for the rest of their lives. I think, however, that recent experiences may have shown that campaigner-implanted impressions, thought to be deep-seated, may later be discarded. For example, I imagine there will be consumers out there who, having reached adulthood and found themselves financially secure in Asia's growing economies, have begun to show interest in their nation's culture and history and have become, perhaps to their own surprise and almost overnight, the buyers and owners of ivory carvings in a way unimaginable a few years ago. I think, too, of the young men and women of Viet Nam, presumably well-educated and well-informed, who nonetheless are allegedly willing to buy and swallow crushed rhino horn as a hangover remedy. It is sometimes the sheer act of engaging in an illegal activity that makes it attractive to some in society. I recall, for instance, rumours that circulated in the early 2000s describing parties among the jet-set and fashion leaders of London and Paris, at which young merchant bankers and successful entrepreneurs served illegal-origin caviar, much as the next party host might serve cannabis joints or lines of cocaine. I suspect it may be difficult to design campaigns that will reach this kind of foolish individual.

So what might we do better? I believe an interesting development in policing in recent years has, potentially, much to offer, especially as its central theme is based around that very question. I have in mind the cold case, a term used by the law enforcement community to describe a crime which remains undetected. Increasingly, in recent years, it is also commonly associated with the reviews conducted by enforcement agencies to determine whether anything can be discovered which might identify the perpetrator, perhaps using techniques developed since the crime was committed, or else assessing how the original investigation was carried out and learning lessons that may improve current approaches.

I have repeatedly expressed my frustration at the failure to exchange information between relevant agencies at national, regional and international levels. This leads to inadequate investigations but also means that, usually, only one agency's perspective will have been brought to bear on the incident in question, be it a poaching, smuggling or illegal trade case. It also, though, means that the information and intelligence which could be extracted from the case has not been used to consider strategies that could lead to preventing, or solving, others. In my opinion, we ought to consider this information and intelligence as data which can be captured, and it ought to be possible to capture the data retrospectively, through the cold case approach.

Were that to be done and the data mined effectively, a greater understanding could be obtained of elements such as:

- How poachers and illegal harvesters of wildlife are identified, recruited and paid. (Illegal harvesting is taken in this context to include marine and plant species, especially timber, and also live animals)
- How poaching and illegal harvesting operations are planned, targeted, funded, equipped and conducted
- How the specimens obtained during such operations are treated and prepared for shipment and who is involved in these preparations
- How wildlife smuggling is planned, managed and funded, including how the modes of transport and concealment are chosen and the routes and ports selected
- How import of contraband is achieved at the final destination
- How the wildlife is processed, prepared, distributed, delivered and marketed to consumers
- What uses the profits made are put to and what level of money laundering takes place
- What role, at each stage, is played by organized crime, either directly or indirectly
- What involvement there is, at each stage, of any corruption of officials

This, in turn, would allow for strategies to be designed to:

- Prevent poaching and illegal harvesting
- Combat exploitation of communities living in areas of relevant biodiversity, which may involve alternative employment or poverty reduction policies
- Improve operations against poaching and illegal harvesting
- Target post-poaching activities conducted in countries of origin and reduce opportunities for contraband wildlife and wildlife products to exit those countries
- Improve current risk assessment, targeting and profiling directed against smuggling in countries of origin, transit and destination
- Improve detection of processing and marketing in final destination countries or others en route
- Engage in demand reduction, which may involve identifying product alternatives alongside raising consumer awareness
- Intercept money laundering of illicit profits and undertake asset recovery

- Identify inadequacies in current levels of human, logistical and financial resources
- Identify inadequacies in national legislation
- Combat corruption
- Deliver training and capacity building in targeted and measurable fashions
- Improve communication, collaboration and co-ordination at national, regional and international levels
- Improve current wildlife management and conservation policies

Neither of the above lists is intended to be exhaustive.

Cold case reviews should not become too focussed purely on the incident itself and on capturing intelligence relating to it, but should look at the circumstances surrounding it. If varying perspectives are brought to bear, as wide a range of strategies as possible can be considered. For example:

In a poaching incident:

- How did poachers access and exit the areas? Can this be prevented in future or could their presence have been detected earlier?
- What enforcement resources were available to respond? Were they adequately equipped? Was a scenes-of-crime examination conducted?
- What resources were available to pursue poachers in the immediate aftermath of a poaching incident? Was back-up available to the first-responders? If poachers were detained, were they questioned effectively? What penalties were imposed on any poachers who were prosecuted?
- How were tusks/horns/skins/bones to be transported from the scene? What would have happened to them thereafter? Were residents of the area involved? Could local residents be encouraged to assist in poaching prevention?

In a seizure incident:

- How was the contraband detected? Risk assessment, profiling, informant, confidential hotline?
- Was adequate or sufficient screening equipment, X-ray, detector dog available? Are there adequate human resources at the port? Have security staff, i.e. at an airport passenger terminal, been alerted to wildlife crime and smuggling methods? Have staff at cargo terminals been similarly alerted? Have managers of express courier, mail and parcel services been advised of how their facilities are used to transport contraband?
- What could be done to prevent further smuggling? Is there potential to train airline or shipping company staff? Is public awareness conducted at the port?

- If a courier was detained, was he questioned effectively? Was he prosecuted? What information was exchanged with other national agencies or counterpart agencies abroad?
- Could a Controlled Delivery operation have been initiated?

In a wildlife sales incident:

- How did the dealer obtain the items? What was paid for them? What penalty was imposed on the seller?
- What type of customer purchases the items? What are the items used for? Do customers understand that they are participating in illicit trade?
- What could be done to prevent or discourage future trade? Do relevant agencies have sufficient inspection personnel? Do they have sufficient training in fields such as product recognition and species identification?
- What demand reduction opportunities exist?

Cold case reviews appear to be achieving considerable success in the realm of mainstream crime and it is surely sensible to deploy them in relation to past wildlife crime incidents too.

RIDING OFF INTO THE SUNSET

My riding range having been the globe, I found myself rather saddle-sore after 14 years. Conscious that I also seemed to be running out of silver bullets, at least in terms of flashes of inspiration for improving the response to wildlife crime, it seemed the time had come for the Lone Ranger to hang up his hat and put his holsters away. Working for CITES had been the most incredible experience, bringing me into contact with some fascinating people and places and allowing me to influence international law enforcement in a manner that would have been beyond the imagination of the young fellow who put on a police cadet uniform in 1973, but it really did seem to be time for a new sheriff in town. I rode into early retirement at the end of September 2011 but it is hard not to look back over my shoulder, especially as the view from the saddle can offer a good perspective.

Having spent almost four decades in law enforcement, including almost a decade and a half focussed on wildlife law enforcement, it is impossible to leave it all completely behind. My interest in this field remains with me and will undoubtedly do so to the end of my life. Now reduced to looking in from the outside, I see progress being made, but it also seems that many of the gaps which I noted again and again continue to exist. Consequently, I still feel some frustration, as I continue to believe that it should not to be too difficult to close those breaches in combating wildlife crime, or at least some of them.

I regret having to say that those of us who worked in international organizations had a tendency, occasionally, to take ourselves far too seriously. I was certainly guilty of this from time to time. Some people did so more frequently than others. I also believe we failed sometimes to remember how remotely we operated from the daily, routine, on-the-ground operations which actually implemented whatever subject matter our activities were linked to. Did one less individual of an endangered species die as a result of my 14 years work with CITES? I doubt it.

Particularly in the field of wildlife crime, I firmly believe and must re-emphasize that international agencies must do more to connect with those on the frontline, and especially to connect more with their managers. While I realize that some will regard the following remarks as bordering on sacrilege, I think it needs to be recognized that there is a very significant gap, essentially a communication cavity, between what international agencies are producing or saying and the audience that really needs to hear what is being said. Additionally, the message is regularly provided in an ineffective format or sent along channels that the audience is not tuned into or cannot tune into. Just now, for example, I read a news item reporting that several car manufacturers were to start fitting only digital radios to their new vehicles. While that might be appropriate for large parts of the United Kingdom, the area of

Scotland in which I live cannot receive digital sound broadcasts. There may be fascinating and informative programmes available on digital channels, but none of them reach the Sellar household.

The United Nations Environment Programme (UNEP) has in recent years published a number of Rapid Response Assessment Reports. These publications, invariably of high quality, are attractive to look at, using excellent illustrations, are reader friendly, avoiding technical terms or too much detail, and provide a first-rate overview of current or emerging issues that warrant attention. Reports have been prepared, for example, on subjects such as the illegal trade in great apes and the poaching of elephants. I was responsible for supplying text for inclusion in at least one of these publications. I never, however, saw any of these reports on shelves in the office of any senior customs or police officer that I visited. It might be argued that I should have carried a constant supply of them as I travelled around the world and, in failing to do so as often as I might have, I may be guilty of maintaining or widening a gap.

The United Nations Office on Drugs and Crime prepares regional trans-national organized crime threat assessments, providing an overview of emerging crime types, describing the forms of criminal activity that are being conducted in regions throughout the world, how they are committed, the scale and profits associated with each, the threats to human and national security represented by these activities, the risks posed to the environment and the nature of the groups or networks suspected of organizing and controlling the crime. These assessments take many months of work by UNODC staff and consultants and I imagine the costs involved in preparing and publishing them are substantial. These, like the UNEP reports, are of a very high standard and I have been delighted and honoured to have peer reviewed several of them. While many law enforcement officers will benefit from the capacity building which UNODC provides in many developing countries, it is not an organization that is particularly known among frontline customs or police officers. Throughout my police service in Scotland, I was unaware of the work being done by UNODC to promote law enforcement across the globe and I suspect a similar ignorance was shared by most of my colleagues.

The average police officer will have no contact whatsoever with Interpol during the course of his or her working life, which will probably cover at least 30 years. Those who do are usually prompted to seek Interpol's assistance to make contact with the relatives of a dead person who either live or are on holiday abroad. Interpol does not send detectives around the world to track down wrong-doers: it is primarily a support body to national police agencies. Interpol's national bureaux are staffed mainly by office-bound enforcement officials who, in turn, liaise with their operational colleagues. Most customs officials will never have reason to make contact with the World Customs Organization's Brussels headquarters, although they will, day to day, benefit from the agency's work in establishing the tariff codes that all customs officers use to identify the nature of cargo and determine relevant duties and taxes. In developing countries, they may well profit from the WCO's capacity building activities.

CITES clearly plays an important role in regulating the world's trade in wildlife but it is questionable how closely it should be involved in responding to matters of crime. The majority of delegates to its meetings and conferences have little knowledge of, or direct involvement in, law enforcement. It occasionally struck me that the discussions on wildlife crime responses, which constantly took place at CITES events, were somewhat out of place. It seemed, almost, like a gathering of representatives of the pharmaceutical industry sitting down to debate how to combat the trafficking in narcotics. If more countries had included relevant enforcement officials in their delegations, it would not have been quite so bad, but few did. I recall, in the run-up to one of the regular meetings of the Conference of the Parties, asking the head of a national CITES authority, which was hosting a regional enforcement-related workshop, whether her nation would be bringing any customs or specialized enforcement staff to the event. 'No,' came her answer, 'Why would we do that?' Out of her sight, but within hearing distance, was the head of her country's wildlife law enforcement unit. He looked at me and just shook his head in resignation.

While it is all very well for international agencies and secretariats to work quietly in the background, never seeking recognition for their valiant efforts, if those on the front-line do not know of their existence, understand their relevance or appreciate the potential support they offer, I believe we are looking not at a gap but at a chasm. I have attended several international conferences where, had I brought an operational customs or police officer into the room to listen to the debates, he or she would have been horrified at their lack of relevance to their daily duties. Looking back to my days as a police manager, I am conscious how easy it is for supervisors to get out of touch with what is happening on the street, and we all need to guard against this. I wonder how often, during the weeks and months of international agency report preparation and the subsequent circulation of drafts, a member of, for example, an anti-poaching field unit is ever asked to review it? How often are such operational staff invited to review or revise draft training manuals or other capacity-building material? Were I a gambling man, I suspect it would be odds-on that precious few such requests or invitations have ever been made.

Inter-governmental organization reports and documents, international conference resolutions and statements, together with numerous academic research papers, are littered with footnotes or text referencing other reports, documents, resolutions, statements and papers. I could not help but wonder, now and again, whether it was some select grouping or club that was generating and reading all this, while it was going relatively unnoticed by, or having little impact upon, those on whose behalf the club was supposedly working. I have seen, and continue to see, many resolutions adopted or amended. I have drafted text for umpteen such documents. What made me reluctant to continue drafting was the fact that, apparently all too often, little of significant impact was emerging following the adoption of such well-intentioned and studiously-worded tracts.

Towards the end of my career, I increasingly found myself wondering whether the various declarations and statements emanating from gatherings of leading experts, senior civil servants, diplomats and politicians were actually translating into meaningful action or, vitally, support for those whose daily task was to protect nations' natural resources and bring wildlife criminals to justice. I questioned, for instance, whether the ministers of environment who committed their countries to do more to tackle crime via joint declarations, round-table outcome documents and the proceedings of regional or international conferences, subsequently went home and notified, let alone had discussions with, their ministerial counterparts under whose auspices action would need to be taken. The reality is that a minister of environment has relatively little influence upon the law enforcement strategies of his or her country. If a change in existing priorities or policies is to take place in that field, it will be the minister of justice or home affairs, in the case of the police, or the minister of finance in the case of customs who will play the major role in determining whether a modification is made or not. The various surveys indicating that many justice ministries, for example, have little knowledge of wildlife crime appear to indicate that the necessary liaison and collaboration is not taking place.

Most ministers of environment know only too well what impact wildlife crime is having upon their country and the staff of their departments, national parks and nature reserves also need no awareness raising. Many of those staff may be engaged in combating the poaching or illegal harvesting taking place at the very beginning of the illegal trade chain. In many respects, it will be their efforts that will determine whether or not a species tips into extinction. In many parts of the world, for example where high levels of elephant poaching are currently taking place, the resources deployed to prevent these crimes seriously and urgently need to be supported and increased. But field staff cannot win the war on their own. Several nations have hundreds, some thousands, of forest guards, wildlife wardens and rangers devoted to protecting species in their natural habitats. However, if they are not successful, and it is wholly unrealistic to expect them constantly to be so, then someone needs to be at their backs, so to speak, to intercept the criminals who slip through. It is in the towns and cities and at borders where enforcement staff are also needed. Yet relatively few of the departments and agencies which employ anti-poaching personnel deploy resources in those towns or cities or at those borders. Where they do not, and it will often be impractical or inappropriate for them to have such a presence, then counterpart enforcement bodies must play their role and take on the responsibility of tackling the links further up the chain.

If the badly-needed co-ordinated retort to wildlife crime can be likened to a jigsaw, perhaps it is not necessarily the case that pieces are missing; perhaps they have yet to be slotted together. It has become increasingly common for major environmental conferences to include side events in which the judiciary are invited to participate. Some of these sessions have attracted very senior figures, such as Attorneys General or Supreme Court judges. Several UN agencies have organized national and regional awareness-raising seminars and workshops for members of the judiciary. These events have been highly successful and the appreciation among prosecutors and judges of the significance and seriousness of environmental crime has undoubtedly risen in recent years. However, judges, for instance, are at the far end of a judicial chain. Much as they may be prepared to deal with offenders, it is not their role to bring criminals into the dock. Neither are they, in the separation-of-powers constitutional structure of most democracies, in a position to influence policy with regard to operational crime responses. Indeed, they tend strictly and very deliberately to protect their independence from such policy making.

I believe there may be scope, when liaising with the judiciary in these seminars and workshops, to also bring on board enforcement agencies. When I began my police career, my colleagues and I seldom had direct contact with prosecutors and I think there was a lack of understanding and appreciation of each other's role in the justice system. Today, however, there is much more collaboration and, particularly where complex or serious investigations are concerned, prosecutor and police officer work very much hand in hand. A close colleague was able to convene a seminar in Africa in which every branch of the system participated, and was impressed by how successful this was in promoting a greater perception of the individual needs of, and challenges faced by, the investigator, prosecutor and judge. This offers an example to be replicated elsewhere.

The links of the long chain of criminality controlling today's wildlife offences seem to be strong. In contrast, many links in the response chain seem to be weak or, worse, the chain itself is fractured in several places.

I certainly do not intend to be wholly dismissive of what has been done in the past and what continues to be done. I do, though, believe there is considerable scope for more reflection and evaluation. Bureaucracies - and international inter-governmental organizations certainly warrant that description - can, at times, display imaginative and innovative approaches, such as in training materials, and yet in their core activities be stifled by the 'We've always done it this way' mentality. National agencies such as the police or park authorities sometimes fall into this trap too. During my police career, I saw increasing importance being placed upon what it became fashionable to call 'policing by consent', and quite rightly, too. In fact, as an officer who had served most of his time in rural areas, I think that was, historically and traditionally, our approach in any case. Today, one tends to speak of a police service rather than a police force. This style is a long way from being adapted in some other parts of the world, where the police continue to be seen as an arm of the state and where there is a considerable gap between the public and those who are meant to be their guardians. Many of the anti-poaching patrols I saw in Africa and Asia were paramilitary in the uniforms they wore, the weapons they carried, the manner in which they conducted their duty and the manner in which they conducted themselves; it was like visiting some military detachment and there seemed to be more standing to attention and saluting in the presence of a senior officer than I have seen on army and air force bases in the UK.

In several instances, I saw clearly that these individuals appeared to have little interaction with local communities. One often saw patrol staff stationed to parks, forests or reserves hundreds of miles from their home towns or villages. Many did not have their families living with them and so had not integrated into the communities in which they operated. While military-type skills are definitely needed by anti-poaching personnel, particularly when they are likely to encounter heavily-armed illegal harvesters, I saw several instances where local residents seemed to view patrols almost with fear, as camouflaged units walked by in formation with semi-automatic rifles strung across their chests or swept past in dark green 4x4 jeeps or trucks. Rather than projecting an image of working in aid of indigenous populations and protecting their local natural resources, they left the feeling that some occupying force had just gone by. It must be said, however, that some of the training they were receiving simply reinforced this fissure between people that were, after all, citizens of the same country. I read an anti-poaching training manual, developed by an NGO operating in southeast Asia many years ago, which, throughout its text, used the phrase 'the enemy' rather than referring to suspects or poachers.

Several park and wildlife authorities in Africa have designated intelligence officers, whose job it is to seek out information about who may, for instance, be engaged in elephant poaching or ivory trading. But the patrol staff, who would be meeting day to day with villagers and others passing through parks and reserves, appeared to have received little training in this subject and so were not being tasked to exploit these interactions. I saw the very same around the Caspian Sea, where fishery protection staff, whose duties would regularly bring them into contact with those living along the rivers and coastlines and with local fisherman, had not received instruction on the important intelligence-gathering opportunities they would come across each day. Also absent from anti-poaching work in relation to sturgeon were the crime-recording and crime-plotting software packages used extensively in modern policing to map out, often graphically on-screen, where incidents were occurring, so that one could obtain an overview of where and when poachers were operating. In the past, in Scotland for example, it was generally thought that local police officers had, inside their heads, a mental picture of where crime was being committed. But computer-assisted crime analysis has shown that such images were often inaccurate or skewed. Most importantly, they also often demonstrated that police resources were being deployed inappropriately, in terms of geography and in relation to the time and day of the week. Such software is badly needed in relation to anti-poaching activities conducted in many parts of the world.

I recall suggesting, during one of my several visits to the Caspian Sea area, that light aircraft might very usefully be deployed to seek out poachers in the myriad channels and estuaries there. The looks on the faces of those listening made it plain that they thought I was mad. Yet donor agencies might have been willing to fund the initial purchase of such a resource and operating costs need not have been that much higher than those of some of the water-borne craft which were already in use. In 1973, when I joined the police, the thought of forces having air support was unimaginable but today, helicopters are a regular feature in patrol and emergency-response fleets. There must, similarly, be considerable potential for drone aircraft to be used in anti-poaching operations.

In 1999, at a time when I perhaps had yet to hone my diplomatic skills, I co-chaired an international conference held in Xining, China, which was convened to discuss conservation of Tibetan antelope. During discussions relating to anti-poaching work, I spoke at one point, without perhaps thinking enough beforehand, and asked whether China's military satellite capabilities might not be used to look down upon the plateau and identify both antelope and poacher locations. It struck me that such viewpoints would be invaluable, given the vast wilderness of the region. A hush fell upon the meeting hall, especially amongst the Chinese delegation. I began to see faces pondering whether it was appropriate for government officials of China even to admit to the existence of military satellites, let alone whether they could be used for such purposes. Eventually, no one being willing to break the silence, I moved discussions on to another issue. Today, of course, satellite imagery is extensively used for conservation purposes, and has been especially helpful in identifying illegal logging locations.

The structure and organization of anti-poaching work being conducted around the world seldom benefits, in my experience, from anything other than a militaristic input, except, of course, in the specific circumstances described above. The heads of anti-poaching divisions in park and wildlife authorities seem always either to have risen through the ranks, having been appointed as ranger or game warden in their late teens or early twenties, or they are ex-senior military officers. The head of enforcement staff in the Kekexili National Park on the Tibetan Plateau, for example, when I visited in 2003, was a retired general from China's People's Liberation Army. Donor governments and NGOs seem almost invariably to employ ex-military officers to deliver capacity-building efforts for anti-poaching work. The response to recent surges in elephant poaching in parts of Western and Central Africa seems always to be, 'Send in the army!' To my mind, poaching is a contravention of criminal law and, as such, is a matter for the civil authorities. Although there may be a case for deploying troops in times of what might be classed as emergency, I think that should be a last resort. One only has to look at Northern Ireland, Iraq or Afghanistan to see why a clear distinction must be drawn between civil policing and military support. It may, however, once again reflect the general view of wildlife crime that governments, time after time, decide not to deploy police resources to support field staff in parks and reserves. I suspect, too, that it reflects the likely reaction of some police commissioners asked to deploy their officers to such work; they probably would not view it as a matter for the police.

When reflecting upon wildlife crime, I sometimes thought of the ideal co-ordinated response as a recipe for a cake being baked in the kitchen of a large hotel. I believe that it requires a whole range of ingredients including legislation, adequate penalties, weapons for the tiger reserve patrols and training materials. The conference reports and resolutions should also be components in the recipe. Because it may have to be a sizeable cake, a number of cooks will be required. These *sous-chefs* are civil servants, UN officials, international agency staff members, conservationists, NGO employee, activists and, most importantly, anti-poaching personnel and frontline customs, police and other law enforcement officers. The kitchen does not operate in isolation; the hotel's management, in the guise of ministers, diplomats, heads of international agencies and, importantly, accountants and financiers to pay for the ingredients, all need to be present. No matter how good the ingredients, however, and no matter how well-tested the recipe, the cake will only rise and will only be worth eating if the head chef is involved. It is the choices made by the man in the tall white hat which determine whether any restaurant is awarded a Michelin star.

In the law enforcement community, only very specific individuals get to wear the tall white hat. They go by different titles but whether they are called Commissioner of Police, Director General of Customs, Comptroller, Chief, Head of Serious and Organized Crime Agency or Director of Financial Crime Unit, it is they who rule the kitchen. And anyone who knows about kitchens knows that the chef rules with a rod of iron. It is the chef who decides how big or small the cake ought to be. It is also the chef who will ultimately decide upon the ingredients. The *sous-chefs* may offer a particular component, may suggest how long the cake needs to stay in the oven or may recommend how hot the oven should be, but it is the chef who will accept or reject their offerings. And anyone who knows about hotels will know that the general manager, although theoretically in complete control of the premises, will probably take his life in his hands if he enters the kitchen and tries to tell the chef how to bake a cake. The Minister of Justice or Finance, the hotel manager, may advise the chef on what flavours are currently popular and how many cakes need to be prepared, but it will always be the chef who makes the ultimate choices and issues the necessary orders.

I firmly believe that, in the past, we have, to a significant extent, been collecting ingredients and writing recipes without first consulting the chef. Many of us have gone ahead and tried to put the ingredients together by ourselves, or sometimes while working with fellow *sous-chefs*, but what keeps emerging from the ovens is a half-baked cake. Some of us have asked the head waiter for cake, only to be told that it is not on today's menu. Some of us have spoken to the general manager and complained that our cake was burned on the outside. However, what too few of us have done is enter the kitchen and speak to the man in the tall white hat. Too many chefs in too many kitchens do not know that the diners want cake on the menu, a menu that they are already juggling in order to fit in the courses tackling drug trafficking, murder, rape and robbery, and those chefs have not been invited to look at the recipe or approve the ingredients.

What I constantly found irritating was that the cake does not have to be as complicated as some of the main courses; it does not require *cordon bleu* preparation. Although wildlife crime is undoubtedly serious in its impact upon endangered species and in the level of profits made by organized crime, it is nothing compared to some other fields of crime. There is not a man on every street corner of New Delhi trying to sell tiger skins to passers-by. Each bar in Ha Noi does not contain a shady character offering drinkers the chance to purchase rhino horn to cure their hangover the following morning. I was often anxious that some of we *sous-chefs* were crying wolf on occasions. Several of the most serious forms of wildlife crime remain, at least for the moment, highly specialized in nature and with a similarly specialized consumer base. Not every kitchen in the world needs to be baking cakes, or at least not every day. What we must definitely avoid is to tell each chef that he has to have cake on the menu, provide him with the recipe and ingredients and then watch him find that none of the diners orders it. Illegal trade in sturgeon products, for example, warrants attention but I do wonder whether it is justified to seize large amounts of cosmetic goods containing caviar extract, as happened recently? Were those extracts from poached sturgeon? I doubt it. We must not waste the chef's time or that of the other kitchen staff.

When, all those years ago, I was chef in a small kitchen in northeast Scotland, I knew which courses were most popular with my customers. The residents of Royal Deeside wanted to come home each evening, secure in the knowledge that their house was unlikely to have been burgled while they were away at work. They wanted to stroll along the streets of their towns and villages on weekend nights without being mugged or sworn at by drunken louts. It was such main courses that they expected to find on my menu. They did not, however, object when, from time to time, I prepared a starter that involved protecting Her Majesty the Queen when she was in residence. Neither did they complain if some desserts included tracking down someone who had poisoned a golden eagle or illegally caught a badger in a snare. Indeed, I regularly found, for instance, that the media loved stories about wildlife law enforcement, that the public supported such work by the police and that, in turn, the favourable coverage was welcomed by Force Command. About a year after I retired from CITES, I was asked to conduct training for enforcement officers in a group of islands in the Pacific and I subsequently sat down to chat with the police commissioner there, a fellow

Brit. Since I was able to explain to him face-to-face both the seriousness of wildlife crime and, importantly, to describe it in terms of his particular context and jurisdiction, there was no hesitation on his part in agreeing that he and his staff should be giving the subject more attention. I regularly found, at the conclusion of the many presentations which I made to gatherings of senior customs and police officers, that the most common remark made to me was that they had not appreciated the seriousness of such crimes or how they affected their areas of responsibility. If we need to sit down with individual commissioners, then maybe it is time to do so. We can deliver copies of all the reports and other publications while we're there. It may also be more cost effective than some of our past efforts.

I know from my days of police service that if the chief orders that intelligence reports have to be completed and disseminated whenever officers deal with certain types of crime, then the reports will be completed and disseminated. If the chief instructs the reports be disseminated inter-agency and internationally, that too will happen. At one point several years ago, in an effort to increase the flow of information, a major international NGO put up an annual prize for the best wildlife crime-related intelligence submitted by an agency to Interpol. As someone who had held a supervisory rank in the police, I found it well-intentioned but utterly ludicrous. The exchange of intelligence should be seen by all ranks as a basic necessity in policing and not something done to win a competition.

If the Director General of a national customs authority commands that particular forms of contraband interceptions be reviewed to determine whether they are suitable to be managed as controlled deliveries, such reviews will be conducted. If the Director General also instructs that details of such interceptions be shared with counterpart agencies, at home and abroad, the details will be shared. Once again, though, as in the field of policing, one would hope that liaison would occur without the need for specific instruction.

I described earlier how, post 9/11, the subject of wildlife crime had to claw its way back up the political and law enforcement agendas. In recent years, it has also had to compete for a place on the chef's menu alongside a bewildering array of dishes. While the following may be an unfair snapshot, I think it is nonetheless interesting. I recently scrolled through the media releases which Interpol had issued in the first three months of 2013 and the results were rather remarkable. I suspect they might surprise not only the man in the street but also many police officers around the world. Interpol is the world's largest police organization, with 190 member countries. In those three months, it had issued slightly fewer than 50 press releases. Several referred to visits by the agency's chief to member countries, while others described visits to its headquarters by senior law enforcement officials and politicians. Others, not surprisingly, related to significant crimes that had been committed or to the arrest of wanted criminals. However, there were also many releases referring to matters that might be thought of as falling outside mainstream crime. Two, for example, related to illicit trafficking in counterfeit goods, three to the theft of items of cultural heritage importance, two to wildlife, a further two to illegal logging, one to illegal fisheries, one to electronic waste and two to child sexual exploitation. It was pleasing to see environmental crime featuring on the list. What surprised me, however, was that eight media releases during the first quarter of 2013 related to football match-fixing. I find it hard to believe that members of the public would recognize the corrupt fixing of soccer games as a matter of priority for the police forces of the world or for their international body. I also doubt that it reflects the priorities of those police forces.

What it does reflect, perhaps, is that there are certain sectors of industry and other bodies which, to put it simply, are buying the attention of the law enforcement community or paying for it to be focussed in certain directions. FIFA, football's international governing body, for instance, entered into a ten-year agreement with Interpol in 2011, under which Interpol will receive four million euros in each of the first two years, followed by 1.5 million euros in each of the subsequent eight years. I imagine 20 million euros buys a lot of attention. Is this how policing priorities are to be determined in the future? If so, will the conservation community have to place a levy on each person who goes on an African safari or visits a tiger reserve in Asia, so that the world's police can be paid to display an interest in endangered species? A policing world increasingly infiltrated by corporate sponsorship would, I predict, be very different from the one I inhabited for 24 years, and not necessarily for the better. This is not criticism of Interpol but, rather, an illustration of how international intergovernmental agencies struggle to cope with ever-expanding fields of interest alongside budgets and human resources which do not expand apace.

During my period dealing with wildlife crime, I saw international enforcement agencies give increasing consideration to the field of counterfeit goods and intellectual property rights. Although I would not wish to argue against customs and police officers seeking out bogus medicines or fake aircraft parts - and these are all too frequently in trade today - I have less enthusiasm for them spending time tracking down imitation luxury wristwatches or handbags or arresting people selling pirated copies of Oscar-winning films.

Interpol has built up an impressive environmental crime programme but it exists thanks to the financial contributions of a limited number of governments, non-governmental organizations and foundations. There is next to no money within Interpol's core budget that is ring fenced for environmental crime. If the funds from external donors were to dry up, the environmental crime programme would presumably have to be disbanded. One of Interpol's officers, who had put considerable time and effort, to great effect, into helping countries in Africa to combat wildlife crime, lost his post a few years ago. The western government which had been funding the work cancelled the project earlier than had been expected.

The World Customs Organization has conducted an excellent project aimed at combating illegal trade in great apes. It has only been able to do so, though, thanks to funding from the Swedish government.

While my salary was paid from the core budget of the CITES Secretariat, the majority of my activities were undertaken using project-specific monies donated by developed country governments. Many of those projects were species-specific, the particular focus being determined by the donor. My counterparts in the UN Office on Drugs and Crime faced very similar budgetary issues. The existing support to national agencies in combating wildlife crime, coming from international agencies, could cease, not exactly in an instant but within a very short time, should external donor funds disappear. Given the worldwide recession and its impact upon economies, there is good reason to be concerned. Budgetary constraints inevitably also influence governments' priority setting and it is the priorities which decide whether the funding tap is screwed down or shut off altogether. I once listened to a speech made by the Secretary General of Interpol in which he observed that law enforcement around the world could be improved immeasurably if governments were to divert to it even a small percentage of the monies they currently devoted to defence and military budgets. How I wish that governments had listened too. For the moment, however, it appears likely that wildlife crime issues will not come within the core budget of international organizations other than CITES, and that some of the priorities in relation to the delivery of assistance, by ICCWC for example, will be dictated by donors.

One of the observations made by the CITES Tiger Missions Technical Team during its visit to the United Kingdom in 1999 was that it seemed overdue for the country to establish some form of multi-agency centralized unit to oversee and co-ordinate wildlife law enforcement. As the leader of the team, I specifically included reference to this when I prepared the final mission report. I was aware that colleagues in UK customs and police had been of the same opinion for a long time and I thought some external nudging might help. I do not know whether the CITES report made any difference but such a group, called the National Wildlife Crime Unit, was subsequently formed and has now been in existence for over ten years. Throughout its existence, it has struggled from year to year, seldom knowing whether the funding would still be in place from one annual budget to the next. Regular difficulties have been encountered in attracting staff, especially experienced crime analysts, since potential applicants could never have confidence in being employed long-term. In April 2013, I checked the unit's website. It was not functioning properly and the words, 'Website currently under construction' were displayed on the homepage. The same words had been displayed there for months. Prior to the formation of the UK's Serious and Organized Crime Agency in 2006, there was considerable debate as to whether the National Wildlife Crime Unit should be absorbed into the new enforcement body. It was not, which presumably reflected the government's priorities in relation to wildlife crime.

If the genie in the bottle were to grant me just one wish to combat international wildlife crime, I would ask that everyone work more collaboratively. I want to see the turf wars of old set aside and a recognition that the more perspectives are brought to the table, the better. I never believed that I had the answer and I do not believe that any other individual, organization, programme, agency or convention does. Working together, though, they can put together a jigsaw and reveal a picture in which the answer, or answers, will become visible. Every piece of the jigsaw needs to be in place, however. Some pieces will have less detail, perhaps will be mere sections of the background or sky, while others will hold intricate features and detailed parts of the overall image. All, though, will contribute to the final result. We all know how irritating it is when the picture is almost complete, yet pieces of the jigsaw have gone astray or have dropped beneath the table. I was similarly infuriated when individuals or groups insisted that it should be they that set the final piece in place or refused to bring their piece to the table until certain conditions were agreed upon. At the outset of this chapter I spoke of the self-importance trap, and too many jigsaw makers fall into it too regularly. I also saw too much time wasted in debates over which would be the lead agency and who should be in charge. The current need for organizations to seek external funding almost inevitably promotes inter-agency tensions and can lead to empire building but this must be vehemently resisted and avoided. If we create a safe and secure future for the tiger, it will not care who did that. Why should we care either? It does not matter who manages to place the organized crime group members behind bars: what matters is that more of them end up in jail.

If I did leave any legacy behind me when I returned to my native Scotland to spend time with a fly-fishing rod in one hand and a tumbler of malt whisky in the other, I would like to think it was the International Consortium on Combating Wildlife Crime. Its initial steps forward have, perhaps, been small and sometimes unsteady. I will continue to shake bottles on its behalf, in case a genie should be inside one of them.

I am very pleased and honoured to have served as both a police and United Nations officer, an opportunity that does not come to many. I look back very fondly upon, and treasure, the relationships and friendships, hopefully many to be lifelong, which I enjoyed. Whatever successes I had in either career owed as much to the support, encouragement and participation of others, particularly my wife and family, as they did to me. As a nation, we Scots are known for our frank and blunt speaking. I am, if nothing else, Scottish from head to toe. I never set out to offend anyone in my spoken words and I trust my writing, too, has not offended.

I left Geneva in September 2011 because I thought I had done as much as I could do, at least from a position of employment. I continue, however, to try and raise the profile of wildlife crime through lecturing and the writing of articles in professional journals. In retirement, as in my proud and privileged term as the UN's Lone Ranger, I remain convinced, utterly convinced, that we would make major inroads into combating international wildlife crime if we could only get our act together. I do not claim it will be easy but neither do I think that it should be as hard and complex as it is sometimes made out to be.

Oh, in case readers are wondering, I haven't forgotten about the Miss World candidate. But that will have to be a story for another day.

ANNEX

OFFICIAL CITES MISSIONS

Argentina	Namibia
Australia	Nepal
Austria	Netherlands
Azerbaijan	New Zealand
Bangladesh	Nigeria
Belgium	Norway
Bhutan	Panama
Botswana	Paraguay
Brazil	Portugal
Cambodia	Qatar
Cameroon	Republic of Korea
Canada	Russian Federation
Chile	Rwanda
China + Hong Kong + Macau	Saudi Arabia
Czech Republic	Singapore
Democratic Republic of Congo	South Africa
Egypt	Spain
El Salvador	Sudan
Ethiopia	Sweden
France	Switzerland
Germany	Thailand
Guinea	Turkey
India	Turkmenistan
Indonesia	United Arab Emirates
Italy	United Kingdom of Great Britain and Northern Ireland
Japan	
Kazakhstan	United Republic of Tanzania
Kenya	United States of America
Lao People's Democratic Republic	Viet Nam
Malaysia + Sabah + Sarawak	Yemen
Mozambique	Zimbabwe
Myanmar	

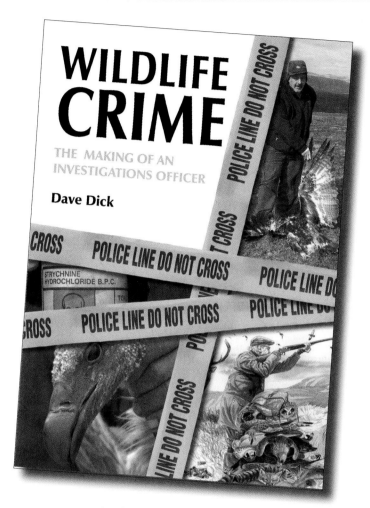

'This is an important book. It is written by an expert who probably knows more about wildlife crime in the UK, and especially in Scotland, than anyone else. It is important because so little is known and understood about a widespread and deeply disturbing illegal practice...'

Extract from Foreword by Sir John Lister-Kaye, OBE

'...is a no-nonsense memoir that weaves 25 years of battling criminals into a gritty account of life on the frontline. ... His forensic accounts make sober, fascinating reading, and revelation is tinged with a hard-won, dry humour. ... hope that the book will "reignite the public debate and media coverage" of illegal bird-killing. Indeed, it must'.

BBC Wildlife

www.whittlespublishing.com

'...What makes his book ... really special is the intimate tone with which Dan writes about the people... ...this is a powerful and evocative collection of stories ... engaging with animals and people on six continents. Dan has observed his subjects with a naturalist's passion for detail, resulting in a book that is engaging, informative and highly revealing'.

Australian Geographic

'...his account of his journey from the bird room of the Natural History Museum to these dangerous swamplands – and many other wildlife havens around the globe – is a hugely enjoyable read'.

BBC Wildlife

'Each chapter begins with a personal anecdote, set around Smith's own encounters with bird's places, and peoples, ranging from the USA to Iceland, Egypt to India, France to Thailand, Libya to Spain, as well as his home ground, ... the chapters evolve into rewarding, energetic explorations of our relationships with birds. ...Smith has sought out an array of lesser-known examples, and his text is worth mining for these alone. ...I can only recommend Malcolm Smith's Life with Birds as a vivid tour through examples old and new, familiar and unfamiliar, and as a valuable introduction to our wider cultural interrelationships with the birds.'

IBIS

'The author has amassed a treasure-trove of facts and figures... ... In a style which moves easily between anecdote, statistic and historic or other truth he succeeds admirably in conveying the breadth and depth of all the things we do to and with birds. ...it is packed with the curious and the thought-provoking. Its fascination itself mirrors the endless fascination that we have for birds.'

ECOS

www.whittlespublishing.com